DAILY LIFE IN

JAZZ AGE
AMERICA

Recent Titles in
The Greenwood Press Daily Life Through History Series

Arab Americans in the 21st Century
Anan Ameri and Holly Arida, Editors

African American Migrations
Kimberley L. Phillips

The Salem Witch Trials
K. David Goss

Behind the Iron Curtain
Jim Willis

Trade: Buying and Selling in World History
James M. Anderson

The Colonial South
John Schlotterbeck

A Medieval Monastery
Sherri Olson

Arthurian Britain
Deborah J. Shepherd

Victorian Women
Lydia Murdoch

The California Gold Rush
Thomas Maxwell-Long

18th-Century England, Second Edition
Kirstin Olsen

Colonial New England, Second Edition
Claudia Durst Johnson

Life in 1950s America
Nancy Hendricks

DAILY LIFE IN

JAZZ AGE
AMERICA

STEVEN L. PIOTT

The Greenwood Press Daily Life Through History Series

GREENWOOD™

An Imprint of ABC-CLIO, LLC
Santa Barbara, California • Denver, Colorado

Library of Congress Cataloging in Publication
Control Number: 2019941331

ISBN: 978-1-4408-6165-9 (print)
       978-1-4408-6166-6 (ebook)

23 22 21 20 19   1 2 3 4 5

This book is also available as an eBook.

Greenwood
An Imprint of ABC-CLIO, LLC

ABC-CLIO, LLC
147 Castilian Drive
Santa Barbara, California 93117
www.abc-clio.com

This book is printed on acid-free paper ∞

Manufactured in the United States of America

To Cindy

CONTENTS

PREFACE

This book, like others in the Daily Life Through History series, seeks to examine a historical period using the approach of more recent social history that looks at people from the bottom up as well as from the top down. This particular volume is focused on the 1920s, a decade that people still commonly refer to as the Jazz Age. The emphasis is on the habits and rhythms of daily life—living, working, playing, and interacting with one another in both rural and urban societies and in racially and ethnically diverse America. It is often the everyday actions of individuals—how they engaged themselves as workers, farmers, consumers, and citizens—as well as the more profound reflections they had on their lives at a given moment that reveal much about a period and its people. This volume is an attempt to show how people during the 1920s tried to give some order to their world and some meaning to their lives.

Daily Life in Jazz Age America comprises seven chapters that try to give some depth to the general premise of the series. In Chapter 1, the focus is on domestic life. What forces were working to transform social relationships in American society during the postwar decade? How did those changes affect especially women in the work they did, the aspirations they had, and the opportunities that were available to them? And, just as important, in what ways did gender relationships change during the decade? The chapter also examines home and family life, child-rearing, marriage and divorce, and the heated debate over contraception. In an attempt to provide some racial and ethnic balance to the discussion, the chapter also casts some light on the domestic life of African Americans in Harlem and Mexican Americans in Los Angeles during a time of significant migration and immigration.

In Chapter 2, the attention shifts to economic life. Did the often-celebrated prosperity of the 1920s reward all Americans evenly? If not, why not? What specific problems confronted those engaged in agricultural and industrial production? This chapter includes a brief discussion of the historical context that preceded the decade: the impact of war, antiradical paranoia, and labor unrest that continued to strain relationships between capital and labor throughout the 1920s. A closer look at Mexican migrant workers and black Pullman porters provides a glimpse of the economic struggles of two minority labor groups. The ethnic and racial bias exhibited toward those groups was symptomatic of a deep-seated nativism and racism that fueled many of the social tensions and a number of cultural conflicts that marked the period, and these points are discussed here.

Chapter 3 deals with intellectual life and begins with a summary of changes in education. The primary focus of the chapter, however, is on the intellectual influences that seemed to have the greatest impact. Two differing perspectives are involved in this discussion: the elite culture, given expression by intellectuals who generally felt alienated from the business-oriented culture of the 1920s, and the emerging mass consumer culture, best expressed by those who accepted or even celebrated the dominant probusiness ethos. Attention to the first group, the "revolt of the highbrows," involves a consideration of the so-called lost generation and the particular influence of writers like Ernest Hemingway, F. Scott Fitzgerald, Sinclair Lewis, and H. L. Mencken, while the second looks more closely at the "popular" literature of the period. This chapter also details the cultural flowering that occurred in New York City during the 1920s, known as the Harlem Renaissance.

Chapter 4 focuses on material culture during the 1920s and employs a case-study approach of Muncie, Indiana, and Southern California to explore housing and class-stratified neighborhoods, suburban growth, and the impact of the automobile on the material landscape. In addition, this chapter investigates the ways in which the American diet changed in the 1920s as families, guided by a new breed of scientific nutritionists, moved in the direction of lighter, simpler, healthier meals; how they became more reliant on commercially processed food products; and how, as lifestyles became more hectic, they increasingly embraced the appeal of commercial, "fast-food" eating establishments. Chapter 4 also examines material culture from the vantage point of changes in the style of clothing and fashion for women and men.

Chapter 5 shifts to political life and explores the state of political activism during the 1920s. Contrary to the stereotype that has tended to characterize the decade as one of political passivity, citizen activism remained vibrant, especially among women, white and black. But as female activists struggled with issues like federal funding for programs to combat infant and maternal mortality, an Equal Rights Amendment, and federal legislation against lynching, they met stiff resistance. The chapter also examines the conservative policies of Presidents Harding, Coolidge, and Hoover in the areas of taxation, tariff revision, the relationship between government and business, and the overall response to the Great Depression and how these policies affected the lives of all Americans. Politics in an era of Prohibition, political scandal, and low voter turnout is also considered.

Chapter 6 examines the various popular forms of commercial entertainment—radio, motion pictures, music (blues and jazz), and dance—that captured the attention of most Americans during the 1920s. It also looks at the ways in which Americans actively participated in various forms of physical recreation and watched or listened to amateur or professional sports contests. As Americans increasingly embraced leisure and consumption as vehicles for individual satisfaction, they also found that vicariously participating in the lives of Hollywood celebrities and sports heroes had become a major part of their everyday life. In a society seemingly fascinated by entertainment of almost any type, the chapter, in addition, assesses the popularity of a number of fads and crazes.

Chapter 7 explores religious life and pays special attention to what appeared to be a rise of religious uncertainty during the 1920s. Central to this feeling was the impact of Charles Darwin's theory of natural selection (evolution) and the debate that it triggered, not only between traditionalists and modernists, in general, but also between "modernists" within the Protestant church—who sought to reconcile science and faith—and "fundamentalists" who saw no room for accommodation. During the celebrated Scopes Trial in 1925, the entire nation became part of a debate that had narrowed to that of Darwin versus the Bible. The chapter also considers the westward migration of religious fundamentalism, the rise of Pentecostalism, and the career of evangelist Aimee Semple McPherson. It concludes with a brief look at religion in the African American and Hispanic communities.

INTRODUCTION

Most historians would agree with the general statement that the "tremendous social forces transforming American life—industrialization, immigration, urbanization, and changing patterns in work, politics, religion, leisure, and the family were in place well before 1914–18" (Dumenil 1995, 10). But those same historians continually refer to the "Twenties" as a "New Era." This apparent incongruity can be explained, at least in part, if one considers that for many Americans the 1920s was a time when old habits seemed to dissolve faster than ever before. As urban growth (the 1920 U.S. Census proclaimed for the first time that more than half of all Americans lived in towns or cities of 2,500 people or more) continued to add to the complexities of life, impersonal relationships came to supplant the more personal associations that had characterized smaller, rural communities. Contesting the moral standards set by local communities and churches were more modern attitudes toward sexual morality, gender relationships, dress, and behavior that became a hallmark of the younger generation. But age was not the final arbiter as older women could also generate widespread consternation as they assumed the role of political activists, candidly discussed the merits of birth control and the idea of a companionate marriage, or debated the need for an Equal Rights Amendment. Especially upsetting to many was the "flapper," who flaunted her rejection of the Victorian code of proper female behavior. Abandoning traditional constraints, the flapper talked openly about sex, laughed and danced gaily, and, to many, dressed immodestly. She bobbed her hair, flattened her chest, abandoned her corset, shortened her skirt, rolled her stockings, painted her cheeks, and assumed a much more casual approach to dating and marriage.

Joining the assault on older habits was the "lost generation," the group of young artists and writers who ushered in a new era of intellectual criticism in the way they reacted against a style of life that had been esteemed before the war. Poet Edna St. Vincent Millay's work reflected post–World War I thinking regarding women with witty female characters who were independent and sexually liberated; writer F. Scott Fitzgerald chronicled the decadent rich, the self-indulgent pleasure seekers, and the anti-Puritanical college students; novelist Ernest Hemingway articulated the feelings of a cynical, disillusioned, and rootless postwar generation; and iconoclast H. L. Mencken showed disdain for just about everyone and even had the audacity to lampoon the formally noble yeoman farmer. But, according to Frederick Lewis Allen, it was two books by Sinclair Lewis that really brought focus to the general intellectual critique that followed. In *Main Street* (1920), Lewis revealed the ugly side of small-town America: its cultural barrenness, its prejudices, its insularity, and narrow-mindedness. The literary portrait was merciless, the satire searing, and the approach overdrawn, one-sided, and offensive to many, but the novel sold 390,000 copies by the end of 1922. With the publication of *Babbitt* that same year, intellectuals only had to read Lewis's books "to realize that the qualities in American life which they most despised and feared were precisely the ones which he put under the microscope for cold-blooded examination. It was George F. Babbitt who was the arch enemy of the enlightened, and it was the Main Street state of mind which stood in the way of American civilization" (Allen 2010, 198).

At the same time, Protestant religious leaders were finding they had to confront "modernists" within the church as well as the defenders of modern science outside it. After the war, many urban, white-collar congregations moved toward theological liberalism or "modernism." Looking to reconcile science and faith, they took the position that the Bible used symbols and allegory to convey God's meaning. They tended to accept scientific discoveries (including the theory of evolution) and regarded these findings as part of God's ongoing revelation to his followers. Following the literal words of the Bible was not as important as discerning the "spirit and purpose" of God's teachings. Conservative Protestants or fundamentalists disagreed. The Bible was the word of God and should be accepted as divine authority. Anything short of that would leave society on the verge of moral anarchy. And, as American life became more and more secularized and it began to look like religion might no longer be regarded as the ultimate source of moral authority for many, there was ample cause for concern. The perceived increase in immorality and the turning away from active participation in the church, especially by the young, seemed to confirm that, for many Americans, the messages of the Bible had lost their meaning.

On the economic front, after a brief postwar recession, the country recovered and entered into a period of booming industrial productivity symbolized by Henry Ford's use of mechanization and innovative management to produce affordable automobiles at a fantastic rate. Most Americans enjoyed a higher standard of living, although that new prosperity bypassed many. The glow of greater wealth, however, obscured an increasingly skewed distribution of income in which more and more of the nation's riches were falling into the hands of only a few. Nevertheless, the outward appearance of affluence helped to foster a get-rich-quick mentality that was apparent in land speculation in Florida and in Southern California as well as financial speculation in the stock market. It seemed as if the country had reached a new era of unlimited material possibilities.

This optimism carried over into the realm of politics as the more traditional conservative policies of the Harding and Coolidge administrations—lower tax rates, protective tariffs, and minimal government regulation—gave way to a new era of political conservatism under the guidance of Herbert Hoover (often referred to as the architect of the "new economic order"). Hoover believed that government could do more than just create a favorable climate for business and that it could actively assist the business community through the distribution of economic information (e.g., statistics on prices, costs, markets, and volume of production), alerting it to potential economic problems and suggesting ways to enhance economic productivity. Thus, first as secretary of commerce and then as president, Hoover crafted an economic policy that promoted business–government cooperation, encouraged the growth of trade associations, refrained from the rigid enforcement of antitrust statutes, and further enabled the formation of oligopolies and the growth of corporate power.

Persistent troubled notes, however, marred the decade. Racism had always been an issue in American society. The lynchings, political disenfranchisement, and "Jim Crow" segregation laws had certainly heightened racial tensions during previous decades. The Great Migration of African Americans from the South to northern cities before, during, and after World War I further strained race relations and saw its most violent expression in a number of post-war race riots like the one in Chicago in 1919 in which 23 blacks and 15 whites died and 500 people were injured. But migration to the North as well as wartime military experience for many seemed to create a new spirit among African Americans. The "new Negro" was more self-assertive, no longer willing to accept an insult or to turn the other cheek. When confronted with violence, he would, as demonstrated in Chicago in 1919, fight back. Helping develop this new race consciousness were black intellectuals, black newspapers, organizations like the National Association for the Advancement of Colored People (NAACP), black entertainers, black nationalists like Marcus Garvey and his Universal Negro Improvement Association (UNIA), the writers and artists of the Harlem Renaissance, and labor organizers like A. Philip Randolph who worked to unionize black workers for the first time. The new spirit empowered blacks but proved unsettling to whites who had hoped to maintain the racial status quo.

Also unsettling to white Anglo-Saxon Protestants was the rising influence of immigrants, Catholics, and Jews. Nativism had certainly been an issue in the late nineteenth and early twentieth centuries and intensified as the annual number of immigrants reached into the millions. The fear that the Bolshevik Revolution in Russia might have repercussions in the United States, a wave of postwar strikes, and unspent wartime nationalism created a situation in which older anxieties became exacerbated. In response, the Justice Department hunted alien radicals and targeted them for deportation; employers conducted "patriotic" open-shop campaigns and charged that unions were "un-American"; Congress passed a series of laws that severely restricted immigration from southern and eastern Europe and excluded Asians entirely, while the state of California created a commission to oversee efforts to "Americanize" Mexican immigrants. Joining in this reaction and contributing to the mood of apprehension was the Ku Klux Klan. The new Klan, modeled after its nineteenth-century Reconstruction predecessor, targeted not only African Americans but also foreigners, Catholics, and Jews as it spread a xenophobic ideology that made it a social and political force until scandals devastated the organization in the mid-1920s. It seemed like the modern notion of a pluralistic order that recognized the intrinsic value of minority cultures was an impossibility.

The passage of the Eighteenth Amendment outlawing the manufacture and sale of intoxicating beverages also added a component to the rise of nativism and greatly contributed to the social tensions and cultural wars that strained society until its repeal in 1933. Supported as a means of promoting morality through sobriety, Prohibition caused critics to see the effort as a way to reaffirm white Anglo-Saxon Protestant cultural values. Some saw the new law as a violation of personal liberties, while ethnic groups regarded it as a blatant attempt at "cultural imperialism." The issue continued to fracture politics throughout the decade as Republicans became the party of the "drys" and Democrats the party of the "wets." The issue finally reached a culmination of sorts in the hotly contested presidential election of 1928 when Al Smith's immigrant background, Catholicism, and opposition to Prohibition became the focal point of a lively campaign filled with negative ads.

Most historians of the Jazz Age view the 1920s as one where there was a pronounced shift in values and behavior. As historian Lynn Dumenil has noted, Americans moved away from "the Victorian 'production' ethos of work, restraint, and order" toward one that embraced "leisure, consumption, and self-expression as vehicles for individual satisfaction" (Dumenil 1995, 57). As work became increasingly regimented for blue-collar workers on the assembly line and more routinized for white-collar workers trapped behind an office desk, it became more alienating. As it did, and as Robert and Helen Lynd found in their sociological study of Muncie, Indiana (*Middletown*), workers increasingly sought satisfaction outside the "job" in consumption and leisure. And those choices seemed limitless. One could tune in to a radio program, attend a motion picture presentation, listen to blues records, go out to a nightclub, dance to jazz music, play golf or tennis, attend a variety of mass spectator sporting events, or become totally caught up in a number of fads and crazes.

As the new cosmopolitan mass consumer culture of magazines, advertising, and motion pictures spread to the countryside, it helped promote new social values. At the same time, mass production and advances in technology generated a flood of affordable consumer goods, which helped drastically alter daily lifestyles. But, as historian Michael Parrish has noted, a "consumer society that sanctioned perpetual technological change, the generation of new fashions and desires, and the ultimate sovereignty of the market did not respect inherited values or the social status quo. It produced as much social conflict as consensus" (Parrish 1992, x). Those who embraced modernity tended to regard the changes as liberating and a mark of progress, while those who felt alienated by modernity tended to see the changes as corrupting and a sign of decline. As one historian commented: "The central paradox of American history . . . has been a belief in progress coupled with a dread of change; an urge towards the inevitable future combined with a longing for the irretrievable past. . . . This duality has been marked throughout most of America's history but seldom has it been more central than during the decade after the First World War" (Levine 1993, 191). Ironically, much the same could be said for our own present day.

TIMELINE

1919–1920	Anti-Bolshevik paranoia turns into mass hysteria and deportations of alien radicals that is known as the Red Scare.
1920s	Harlem on New York City's Upper West Side becomes a mecca of black cultural and intellectual life.
	Marcus Garvey's Universal Negro Improvement Association (UNIA) becomes the largest and most prominent social organization in Harlem.
	Promoting a program rooted in nativism, racism, anti-Catholicism, and anti-Semitism, a revitalized Ku Klux Klan is able to attract nearly four million members until scandal hastened its decline in 1925.
	Prohibition settles in as national policy and triggers a debate over its merits.
1920	The Nineteenth Amendment granting women the right to vote is ratified.
	The League of Women Voters is founded.
	The Department of Justice conducts the "Palmer Raids" (named after Attorney General A. Mitchell Palmer) as part of its campaign to round up and deport suspected alien radicals.
	Radio station KDKA launches the first commercial radio broadcast from Pittsburgh, Pennsylvania.

The federal census reports that population in the United States tops 100 million and that more Americans live in urban areas than in rural areas.

The Eighteenth Amendment prohibiting the manufacture, transportation, and sale of alcoholic beverages goes into effect.

Sinclair Lewis's new novel *Main Street* shatters the image of rural American small towns.

F. Scott Fitzgerald publishes *This Side of Paradise* and calls attention to the emerging cultural rebellion among America's college-age generation.

Nicola Sacco and Bartolomeo Vanzetti, two Italian anarchists, are arrested for the murder of two employees of a shoe factory in South Braintree, Massachusetts.

Promising voters a "return to normalcy," Warren G. Harding (R) defeats James M. Cox (D) to become twenty-ninth president of the United States.

The American Civil Liberties Union (ACLU) is founded by Roger Baldwin.

1921   Congress enacts a quota system limiting the number of immigrants allowed into the United States.

Rudolph Valentino stars in *The Sheik* and becomes a dashing screen idol.

The Sheppard-Towner Maternity and Infancy Protection Act is passed.

Margaret Sanger forms the American Birth Control League.

Shuffle Along becomes the first musical to be written, produced, directed, and performed entirely by African Americans.

1922   Sinclair Lewis publishes *Babbitt* and satirizes middle-class conformity.

The U.S. Senate launches an investigation into the actions of Secretary of Interior Albert B. Fall in what became known as the Teapot Dome Scandal.

1923   The Harding scandals begin to dominate the national news.

The Chinese tile game mah-jongg becomes a national fad.

A Broadway adaptation of an African American folk dance, the Charleston, sets off a dance craze.

Bessie Smith, regarded by many as the best female blues singer, records "Down-Hearted Blues" and "Gulf Coast Blues."

French self-help guru Emile Coué publishes *Self-Mastery through Conscious Auto-Suggestion* and encourages Americans to seek self-improvement by repeating optimistic phrases.

The first dance marathons are held.

Harold Lloyd's best-remembered silent film, *Safety Last*, is released.

Bobbed hair becomes the rage.

The U.S. Supreme Court in *Adkins v. Children's Hospital* blocks minimum wages for women.

The Women of the Ku Klux Klan is formed as an auxiliary of the KKK.

The discovery of Tutankhamen's tomb in 1922 ignites "Tutmania" and spawns a wide range of fashion and objects decorated in Egyptian motifs.

The Equal Rights Amendment (ERA) is introduced in Congress for the first time.

President Warren Harding dies in office and is succeeded by Vice President Calvin Coolidge.

1924   George Gershwin's *Rhapsody in Blue* is first performed at New York City's Aeolian Hall.

Congress passes the National Origins Act and drastically reduces the number of immigrants entering the country.

Richard Simon and Max Shuster publish *The Cross Word Puzzle Book* and start a nationwide craze.

Calvin Coolidge (R) defeats John W. Davis (D) and Robert M. La Follette (P) to become thirtieth president of the United States.

Flagpole sitting becomes a national fad.

The Loeb and Leopold Trial captures national attention as another "crime of the century" and triggers a discussion over the merits of capital punishment.

Henry Ford announces the production of the ten millionth Model T and lowers the price to under $300.

1925   John Thomas Scopes is tried for teaching evolution in Dayton, Tennessee, in violation of state law.

F. Scott Fitzgerald publishes *The Great Gatsby* and captures the romance and glitter of the Jazz Age.

The Florida land boom reaches its frenzied peak.

Bruce Barton publishes *The Man Nobody Knows*, a soon-to-be best seller, that cleverly reconciled Christianity with the pressures of modern consumerism.

A. Philip Randolph organizes the Brotherhood of Sleeping Car Porters.

Trumpeter Louis Armstrong begins leading his own bands and changing the face of jazz music.

Alain Locke publishes his influential Harlem Renaissance book, *The New Negro*.

Grand Dragon D. C. Stephenson is convicted of second-degree murder in a case involving kidnapping and sexual assault. The trial does irreparable damage to the Ku Klux Klan.

The hemline is the shortest in history.

1926   The Book-of-the-Month Club is founded.

Charlie Chaplin's silent comedy *The Gold Rush* premiers.

Ernest Hemingway publishes *The Sun Also Rises* and gives meaning to the term "lost generation."

Evangelist Aimee Semple McPherson is allegedly abducted in Los Angeles. But her "Foursquare Gospel" suffers a serious blow when it is revealed that the "kidnapping" was most likely a hoax.

A hurricane devastates Florida killing 372 people and effectively ending the Florida land boom.

Buster Keaton's film *The General*, considered by many movie historians to be the greatest silent film ever made, premiers.

Nineteen-year-old Gertrude Ederle becomes the first woman to swim the English Channel.

1927   Charles A. Lindbergh makes the first solo flight across the Atlantic in an airplane called *The Spirit of St. Louis*.

Nicola Sacco and Bartolomeo Vanzetti are executed in Boston, Massachusetts.

Al Jolson stars in *The Jazz Singer* as Warner Brothers launches the era of the "talkie."

Judge Ben Lindsey publishes *The Companionate Marriage*.

Clara Bow stars in the "It Girl" and becomes the embodiment of the flapper ideal.

Henry Ford introduces the Model A to compete with more innovative carmakers.

The *Amos 'n' Andy* radio program debuts on Chicago's WMAQ and soon reaches 40 million listeners over the NBC network.

At the peak of its popularity, H. L. Mencken's *American Mercury* magazine reaches a circulation of 77,000.

Bandleader and composer Duke Ellington transforms the Cotton Club in Harlem into a jazz mecca.

Gene Tunney defeats Jack Dempsey in the heavyweight championship boxing match remembered for its famous "long count."

1928   Herbert Hoover (R) defeats Al Smith (D) to become thirty-first president of the United States.

1929   Ernest Hemingway publishes his notable World War I novel, *A Farewell to Arms.*

Sociologists Robert and Helen Lynd publish *Middletown* and show that the ideals of egalitarianism and individual freedom had fallen victim to class structure and uniformity.

The stock market crashes in late October.

1

DOMESTIC LIFE

TRANSFORMATIVE SOCIAL FORCES AND THE PACE OF SOCIETAL CHANGE

The Impact of World War I

In his very popular informal history of the 1920s, *Only Yesterday*, Frederick Lewis Allen listed a number of forces that were working to transform social relationships in American society during the post–World War I decade. At the top of his list was a state of mind, a general disillusionment, brought about by the war. As Allen saw it, traditional "restraints," "reticences," and "taboos" had toppled under the pressure of wartime conditions. It was quite understandable to Allen that many had returned from the ordeal in a different frame of mind. They had "acquired under the pressure of war-time conditions a new code which seemed to them quite defensible" and had been "provided with an emotional stimulant from which it was not easy to taper off." "They found themselves expected to settle down into the humdrum routine of American life as if nothing had happened, to accept the moral dicta of elders who seemed to them still to be living in a Pollyanna land of rosy ideals which the war had killed for them. They couldn't do it" (Allen 2010, 82). Novelists like F. Scott Fitzgerald and Ernest Hemingway often instilled in their main characters feelings of alienation, cynicism, and disillusionment, suggesting an explanation for much of the escapism that fueled the excesses of the Jazz Age.

An Expanding World for Women

Postwar social change seemed to impact women more than men. With the Nineteenth Amendment, ratified in August 1920, women finally won the right to vote. The ability to participate in politics gave women an increased sense of independence and a new status as man's equal. Domestic life was also changing, and Madison Avenue's ad men were quick to point out that this growing sense of independence carried over to homelife as well. Heralding the arrival of the electric washing machine, the electric iron, and the vacuum cleaner, advertisers proclaimed that a technological revolution in the home was transforming the conduct of daily life and, in the process, "emancipating" women from their humdrum routine and enabling them to live their own lives.

For many women change came in the form of an increased presence in the workplace. By 1927 one in five wage earners was a woman. Just as women were able to take advantage of the wartime emergency to move into jobs that had been previously closed to them, many white women were able to continue that trend after the war and transition into new areas of white-collar employment. Banks, real estate and insurance offices, and publishing houses all required a legion of clerks to handle the rising volume of paperwork. By 1930, women filled over 52 percent of these clerical positions. As historian Alice Kessler-Harris has noted, "By 1920 . . . a larger percentage of employed women worked in these jobs (25.6 percent) than in manufacturing (23.8 percent), in domestic service (18.2 percent), or in agriculture (12.9 percent)" (Kessler-Harris 1982, 224). There was, however, a large wage differential between men and women. Roughly, during the 1920s white women, on average, earned about half of what men earned for similar work. Black women earned about half of what white women did. Barriers to advancement based on gender and race remained high, and many women worked with little hope of a raise or a promotion.

Disappointingly, the majority of the new clerical jobs that opened for women were available only to white and native-born women. Although African American women and recent immigrants comprised 57 percent of all employed women, they were largely relegated to domestic service, laundries, or the garment trade. Black women who found work in southern tobacco plants were often barred from the process of actually making cigars and cigarettes, which was reserved for white women, and, instead, offered seasonal jobs preparing the tobacco for the manufacturing process. For Chicana women in the Southwest, employment opportunities were often limited to agricultural labor in the fields or to work in canneries or food processing plants. Job segregation based on race and ethnicity persisted throughout the decade.

By the 1920s most women no longer looked on work and home as mutually exclusive preserves. Whereas the typical female worker in 1900 had been single and under the age of twenty-five, by 1930 she was over thirty and married. Although the percentage of women in the workforce rose only modestly between 1900 and 1930, the employment rate among married women doubled, motivated in part by rising expectations. While for many married women, paid work enabled their families to meet basic needs, for others, it opened the path for the purchase of an ever-expanding array of consumer goods. As one commentator noted: "As our pleasure philosophy takes deeper hold, as the demand for luxuries, artificially stimulated by advertising, mounts giddily higher, there is no help for it—the women have to go to work . . . the manufacturers need the women as consumers, need the two-wage family and its demands to keep the factories going" (Buhle 2009, 514). As one Muncie, Indiana, cleaning woman married to a pipe fitter commented: "I have felt better since I worked than ever before in my life. . . . We have an electric washing machine, electric iron, and vacuum sweeper. I don't have to ask my husband any more because I buy these things with my own money" (Rosenberg 1992, 94). But the new role of female, wage-working consumer had its downside. Many employers were of the opinion that women worked only for "pin money," extra spending money for nonessential expenses, and this justified the lower pay that women received in relation to men.

Rising aspirations affected other women as well by placing a new emphasis on college and a career. Female college graduates tripled during the 1920s, while the number of women professionals doubled. Although three out of four women professionals still worked in areas that had been traditionally dominated by women—teachers, librarians, nurses, and social workers—others were finding new opportunities as journalists, civil servants, businesswomen, lawyers, accountants, and college professors. By 1930 women earned one-third of all graduate degrees and comprised 30 percent of the nation's college and university faculties. Writer Gail Collins found that in the early days of radio "a lot" of women were involved in producing,

A home economics class, 1926. Led by the American Home Economics Association and the Bureau of Home Economics in the U.S. Department of Agriculture, home economists pushed the idea of applying scientific management to the home and encouraged housewives to see themselves as expertly trained, efficient, economical, new-age professionals. (Library of Congress)

writing scripts, emceeing the programs, and serving in various performance roles as well. As Collins humorously noted: "It would have been surprising if they hadn't been active, since early radio was exactly the sort of operation—disorganized, badly paid, and in great need of multitasking—that welcomed creative women" (Collins 2003, 340). Certain fields, however, remained male-dominated. In the fast-growing field of advertising, for example, only about 10 percent of advertising professionals ("admen") were women.

To contemporary observer Frederick Lewis Allen, these new opportunities for women brought a feeling of "comparative economic independence" and with that a "slackening of husbandly and parental authority" (Allen 2010, 84). It might be noted, however, that more recent studies of wage-earning women during the 1920s have shown that although they challenged the doctrine of separate spheres in the area of employment and "broke some barriers," "the portion of the marketplace allocated to women became increasingly credentialized, segmented, and hierarchical." Even in radio, once the business became a moneymaking success, women saw their on-air roles diminish when polls showed that listeners preferred to hear a man's voice. "That was the paradox of the twenties. . . . Women were invited into the work force and again invited not to expect too much of it" (Kessler-Harris 1982, 248).

The Influence of Sigmund Freud

Another item on Allen's list of transformative forces was the influence of Sigmund Freud. Although Freud had come to the United States in 1909 to give a series of lectures billed as "Concerning Psychoanalysis" at Clark University in Massachusetts, Americans seemed to pay little attention to his ideas until the 1920s when they gained popularity among the educated middle class. Freud boldly challenged existing explanations of social behavior and posited that the source of human motivation was sexual desire rooted in the unconscious mind. As historian Michael McGerr noted, "Whatever their misunderstanding of repression, sublimation, dreams, or infantile attachments, Americans recognized that psychology undermined the Victorian concept of the self. Inside the human being was a vast, uncharted, and powerful inner world" (McGerr 2003, 242–43). As Freud's ideas spread in overly simplified form, many concluded that the message was simply that sex was good and sexual inhibition, repression, and social control were bad. Thus, if inhibition was seen to be the primary cause of mental sickness, then self-expression and self-gratification must be the road to improved health and greater happiness. For many, Freud offered a rationale for rebelling against social conventions, especially those related to sex. For others, Freud's ideas provided a simple explanation for a complex set of anxieties that seemed to grip postwar American society.

Prohibition

Three other factors appeared to Allen to accelerate the pace of societal change. The first of these was the advent of national Prohibition. When Congress passed the Eighteenth Amendment in mid-January 1920, it appeared to have solid popular support behind it. But the new law proved difficult to enforce, and evasion of the law quickly gathered momentum, especially in the larger cities. The public soon learned about the "bootlegger" who made, transported, or sold liquor illegally and the unlicensed "speakeasy" that replaced the saloon or nightclub and sold illegal booze and, shockingly, catered to both men and women. Imposed as social control, the law also triggered a spirit of deliberate defiance that, especially among the younger set, made drinking the "in" thing to do.

The Automobile

Yet another factor quickening the pace of change was the automobile. Henry Ford, the industry's pioneer in the art of mass production, thought that the car would usher in a new age of personal freedom. An inexpensive vehicle like the Model T would allow a worker to consider a wider range of employment opportunities, provide a psychological sense of self-fulfillment for the proud owner, and allow families to experience an entirely new realm of pleasure on the open road. Ford thought this could all be achieved without upsetting the traditional values of his youth. But Henry Ford naively failed to grasp the broader implications of his brilliant achievement. The increasing availability of the automobile offered an entirely new sort of freedom in the sense that it provided a means for young people to escape the supervision of their parents and the watchful eyes of gossipy neighbors. Ironically, even though Ford hated cities as zones of congestion, crime, and moral debauchery and his newspaper, the *Dearborn Independent*, regularly condemned the new dance crazes, jazz music, smoking, and drinking, his car "helped to put sex, booze, and music on wheels" (Parrish 1992, 42).

The Cinema

The final item on Allen's list of factors propelling the pace of change was the cinema. Even in silent movies produced before World War I, sexual titillation had been the industry's most popular box office commodity. This preoccupation with sex on the screen persisted throughout the 1920s despite a number of sensational Hollywood scandals, continued denunciations from religious leaders, and even the creation of a special office to monitor immorality in film. Sensing that it was time to repair its libidinous image, Hollywood's studio executives hired former Indiana congressman and former chairman of the Republican National Committee, Will H. Hays, to head the effort. The Hays Office quickly purged the industry of hundreds of individuals who were dismissed on morals charges and allowed studios to insert a "morals clause" in their star's contracts, thus enabling them to fire actors for conduct that placed the industry in a bad light. Hollywood also adopted an official Hays Code enumerating actions that were banned from the screen: for example, no kiss should last longer than seven feet of film, adultery was not to be portrayed in an attractive manner, and complete nudity was forbidden. But righteous pronouncements against adultery and illicit sex, and sermonettes about following "the dictates of good taste" and maintaining a high regard for "the sensibilities of the audience," did not alter the "final cut" very much as producers and directors got around the censors by merely being a bit more creative in how they presented passion on the screen. Hollywood may not have created the sexual revolution, but it openly promoted the idea of individual sexual gratification.

HOME AND FAMILY LIFE

Although the pressures toward social change seemed to be constantly intensifying during the 1920s, most Americans held tightly to traditional values. The home was still the sanctuary, and a woman's primary duty was to maintain it. There were, however, significant changes in home and family life as well as in courtship and marriage that impacted gender relationships especially for the white, middle class. As mentioned earlier, inventions and new advancements in technology were making housework less arduous. By 1920 more than half the homes in the country had electricity, which enabled many housewives to begin to take advantage of an ever-increasing array of new appliances—electric irons, washing machines, refrigerators, sewing machines, toasters, and percolators. It has been argued, however, that rather than lessening the tasks, the new appliances actually "provided 'a silent imperative to *work*'" (Brown 1987, 108). As historian Ruth Schwartz Cowan has noted, although housework became "easier," it did not necessarily become less time consuming. It has been suggested that these new advancements actually served to increase the expectations placed on housewives and push standards for living conditions (in terms of household care and cleanliness) to a higher level. There seemed to be a new emphasis on good health and a heightened concern for the importance of a hygienic living environment, and a greater concern for proper diets, fewer calories, and the importance of vitamins. In fact, as various time studies have shown, housewives with the latest conveniences in the 1920s were spending just as much time on household duties as housewives without them. As one historian put it, it seems that "housework, like so many other types of work, expands to fill the time available" (Cowan 1976, 14–15).

At the same time, women's magazines, such as *Ladies' Home Journal*, *Good Housekeeping*, and *Woman's Home Companion*, and a legion of home economists were hard at work convincing homemakers that housework and cooking were the means by which to nurture the family and reaffirm self-worth. A spate of new textbooks, a surge in the number of new home economics courses in high schools and colleges, and advice columns in popular magazines inundated the wife/mother with tips on how to be efficient and economical. Home economists, led by the American Home Economics Association and the Bureau of Home Economics in the U.S. Department of Agriculture, increasingly pushed the idea of applying scientific management to the home and encouraged the housewife to see herself as a diligent, expertly trained, new-age professional. But these same home economists were also quick to remind her that it was important that she strive to be the expert hostess in order to promote her husband's career and realize her own social expectations. "The wife in the middle class who cultivated the right people, belonged to clubs, played bridge and outdoor sports, and made herself agreeable was the best helpmate to her husband" (Brown 1987, 105).

Other changes affected family life as well. As women watched their roles as producers give way to their new responsibilities as the primary purchasers of consumer goods, advertisers perceptively pitched their ads to them as the family's primary home manager and purchasing agent. One advertisement described a woman's new, expanded role by stating: "She is the active partner in the business of running a home. She buys most of the things which go to make home life happy, healthful and beautiful. Through her slim, safe fingers goes most of the family money" (Dumenil 1995, 129). As historian Dorothy Brown has noted, "As the emphasis changed from making a living to 'buying a living,' columns in women's magazines gave tips on managing budgets that would enable the prudent to plan and paradoxically scrimp and save in pursuit of the rising American standard of living" (Brown 1987, 106). Advertisements also encouraged women to identify themselves with the products they bought. But by exaggerating the importance of the choices women made in the marketplace, advertisers also gave women a false sense of freedom.

Child-Rearing

Child-rearing was another area of fundamental change within the home. As family size continued to shrink during the 1920s, especially among members of the urban, middle class, the nature of the family shifted toward what was known as the "affectionate family." The "new" family would become less patriarchal and more democratic. It would bind its members by affection rather than rules and place a greater emphasis on nurturing the individual potential of each child. Advice on expert child-rearing became a new cottage industry, with psychologists like John B. Watson, the leading American behaviorist, writing articles and books on the topic and emphasizing child-centeredness and individuality as the recommended focus of the new family. Watson's ideas served as the basis for the advice offered in the U.S. Department of Labor's best-selling twenty-five cent booklet *Infant and Child Care*. Family functions changed as well. Families continued to operate less as productive economic units as family life increasingly centered around consumption. At the same time, family-directed social and educational activities increasingly became absorbed by outside agencies.

Marriage and Divorce

Accompanying changes in child-rearing was a shifting conception of marriage and divorce. As a general trend in the early twentieth century, the age at which couples married was dropping, while the percentage of married couples was increasing. But the rate of divorce, which had been on the increase in the prewar period, rose even faster in the 1920s. In 1922, there were 131 divorces for each 1,000 marriages. Six years later, that number had risen to 166. By the end of the decade, slightly more than one in six marriages ended in divorce. Suggested explanations for this trend were numerous. Some experts pointed to the "mood of the age," with its "yeasty unrest" as being the primary cause (Buhle 2009, 511). Others blamed the "new" woman and her new freedom and independence. Another explanation suggested that as American society became more secularized, religiously sanctioned weddings (85 percent of those married in 1890 but only 63 percent of those married in 1923) became less important. As marriages increasingly took place in secular offices and away from the sanctity of the churches, it seemed as if marriage was becoming less sacred as an institu-tion. Yet another hypothesis offered the notion that couples in the 1920s were coming to view marriage as a source of personal satis-faction in contrast to the late nineteenth-century notion that mar-riage was a duty and a bad marriage was something to be endured. If economic difficulties arose or emotional demands intensified and compromised expectations, the decision to divorce simply became easier. Although the causes of divorce varied among middle-class and working-class families, there seemed to be a deepening gen-erational divide in both groups. As one contemporary observer put it, "The age believes in divorce, thinks reticence old-fashioned and false, holds that getting married is 'only getting married'" (Brown 1987, 124).

One individual who had something to say on the topic of mar-riage and divorce that attracted a good deal of attention in the 1920s was Ben Lindsey. Judge Lindsey, who had achieved a degree of notoriety during the Progressive Era as pioneer of the juvenile court system in Denver, Colorado, published two books during the decade in which he sought to save the troubled institution of mar-riage and reverse the climbing divorce rate. The books, *The Revolt of Modern Youth* (1925) and *The Companionate Marriage* (1927), were actually written by ghostwriter Wainwright Evans in collaboration with the judge. The first volume was a response to the heated reac-tions of parents and the influential members of churches and wom-en's clubs to reports of increased sexual activity among the young. In it Lindsey boldly advocated sex education, the dissemination of birth control information, and instruction on venereal disease. The second volume was even more provocative. Although Lindsey was influenced by British essayist and physician Havelock Ellis, the then current authority on human sexuality and the author of an ongoing seven-volume study, *Studies in the Psychology of Sex*, the idea of "companionate marriage," actually originated with Melvin M. Knight, a social scientist at Barnard College. As described by Lindsey, a companionate marriage (one based more on partnership than patriarchy) would be a legally binding union entered into for the purpose of companionship, with no intention of having chil-dren. It would allow men and women to live together before mar-riage and enjoy sexual relations. Couples could separate by mutual consent at any time but only after a court of human relations had failed to reconcile their differences. The proceedings of the court in such cases would be in private. There would be no high-paid divorce attorneys. The arbitrary legal right of a wife to alimony would be abolished and awarded only when circumstances (if children were involved) justified it, while property rights in cases of separation would be determined based on the economic standing of both parties. A traditionalist at heart, Lindsey claimed to idealize the nuclear family and hoped to strengthen it by calling for the state to undertake "the education of youth in the art of love, the laws of sex and life, to better equip them for the serious duties of marriage and parenthood" (Borough 1968, 374). The judge tried to make a distinction between a companionate marriage and a trial marriage, but outraged religious and social conservatives were unable to see the difference.

The Importance of Sexuality in Marriage and the Change in Female Sexuality

One new trend that was becoming increasingly pronounced in the 1920s was the growing assumption on the part of experts as well as the general public that sex was a vital part of a good marriage. As a 1930 sociological study described the change, "After hundreds of years of mild complaisance to wifely duties, modern women have awakened to the knowledge that they are sexual beings. And with this new insight the sex side of marriage has assumed sudden importance" (Dumenil 1995, 131). Accompanying the new importance of sexuality in marriage was an equally significant change in female sexuality. In the Victorian era women were seen as chaste and "pure." Lacking sexual natures, so the argument went, they made no demands under the marriage relationship. Women fulfilled their passive roles by submitting, either to satisfy their husband's sexual desires or to conceive. Contraception changed this relationship and the woman's position in the family by enabling a new equality in marriage roles. But the use of contraception carried with it distinctions based on class. One study done in 1925 found that among young married women between the ages of twenty-five and twenty-nine with one child, approximately 80 percent of middle-class women but only 36 percent of poorer women used contraception. But for an increasing number of women, freedom from prior constrictions meant that they could now experience a fuller expression of their personality. As Paula Fass has noted, "In the twenties, sex for married women was no longer a matter of submission but a basic expression of personal right. . . . In large part, the sexual revolution of the twenties was not a revolt against marriage but a revolution within marriage, and as such it recharged

the momentum toward marriage as the consummation of love."
According to Fass, dating became sexually oriented as well, but it
was actually restrained as couples tended to look ahead to sex and
marriage. "The result," she noted, "was sexual exploration without
sexual consummation, with the corollary that intercourse between
engaged or 'serious' couples was both much more likely to occur
and more acceptable" (Fass 1977, 73, 75).

Birth Control

One individual who pioneered in making birth control more
acceptable and available was Margaret Higgins Sanger. Deeply
affected by her mother's death at age forty-nine from tuberculosis, Sanger was convinced that her mother's tragic death was the
result of being worn out from the effects of childbearing and raising eleven children. Sanger believed that control over childbearing
was an essential factor in freeing women from domination by men
and that labor and economic reforms would do little for women
without sexual reform. Sanger, with training as a nurse, began to
share her philosophy on birth control and provide explicit information about contraception in two publications that appeared before
the war—a journal called *Woman Rebel* and a brief pamphlet entitled *Family Limitation*. Her basic argument was that women who
were financially secure had access to effective contraception and
safe abortions but that poor women did not. Trapped in a vicious
cycle, poor women would continue to have unwanted pregnancies
that they would increasingly be unable to support. For her views,
Sanger was charged with violation of the so-called Comstock Law,
which deemed the publication of information on contraception
to be pornographic. As a result, Sanger's publications fell under
the existing ban that outlawed the mailing of lewd, lascivious, or
obscene literature. After the publication of *Family Limitation*, Sanger
fled to England in 1914 to avoid jail. It was there that she met British sexologist Havelock Ellis, who supervised research that she was
doing on sexuality and contraception at the British Museum. At
Ellis's suggestion, Sanger traveled to the Netherlands where she
spent two months visiting birth control clinics run by midwives.

After her return to the United States in 1915, Sanger and her sister fell afoul of the law for operating a birth control clinic in the
Brownsville section of Brooklyn, a poor immigrant neighborhood.
Although the clinic was only in operation for ten days before the
police shut it down, 464 women visited. Arrested and convicted,

Margaret Sanger spent thirty days in the workhouse. She appealed her conviction by arguing that the law was unconstitutional, in that it forced women to risk death in pregnancy against their will. Although the judge did not overturn Sanger's sentence, he did alter the meaning of the law by ruling that licensed physicians could prescribe contraceptives to married women in order to prevent or treat disease. The decision convinced Sanger to join forces with the male-dominated medical profession and abandon her previous direct-action approach through clinics run by midwives and nurses. Her decision, however, also had the effect of limiting easy access to birth control only to patients who could afford to have private doctors.

In November 1921 Sanger organized the first national birth control conference in New York City. Capitalizing on the momentum gained from the conference, Sanger formed the American Birth Control League (ABCL) in December 1921, remaining as the organization's president until 1928. As the decade progressed, Sanger continued to write and lecture on birth control as the source of freedom for women. In doing so, she increasingly directed her advice at middle- and upper-class women who appeared keenly interested in learning about methods that would allow them to control reproduction and in exploring eroticism. Influenced by Havelock Ellis's romantic view of sexuality and his belief in sexual liberation, Sanger argued that birth control made sex "a psychic and spiritual avenue of expression" (Dumenil 1995, 133).

At the same time, Margaret Sanger also found herself being drawn to the topic of eugenics. Eugenicists looked to improve the human race through heredity or better breeding. Those attracted to the eugenics movement during the Progressive Era had been drawn by the argument that the superior white, Anglo-Saxon race was committing a form of racial suicide by not producing enough offspring. In her 1922 book, *The Pivot of Civilization,* Sanger lamented "the lack of balance between the birthrate of the unfit and the fit." Two years later in an article entitled "The Case for Birth Control," Sanger commented: "We see that those parents who are least fit to reproduce the race are having the largest number of children; while people of wealth, leisure and education are having small families." But where the eugenicists tended to want more children from the rich rather than fewer children from the poor, Sanger and her organization "sought first to stop the multiplication of the unfit" (Brown 1987, 116). In joining with the eugenicists Sanger brought the cachet of "science" and a good deal of monetary support to the ABCL, but in doing so she appeared to abandon her initial concern for the poor, and later arguments about freedom and romance for women, to join in a much broader discussion of racial and ethnic inferiority that was so much a part of the emphasis on social control during the 1920s.

The Cinematic Image of Womanhood

Caught up in the discussion of the changing nature of womanhood, female sexuality, and marriage were Hollywood's film producers. As self-appointed custodians of social change, the studios attempted to project a new image of womanhood in film during the 1920s but could never completely ignore the staying power of traditional values. Young female stars in the 1920s, like Clara Bow and Joan Crawford, increasingly personified the new woman with an exuberance of freedom, energy, and independence to accompany their sexual attractiveness. They also had to have what British novelist Elinor Glyn called "It," an inexplicable charisma or sexual attraction akin to animal magnetism. The plots that featured such stars evoked the new sexuality, with risqué scenes designed to titillate fans. As one movie advertisement put it, viewers could expect to see "beautiful jazz babies, champagne baths, midnight revels, petting parties in the purple dawn, all ending in one terrific smashing climax that makes you gasp." But there were limits to such revelry. Adultery and promiscuity were rarely condoned in the movies. As one historian has noted, "Movie adulteresses invariably paid for their sins, and heroines ultimately resisted temptation and were rescued by marriage or renewal of their marital commitment. . . . The purveyors of mass culture recognized changing sexual morality and, moreover, promoted it, but they nonetheless reveal a persistence of traditional values, especially the double standard" (Dumenil 1995, 134).

Middletown

One of the richest and most complete pictures of daily life in an American community in the 1920s has come from Robert and Helen Lynd, two Columbia University sociologists. Looking to analyze a contemporary American community that they felt would be representative of the changes taking place in American society by the late 1920s, they selected Muncie, Indiana. Muncie, a medium-sized, midwestern city of approximately 35,000 inhabitants, was in the process of being transformed from a commercial center for the surrounding rural countryside into a modern, manufacturing city. In an effort to limit the variables necessary for their assessment of social changes taking place, the Lynds made the conscious decision of choosing a city with little ethnic or racial diversity. Having said that, what the Lynds accomplished remains a notable achievement that captured changes impacting the economy, the nature of work, leisure, religion, sexuality, and the family, as well as the value adjustments accompanying those changes. They called their study *Middletown* (1929).

Central to any such sociological study is the family, and the trends uncovered by the Lynds in Muncie match closely the social trends about which others have generalized in a broader context. The Lynds discovered that families in Muncie were shrinking in size (from 4.6 persons in 1890 to 4.2 in 1900 to 3.9 in 1910 to 3.8 in 1920). They also found that a smaller percentage of the sample studied were unmarried in 1923 than in a generation earlier and that couples were marrying at a younger age. The reasons given to explain the data included increased opportunities for wives to supplement the family income by working, the diffusion of knowledge on contraception, the increased tendency for couples to engage in leisure-time pursuits than in a generation earlier, and the greater ease of dissolving a marriage and the reduced social stigma attached for doing so. On this last point, the Lynds noted that, as the population of Muncie increased by 87 percent between 1890 and 1920, the divorce rate more than kept pace—rising from eighteen divorces for each one hundred marriage licenses issued in 1895 to twenty-five per one hundred in 1909 to fifty-four in 1918 to thirty-three in 1920 to fifty-five in 1922 to forty-two in 1924. They also found that the increasing number of women working was less likely to continue in an unsatisfactory marriage relationship. And, as the Lynds noted, the divorce process seemed to be getting easier. A commonly heard remark in 1920s' Muncie, in stark contrast to a generation earlier, was that "Anybody with $25 can get a divorce" (Lynd and Lynd 1956, 121).

The Lynds also examined the topic of birth control and noted: "Traditionally, voluntary control of parenthood is strongly tabooed in this culture, as is all discussion of sexual adjustment involved in mating, but this prohibition is beginning to be somewhat lifted." However, the Lynds were surprised to find such divergent attitudes toward contraception between different groups (classes) of people living in the same community. In their sample, every one of the twenty-seven women defined as being in the business class used or believed in the use of some method of birth control and accepted it as standard practice. At the same time, however, less than half of the seventy-seven working-class wives studied said they used any means of birth control. The Lynds concluded that the behavior of the community on this topic presented "the appearance of a pyramid. At the top . . . the use of relatively efficacious contraceptive methods appears practically universal, while sloping down from this peak is a mixed array of knowledge and ignorance, until the base of ignorance is reached." At that point, they noted that fear and worry over pregnancy "frequently walk hand in hand with discouragement as to the future of the husband's job and the dreaded lay-off" (Lynd and Lynd 1956, 123, 125).

The Lynds also gave a great deal of attention to the topic of child-rearing. What they found was that parents were having increased difficulty holding their children to established "sanctions" or norms and in keeping up with the "shifting of the sanctions themselves" (Lynd and Lynd 1956, 146). As radios, movies, and automobiles transformed the culture of the young, the values of restraint and self-denial that had directed their parents' generation gave way. The constantly multiplying opportunities for contacts outside the home worked to undermine parental authority as well. As one historian has commented: "Young women whose mothers had entertained suitors on their back porches, within parental earshot, were now 'dating' far from home, lured by a growing array of commercial entertainments and abetted by the automobile" (Rosenberg 1992, 92). With educational enrollments on the rise, young men and women increasingly spent time with those their own age in either high school or college. As a result, their behavior was being shaped more by their peers than by their parents.

As the importance of the home in the life of the young diminished, parents found they were confronted with a new problem (described as "early sophistication"). Mothers of both the business and working classes detected a greater frankness between the sexes and a greater assertiveness on the part of girls. The Lynds noted that nine out of ten of boys and girls of high-school age surveyed said they attended "petting parties," while the remarks of mothers seemed to confirm the trend—"Girls," said one, "are far more aggressive today. They call the boys up to try to make dates with them as they never would have when I was a girl." "Girls have more nerve nowadays," said another, "look at their clothes!" (Lynd and Lynd 1956, 140). Despite the difficulties and the apparent widening gap between parents and children, the Lynds found that many Muncie mothers, especially among the business class, were more likely to devote a part of their increasing leisure to their children. At the same time, however, working-class wives found that the pressures of outside work or the burden of unending housework duties prevented them from giving the same kind of time and attention to the daily lives of their children.

THE AFRICAN AMERICAN EXPERIENCE

The Great Migration

Ironically, in seeking to select a relatively homogeneous community in which to gauge the trend toward "modernity," the Lynds excluded an increasingly important factor in the making of modern society—its pluralism. One of the truly remarkable features of the 1920s was the continued exodus of hundreds of thousands of African Americans from the South to the North, from the countryside to the city. Historians have come to call this demographic shift the Great Migration. Black Americans had been leaving the South since Reconstruction, but during the years surrounding World War I the process accelerated. Between 1915 and 1918, roughly 500,000 African Americans left the South for Harlem and other major urban-industrial centers in the North. Another 700,000 black migrants from the South followed during the 1920s. The boll weevil infestation of the southern cotton crops prior to the war and the elimination of the European market for southern cotton with the outbreak of the war caused a precipitous drop in cotton prices and the impoverishment of southern cotton farmers, especially black tenants and sharecroppers. When the outbreak of World War I effectively ended European immigration, the demand for workers increased. War production offered new economic opportunities to men and women who were bold enough to move North and try to remake their lives. Pushed out of the South by poverty, discrimination, and persistent racial violence, and pulled to the North by the promise of jobs, better education, and more freedom, blacks increasingly decided to make the move. Often the balance of those who came North shifted—between men and women, between young and old, between individuals and families both nuclear and extended. No matter how they came, the dominant idea was to reconstruct the family and join neighbors, the very people with whom they had lived and worked. As historian Ira Berlin noted:

> In some places, entire communities mobilized, forming emigration clubs, sharing knowledge, sending a few men and women ahead to establish a beachhead, and then—when all seemed secure—calling

for family and friends to join them. Church congregations and congeries of neighbors also collectively agreed upon how, when, and where
they would move. In various places, they transported themselves and
took up residence in the same neighborhood or even the same tenement building. For many, doing so fulfilled the entire purpose of the
move—maintaining the sanctity of familial and communal ties that
had been threatened by the transformation of the Southern economy.
(Berlin 2010, 171)

On arrival in the North, many blacks found their grand hopes for
a better life tempered by a persistent racism. In prewar America,
most in the North were relegated to what was known as "negro
work." In 1910, almost one-half of black male workers in Chicago
toiled at just four occupations—janitor, porter, servant, or waiter,
while approximately two-thirds of employed black women labored
as cooks, laundry workers, maids, and other domestic servants.
The jobs were hard, poorly paid, and often demeaning. With the
wartime emergency, the pressing need for labor allowed some
black Americans, both men and women, to break the color line
and find work on the assembly lines. But even here black workers
encountered racial bias on multiple fronts: from white employers
who thought black workers were inherently unqualified for more
skilled tasks, from white workers who resented working alongside
black men and women, and from white unions who barred black
workers from membership. Needing places to live as well as jobs,
the new arrivals quickly encountered residential segregation and
found themselves being channeled into areas that were already
densely populated by African Americans. Like immigrants before
them, however, ghettoization had an upside. Residents were able
to create exciting areas (cities within a city) where they could find
their own food, religion, and music. It has been said that jazz and
the blues migrated from the South along with the people. Many
of these urban enclaves attracted ambitious businessmen, preachers, novelists, musicians, and artists of all types. One of the most
famous of all these cultural meccas was New York City's Harlem,
which would foster an intellectual and cultural resurgence in the
Jazz Age known as the Harlem Renaissance.

Harlem

The era of the Great Migration from the South was also a
time of black immigration to the United States from other countries. Between 1910 and 1920, 33,464 people of African descent

emigrated to the United States. By 1920, most of the 73,803 foreign-born blacks living in the United States had come from the Americas, most notably from the West Indies and Cuba. And it was to Harlem in New York City that many came—over 200,000 by 1930, with almost one-fifth of that number coming from the West Indies. By 1930 those numbers had "spilled over Eighth Avenue to Amsterdam Avenue and the heights overlooking central Harlem as far south as 130th Street, moved north to 160th Street, and had begun to settle as far south as 110th Street" (Robertson et al. 2010, 98). Migration and segregation had forced up rents to a point where many families could only get by if they took in boarders. The resulting overcrowded apartments made some blocks in Harlem among the most densely populated in the city and contributed to rates of disease and mortality that were far above those of the city's whites. Employment opportunities were scarce, with only a small number of manufacturing jobs available for the fortunate. Blocked by unions and employers from obtaining skilled jobs, most blacks ended up doing low-paid service work. There was, however, another employment opportunity available to some blacks living in Harlem—numbers gambling. It was estimated that the illicit business employed about 1,000 men and women who collected bets for the "money-men" running the games. But the risk of arrest or of bodily harm from gangsters seeking to control the profits was great. The numbers racket, along with the thriving trade in illegal liquor and entertainment that drew many affluent whites uptown during Prohibition, worked to tarnish Harlem's image and link it with criminality.

Social Organizations

But Harlem as a "neighborhood" also offered a network of supports that enabled residents to establish and sustain their lives. The largest and most prominent social organization in Harlem in the early 1920s was Marcus Garvey's Universal Negro Improvement Association (UNIA). Influenced by the self-help philosophy of Booker T. Washington, Garvey had come to New York City from Jamaica in 1916 and founded the UNIA the following year. At quick glance, the UNIA looked like any other fraternal order with exotic titles, colorful uniforms, and elaborate ceremonies and parades. Like other fraternal orders, the organization also offered modest health insurance and death benefits. Looking to broaden its base, however, the UNIA established a separate women's auxiliary to enhance its appeal and used its own publishing house and newspaper, the *Negro World*, to communicate directly to ordinary black men and women.

Savvy as a publicist, Garvey used his new forum to craft a message that was simple and straightforward—black people were once a noble race and could be so again. In planting the idea of their collective potential, Garvey gave marginalized people hope and offered them the opportunity to experience the emotional satisfaction that would come through the organized promotion of racial solidarity. In the process, Marcus Garvey generated a true mass movement, something other black leaders and intellectuals at the time were unable to do. The UNIA soon had several thousand members in Harlem who rallied behind Garvey's call for black pride and self-determination. At the 1920 UNIA convention, 25,000 people turned out at Madison Square Garden to hear Garvey speak. Garvey's commitment to racial uplift had an economic component as well. Believing that blacks could expect no help from whites and must create their own economic institutions, the UNIA established the Negro Factories Corporation and was soon operating a string of cooperative grocery stores, a restaurant, a millinery store, a tailor shop, a company that produced phonographs, and a factory that made black dolls. As part of his larger plan to promote black capitalism and achieve economic independence, Garvey also envisioned establishing a triangular trade between black America, black Africa, and the black Caribbean on ships purchased through the UNIA-owned Black Star Steamship Line.

But the UNIA was only one of dozens of voluntary organizations that comprised Harlem's social fabric. Literally hundreds of small clubs gathered in apartments or meeting rooms to socialize, play cards, organize dances, and plan excursions. Popular fraternal orders like the Prince Hall Masons and the Elks set up a number of elaborate lodges in Harlem with auditoriums, meeting rooms, and practice facilities for talented local orchestras and bands. Religious organizations probably outnumbered voluntary associations with scores of church buildings and hundreds of storefronts and apartments that had been converted into houses of worship scattered throughout the neighborhood. Some of the larger churches also organized athletic and social clubs, offered classes in vocational training and art, and conducted their own choirs and musical groups. Harlem's vibrant YMCA and YWCA offered a similar range of social activities.

Family Life

Most studies of Harlem as a neighborhood in the 1920s have focused on the writers, artists, and intellectuals who comprised the Harlem Renaissance and the high society in which they moved. Pictures of the everyday lives of ordinary residents of Harlem appear only dimly in the historical record. One of the few books to focus on the black family was Herbert Gutman's influential *The Black Family in Slavery and Freedom, 1750–1925*. What Gutman discovered, contrary to previous studies, was how resilient the black family had shown itself to be over time and how adaptive it had been in maintaining cohesion despite the traumas associated with drastically changed circumstances and persistent economic hardship. In his brief examination of Central Harlem in 1925, Gutman took special issue with an earlier assertion made by historian Gilbert Osofsky in his "standard" account, *Harlem: The Making of a Ghetto*, that "the slave heritage, bulwarked by economic conditions, continued into the twentieth century to make family instability a common factor in Negro life." What Gutman found was that large numbers of black migrants to Harlem during the period of the Great Migration "adapted familial and kin ties . . . to life in the emerging ghetto" (Gutman 1976, 455).

The story of one family of the immigrants who moved to Harlem during this period was possibly the story of many and serves to illustrate the "adaptive capacities" of the black family. Malcolm Thompson had roots in the Caribbean island of Montserrat and a West Indian accent that suggested his area of origin. Leaving school at the age of fourteen, Malcolm joined thousands of other West Indians who migrated to Panama to work on the canal. It was there that he met Margaret Franklin, another native from Montserrat, and married her in 1911. By the time the canal was completed six years later, the couple had a son, George, and a daughter, Elizabeth, and decided, like many other West Indians, to emigrate to New York City. The couple had a third child in New York City in 1926, but the boy, named James, died at the age of two years. Malcolm found work as an unskilled laborer for a construction contractor based in the borough of Queens, while Margaret worked as a domestic servant. Both Malcolm and Margaret relied on day work rather than steady jobs, and Malcolm was able to pick up odd jobs during the winter to bolster their income. Patching together a regular income, the couple had managed to accumulate $100 in savings by 1928 and was able to maintain the same stable domicile (a four-room apartment on West 144th Street) for their first eleven years in New York City.

Malcolm and Margaret Thompson's immediate support group was rooted in their West Indian background. Three-quarters of the thirty-one households who occupied their apartment building had emigrated from the British West Indies. This bond also influenced Malcolm's limited involvement in organized social activities. He was a member of the Victoria Society, a West Indian social club with rooms on West 137th Street that held bimonthly dances and luncheons. When he attended church, it was an Anglican church on 140th Street where he would have also been in the company of West Indians. These activities, however, played only a limited part in his life. For the most part, Malcolm socialized with his wife and children by going to the movies or by visiting friends and relatives who lived nearby. Spending most of their time at home, the Thompsons frequently entertained family relatives and other visitors. Joining together in this fashion was typical of blacks living in Harlem in the 1920s. Such social ties helped immigrants like the Thompsons retain a sense of their identity through language, distinctive modes of worship, cuisine, and dress. But those same ties could create friction with the larger African American community. Color prejudice against dark Caribbeans could prove contentious as could the competitive resentments that surfaced when many West Indians showed prominence as business owners.

By the late 1920s life had started to become more difficult for the Thompsons. Employment was always hard to find and even harder to retain, while housing became ever more difficult to afford. In January 1929, while hoping to maintain four days of work each week on his construction job, Malcolm severely sprained his ankle and was sidelined from work for three months. With weekly payments from workmen's compensation, Margaret's wages obtained from sporadic employment as a housekeeper, savings, and assistance from Malcolm's brother, who was now lodging with them, the family managed to eke out a livelihood. The Thompson's story was not dissimilar from that of their neighbors. Almost half of the other families in their apartment building had been forced to take on boarders as early as 1920, a rate that rose to three out of five by 1925 and then to three out of four by the Depression year of 1930. An Urban League study done in 1927 found that one in every four Harlem households included a lodger, which was twice the rate among whites living in Harlem. Not all lodgers shared family ties with their renters, but many did come from the same community and as such were not total strangers.

Belt-tightening measures were not enough, however, to allow the Thompsons to keep up with their rent payments, and they were evicted from their home in April 1929. Borrowing money to move their few possessions, the family relocated to a six-room apartment only a couple of blocks away. Although they paid considerably more rent for the larger apartment, it was part of their survival strategy. They could now use the two extra rooms to take on additional lodgers and provide a source of additional income. Although Malcolm's brother moved elsewhere, several individuals and a married couple continued to rent the spare rooms over the next few years. Based on the available evidence, the constant presence of lodgers failed to cause any disruptions to the Thompson's family life.

A month after returning to work in April, Malcolm was injured again, this time when he badly damaged his finger. Then, when Margaret's rheumatism flared up, she had to give up paid work as a housekeeper. Malcolm eventually returned to work, but despite traveling all over Manhattan, Brooklyn, and Queens, he endured long periods of unemployment just as the Depression began to fasten its grip on New York City. This time, with the family experiencing severe financial difficulty, it was the Thompson's two teenage children who stepped in to help. George obtained work in a dress factory, and later as a scarf maker, while Elizabeth secured employment in a hat factory. Both children turned their earnings over to their parents to maintain the household, and, as if to recognize the shift in family roles, George was given a leading role in managing the family funds. When George and Elizabeth suffered periods of unemployment during 1932 and 1933, it was Malcolm, as head of household, who was able to keep the family going by obtaining work through Depression-era relief agencies. The ups and downs that impacted the Thompsons illustrate how one black family negotiated the challenges and drew support from neighbors and local organizations to sustain their lives during the 1920s.

THE MEXICAN AMERICAN EXPERIENCE

"Crossing Borders": Mexican Immigration

During the same period in which African Americans conducted the Great Migration from the South to the North, Mexican immigrants began their own mass migration across the border into the United States in equally great numbers. While there had been roughly 100,000 people of Mexican descent or birth living in the United States in 1900, that number soared to over 1.5 million by 1930. From 1910 to 1930 about 10 percent of Mexico's total population entered this country. The Mexican population of Los Angeles, in particular, tripled during the 1920s, growing from 33,644 to 97,116, while Los Angeles County had a Mexican American population of 167,000 (13.5 percent of the county's population). The Los Angeles barrio was the largest Mexican community anywhere outside of Mexico City. Some of these new migrants had been pushed out of Mexico by the economic, political, and social disruption caused by the Mexican Revolution in 1910, while others were lured North by jobs in industry and agribusiness. Many Mexican immigrants worked in the garment factories, furniture shops, and other small manufacturing plants in the south downtown area, or in agriculture in the citrus groves of Pasadena and on truck farms around El Monte east of the city. World War I created a labor vacuum and added an additional incentive for employers to encourage further immigration. Although this flow of immigrants slowed during the recession of 1921, it regained its momentum for the remainder of the decade as restrictions on European and Asian immigration forced American employers to turn again to low-wage workers from south of the border.

Los Angeles and the Urban Barrio

Los Angeles was a popular destination for these new migrants and often the gathering point for the reunification of extended families. Very often the head of a Mexican household would cross the border first, find a job, and, after getting settled, send for his wife and children. In many cases, brothers, sisters, parents, and cousins would soon follow, creating an extended family network that would help in dealing with the bewildering changes that came with moving to a new country as well as serving to help maintain native customs, values, and institutions from Mexico. The new Mexican American culture continued to be barrio centered and family oriented. This chain migration, however, placed tremendous pressures on existing Mexican communities. Urban barrios like Los Angeles quickly became overcrowded. As barrios rapidly expanded, newcomers no longer entered well-defined, tightly knit communities. Compounding problems was the fact that most Mexican migrants came to the cities from the ranks of the rural poor, placing added burdens on community resources.

The response of Anglo Americans to this burgeoning influx of new migrants seemed to follow three channels. First, there were the "restrictionists" who consisted primarily of organized labor and nativists who hoped to limit the migration. Organized labor, led by the American Federation of Labor, feared cheap labor competition, while nativists looked to further restrict immigrants whom they considered inferior and/or unassimilable. Opposing them were employers, primarily southwestern railroad, agricultural, and mining companies, but also western canneries and garment firms, who understood the economic advantage of utilizing cheap Mexican labor and wanted to allow Mexican immigration to continue unrestricted. A third group, who might be called the "Americanists," believed that society had an obligation to assimilate the Mexican immigrant into American society and, for the most part, hoped to improve the social treatment of immigrants in general. It might be noted that Americanists saw the immigrant question only from an Anglo perspective. In their minds, Mexican culture had little value. In fact, most Americanists regarded old traditions and customs as impediments to integration into American society.

Americanization Efforts

In California, the effort to Americanize Mexican immigrants was directed by the Commission of Immigration and Housing established in 1913. The centerpiece of its agenda was the creation of a home teacher program that would allow school districts to employ teachers to work in the homes of the pupils, instructing children and adults in matters relating to school attendance, use of the English language, proper health practices, food and diet management, the efficient performance of various household duties, and how to manage a budget. Young Anglo women who were recent graduates of the Los Angeles State Normal School taught the classes at either a local school or settlement house and supplemented that instruction with home visits. The goal was to create a home environment that would be well suited to the demands of the modern economy. Their efforts were aimed at the Mexican family but more specifically at Mexican immigrant women as the ones more likely to affect cultural change within the family. The decision to focus on mothers was based on the assumption that the Mexican immigrant father's role in parenting was minimal.

An American citizenship class. Although World War I reduced the numbers of new immigrants, it did not quell the apprehensions of many old-stock Americans who felt that non-English-speaking "foreigners" were unprepared to become good citizens. This growing sentiment led Congress to impose a quota system and also triggered an "Americanization" effort carried out by "patriotic" groups, public schools, and employers that provided English-language training as well as courses in civics and American history. (Library of Congress)

Through the mother, Americanists hoped to program the thinking of the second generation—the sons and daughters—of Mexican immigrant families.

In the end, these Americanization programs never achieved anticipated expectations. Only half-heartedly committed to the program in the first place, the administrators of the program never overcame problems relating to limited personnel and resources and could never cope with the volume of Mexican immigration. The barrios expanded so rapidly that teachers found it impossible to keep up with the number of new families, while newer areas of settlement were usually beyond the reach of established programs. Although the program undoubtedly produced some converts to "the American way of life," it failed to change the fundamental cultural practices of most Mexican immigrant families. There were at least two dominant reasons for this. First, Mexican immigrant mothers tenaciously clung to tradition. Second, naturalization rates continued to be very low. As one Mexican resident who did become a citizen commented, "Most of the Mexican people do not want to be American citizens, though. I can see why they don't. They all think that they will go back to Mexico." Community pressure often reinforced the reluctance to opt for citizenship. As one small businessman commented, "I have a store in the Mexican district. If I became a citizen of the United States the Mexicans wouldn't trade with me, because they wouldn't think that I was fair to them or loyal to my country" (Monroy 1999, 39).

The one area in which some change was apparent was in female employment. Textile factories, laundries, hotels, retail stores, and bakeries all seemed to have good success at recruiting Mexican women as employees. But here, too, it was economic necessity rather than any Americanization efforts that governed that choice. And, not too surprisingly, it was not the mothers but the unmarried, older daughters who had been born in the United States who sought work outside the home and whose wage labor was essential to the economic survival of their families. With the stock market crash of 1929 and the onset of the Great Depression, all attempts at Americanizing Mexican immigrants came to a halt. Instead of looking to assimilate them, American society now wanted to expel them. Under strong pressure from the government, about 500,000 Mexicans left the United States during the 1930s. About one-tenth of those individuals had resided in Los Angeles, which lost one-third of its Mexican residents.

Acculturation

The cultural values of the second generation did change during the 1920s, but those changes were more the result of the impact of American culture rather than the efforts of Americanists. And the change in cultural values among Mexican children born or raised in the United States often led to conflict with their more traditional Mexican immigrant parents.

Young Mexican women gained exposure to American culture in a number of ways. When they took jobs in canneries or packing houses, they often worked alongside female relatives and had the opportunity to develop friendships with other Spanish-surnamed employees. They could share their problems as second-generation ethnic women and chat about the latest fads, fashions, and radio and movie personalities. As one historian noted, "Seductive images encountered in movie houses and in fashion advertising offered compelling new models of behavior for Mexican youth." "In the new land, even with low wages, they could buy commodified things of great iconic value" (Monroy 1999, 165).

Movies, both Mexican and American, were a popular form of entertainment for young women of the barrio, and the ten-cent admission to the afternoon matinee offered them a chance to watch "Latin lover" Ramón Novarro or glamorous Latina actresses like Lupe Vélez and Dolores del Río and dream of becoming a Latina movie star. It was not uncommon to see older adolescents and their friends enjoying an afternoon outing to Hollywood, with the faint hope that they might be "discovered" as they walked down Hollywood and Vine. The influential Spanish-language periodical *La Opinión* promoted ethnic pride by publishing reviews of the latest Spanish-language films, concerts, and plays and was critical of movie stars who distanced themselves from their Mexican origins. However, *La Opinión* also closely followed the "Hollywood scene," kept readers up-to-date on the latest celebrity gossip, featured advice columns that offered instructions on behavior, carried advertisements for recordings to help immigrants learn the English language, and often featured models wearing clothing and makeup that offered a glimpse of the "New Woman."

Although Mexican immigrants retained their cultural traditions, parents constantly sought to find ways to counteract what they considered to be the alarming Anglo acculturation of their children. Knowing that their children were required to speak only English at school, many parents required that they speak only Spanish at home. Often living close to the Mexican border, many parents structured annual visits to Mexico into family schedules in an effort to maintain cultural ties. Parents often received assistance in their efforts to strengthen ethnic awareness through a number of youth-oriented community organizations for young men and women, while the Catholic Church played a role as well by organizing youth clubs and dances aimed at reinforcing an inwardness in cultural focus.

Within families, there existed something of a double standard. Young Mexican women, more than their male siblings, were expected to adhere to certain standards, and parents believed that it was their prerogative to regulate the actions and attitudes of their adolescent daughters. When teenagers did not agree with the established boundaries, tensions flared. One area of disagreement was over personal appearance—whether to bob one's hair or to wear makeup or to wear short skirts. One young girl recalled that when she was young her mother dressed her "like a nun" and mandated "no make-up, no cream, no nothing" on her face. Pushing against this control was Los Angeles-based *La Opinión* that carried sketches of the latest flapper fashions, ads for cosmetics, and testimonials from celebrities. As one historian noted, "The point remains that the Spanish-language press conveyed symbolic American norms and models to a potentially assimilable readership." Temptations were great. Young women in the city had to take only a short streetcar ride from their neighborhood to find escape in the form of dance halls, amusement parks, and other forms of commercial leisure. The generational struggle within the Mexican immigrant family during the 1920s was really one of boundaries. It has been said that Mexican American women engaged in "cultural coalescence" or, as one woman stated, "fusion is what we want—the best of both ways" (Ruiz 1998, 160, 161, 166).

Historian George Sánchez has commented that family life in the barrios of Los Angeles "ranged from conventional to experimental" and noted that these families often lived very close to one another. "Even within a family, certain members could exhibit behavior that others might consider inappropriate or 'un-Mexican.'" One's definition of freedom could be positive or negative depending on one's position in the family. One Mexican mother living in Los Angeles remarked that she had felt oppressed by the protective social customs when she lived in Mexico but that she now enjoyed the freedom to go wherever she wanted without any restrictions. But that same freedom-loving mother also criticized the behavior of young women in this country. "Liberty," she stated, had been "contagious" to her daughters, and this upset her very much (Sánchez 1993b, 143).

But the point of greatest contention within Mexican immigrant families came from a daughter's attitude toward young men. Whether in an urban or rural environment, young Mexican girls were closely chaperoned by a family member every time they went out to a movie, a dance, or even a church-related event. As historian Vicki Ruiz has noted, "While conjuring images of patriarchal domination, chaperonage is best understood as a manifestation of familial oligarchy whereby elders attempted to dictate the activities of youth for the sake of family honor. A family's standing in the community depended, in part, on women's purity." "Chaperonage triggered deep-seated tensions over autonomy and self-determination. 'Whose life is it anyway?' was a recurring question with no satisfactory answer" (Ruiz 1998, 159, 165). For young women seeking greater independence, an early marriage might offer a way to escape overly protective parents. One young woman from the

Belvedere community of East Los Angeles expressed anger that "as soon as I was sixteen my father began to watch me and would not let me go anywhere or have my friends come home. He was born in old Mexico but he has been here long enough to know how people do things." Another young woman from the same community, and feeling similar pressure, used her own knowledge of Mexican mores to gain control over her marital decision. "[My father] said when it was time for me to get married, he would have something to say about who my husband would be. So [my boyfriend] and I fixed that. I ran off with him and stayed with his family. We knew my father would make us get married then" (Sánchez 1993b, 144). For some, elopement often became the way to resolve the conflict between old and new modes of courtship.

According to historian Sánchez, the act of marriage only began "the process of redefining cultural values within the family. The actual nature of the union between husbands and wives varied tremendously, depending on the individuals' perspectives." Sánchez suggests that this flexibility of family roles in given social and economic circumstances has served to modify the image of the traditional Mexican family as a rigid patriarchy. The conclusion one might draw from the sociological data is that even though the barrio could be a "stifling and restrictive" environment for some with its emphasis on strong familial ties and adherence to cultural norms, it also served as a "haven" for Mexican immigrants and American-born Chicanos. It was a place where individuals could adapt to American society while still retaining in their daily lives "much of the flavor of Mexico" (Sánchez 1993b, 146, 150).

Document: Anne Martin, "Women and 'Their' Magazines" (1922)

The following selection is from an article written by Anne Martin, a notable early twentieth-century American reformer and ardent feminist. Her criticism of modern magazines, one that would be reprised more famously in the early 1960s by Betty Friedan in The Feminine Mystique, *is that they encouraged, even admonished, women to focus all their attention and energy on housekeeping, childcare, and marriage rather than aspiring to self-fulfillment or economic and social equality.*

"Women and 'Their' Magazines"

How are women[,] . . . ceaselessly preached at, admonished and advised by male "professional understanders," by male editors, and even by women themselves[,] . . . to be roused to demanding economic equality when "their" magazines, reaching millions, talk down to them in this fashion:

> Where there is the greatest freedom in the world for womenkind, she [the feminist] finds slavery and degradation. Where there is new freedom on an ever expanding scale, she strains a morbid fancy to raise bogies and banshees of man-tyranny that have been buried since the dawn of the nineteenth century.

No wonder many women, constantly administered raw narcotics like this on the editorial pages of their favorite magazines, and subtly blended doses of soothing syrup on its fiction pages, are lulled into forgetfulness of their contemptible economic status, and into complacency over their "new freedom."

Against the incubus of these so-called "women's" or "home" magazines, edited chiefly by men—in a few cases by women who obediently carry on the male tradition—how can our sex be roused to feel that they have not yet even the poor measure of "freedom" that men have? Against this incubus, how can mothers, the unpaid household drudges through the ages, be roused to demand that the economic value of their labor in the home be acknowledged by law and society, which acknowledgment would raise that labor to the status and emolument of a skilled trade, a profession? Authorities agree that the service of mothers in bearing and rearing the new generation is incalculably important, and that no civilization can progress farther than its women progress. Is it not then vital . . . that the status of all women be raised from that of "dependents" to "equals"? But millions of American women, although the vote is won, are still inside the four walls of their houses, "being supported," according to legal and social theory, while doing twelve and fifteen hours a day at unpaid labor. And "their" magazines continue to tell them in honeyed words to stay there.

I hold in my hand the only "organized" housewives' protest I have ever seen, in the form of a printed circular, which reached me by mail:

Membership Many Millions
Branch In Every State
Chapters In Every Community
Association
of
Overworked—Unpaid—Dishwashing
Housewives

Headquarters
By the Cookstove and the Cradle
With the Washtub Nearby

This circular protests against the housewives' 15-hour day and the 105-hour week, as contrasted with the industrial 8-hour day and the 44-hour week. It is signed "Sara Smith, President," and "Matilda Brown, Secretary," and was posted in Brooklyn. Let us hope that Brooklyn housewives will lead us to light.

But meanwhile, by all available evidence, it is the policy of the "home" magazines to keep women, or a majority of them, where they are, at the headquarters mentioned above. Just as these publications did not support equal suffrage until it became popular and inevitable . . . so they are today not urging women to take "the next step," equal economic and political opportunity. While their chiefly male, high-salaried editors are valiantly standing for the most daring doilies, the most revolutionary stitch in knitting, and the most risqué thing in custard pies, some women are fighting for this next step and others are . . . [demanding] motherhood endowment [a monetary allowance for mothers who are bringing up children] and birth control! But to read these magazines "dedicated to women's interests" you would not know any fight was on, except with the housefly, or cockroaches, or the washing-machine. Are the editors women haters? Not at all; I am told that their editorial policy, and even the trend of their fiction, is shaped by their advertisers. . . .

And so we have the development of these enormous "home" magazines, with circulations running into the millions, which are really little more than "trade journals" written for women in their "trade" as housewives. But they are obviously not designed to simplify or improve the life of the housewife. They make it more complicated and expensive of time, labor and money, with their . . . articles about "up-to-date" houses, plumbing and furnishings, guest-rooms and nurseries, fancy-work and fashions. . . .

When will women . . . see clearly enough to protest against the trademark, the brand of these magazines that are called theirs, the pictures of themselves as wives and mothers appropriately arrayed in housewives' uniforms, working oil, gas and electric stoves, furnaces, carpet-sweepers, washing-machines and clothes-wringers, or cooking and serving various foods—all the wares of the advertisers— with sweet, seraphic smiles on their faces? As if they never had, or wanted, another thought! When will they revolt against the stream of editorials, articles, and even fiction designed to keep them satisfied with these endless tasks and their inferior economic status?

Against the editorial policy of criticism or silence toward the vanguard of the woman's movement? Only by individual and organized protests . . . can any impression be made upon these "trade journals," which prosper on maintaining women as housewives—brakes and parasites on the woman's movement!

Source: Anne Martin. "Women and 'Their' Magazines," *New Republic* 32 (September 20, 1922): 91–93.

Document: Leta S. Hollingworth, "For and against Birth Control" (1922)

The following is a summary of the basic arguments put forth in two new books, one by Margaret Sanger and the other by Dr. Halliday G. Sutherland, on the topic of birth control. "Having heard the debate thus earnestly presented by both sides" reviewer Leta S. Hollingworth then turns the topic over in her own mind.

"For and against Birth Control"

Some of us remember how, in the days when we were "too young to understand," mothers of the neighborhood gathered with their sewing on the front porch to exchange confidences. As we played about, we heard terrifying words—the same words they used when they found things in traps—spoken in a whisper. . . . Evidently there was a snare that mothers couldn't escape. . . .

Of course we lived to learn that the terrifying words were vulgar—vulgar in the true sense of the term. Thus common people interpreted the phenomena of their lives. In late years that muted murmur of obstetrical anecdote has risen beyond the bounds of the front porch. Birth control has taken on the dignity of an issue, freely discussed by those who have command of language proper to public debate, as in the case of the two protagonists here brought together in review.

With regard to birth control, these two represent in clear-cut fashion the antipathetic standpoints referred to by Mr. [H. G.] Wells in his introduction of Mrs. Sanger. There exist side by side in our civilization "honest and intelligent people who regard birth control as something essentially sweet, sane, clean, desirable and necessary, and others equally honest and with as good a claim to intelligence, who regard it as not merely unreasonable and unwholesome, but as intolerable and abominable."

Dr. Sutherland represents the latter of these two attitudes. He earnestly declares that Malthus was wrong; that biological fertility does not tend to exceed the means of subsistence; that even if it does, we should still rely upon disease, war and "some natural law" to keep down the population; that famine and poverty are never caused by over-population; that the high death-rate in crowded countries is due to unfortunate customs, like infanticide, rather than to unrestricted birth-rate; that contraceptive methods cause fibroid tumors, sterility and neuroses; that birth control is contrary to the true nature of woman, who is a poor judge of what she really wants; and that birth control, except by abstinence, is a sin, being unnatural.

Mrs. Sanger goes over the self-same ground, but with a different outcome. . . .

The issue of birth control is to Mrs. Sanger paramount because uncontrolled breeding tends to overcrowd the means of living, thus bringing on famine and war; modern peoples can no longer regard war and disease as satisfactory means of holding population in check; over-crowding is the most potent cause of famine, unemployment, poverty, stupidity and ignorance; reckless breeding costs the lives of thousands of women annually, and cripples thousands more; the happiness of women and children depends on knowledge and control of the processes of population; and contraceptive methods are, therefore, not sinful, but highly ethical, and certainly no more unnatural than abstinence is.

Having heard the debate thus earnestly presented by both sides, we begin to think it over for ourselves. It seems unfair, even in a propagandist, that Dr. Sutherland should put the authority of his professional degree behind a statement that contraceptive measures produce sterility, fibroid tumors and neuroses, citing only desultory and possibly prejudiced opinions, without citing quantitative data upon which such a frightening statement should properly be based; and that he does not tell what he as a physician surely knows, since it is set forth in standard texts and journals of obstetrics, that child-birth kills thousands of women each year and injures thousands more. . . . Surely he knows that maternal mortality in childbirth is about two percent. But perhaps that, along with war and disease, is considered a natural and hence desirable method of keeping the female half of the population within limits.

One must object, also, to the logic involved in the argument that the high death rate in China is due to infanticide, and not to uncontrolled breeding. What, then, causes the custom of infanticide?

On the other hand, Mrs. Sanger, like a true propagandist, claims too much for birth control. Very large sections of the population, whom she most pities and plans to aid, will be unable to profit by knowledge, because they lack that "intelligence, forethought and responsibility," which Mrs. Sanger tells us are required to control conception by scientific methods. Human nature being what it is, education for birth control will not cure every ill from which we suffer in the body politic.

But one's thoughts keep going back to the mothers on the porch. . . . Why shouldn't Mrs. Sanger rest on that? Her equipment is unique for piercing clean through the smug fiction that all is beautiful in motherhood. She can alleviate the repressive taboo on mention of its agonies and fears. As an obstetrical nurse, she has seen scores of women undergo childbirth. She has heard what they say. . . . She has developed a power of speech to tell exactly what she has seen and heard, and she is brave enough to do it. Margaret Sanger's real contribution is that she proclaims aloud what women have been taught they must smother to whispers.

Source: Leta S. Hollingworth. "For and against Birth Control," *New Republic* 32 (October 11, 1922): 178.

2

ECONOMIC LIFE

PROSPERITY DECADE?

Histories of the 1920s have commonly portrayed the decade as a time of general prosperity. For the most part, that description is accurate as the economy produced an increasing output of goods and services and higher real wages for many while maintaining a low rate of inflation and relatively low unemployment. After the postwar recession of 1920–1921, the gross national product grew at a rate of about 2 percent per year. The annual average increase in prices was less than 1 percent from 1922 to 1929, and the yearly average unemployment rate never rose above 4 percent over the same period. Between the presidential inaugurations of Warren G. Harding in 1921 and Herbert Hoover in 1929, real per capita income (the total national income divided by population and adjusted for inflation) increased by roughly 30 percent. Americans also experienced a little more leisure time as the average number of hours spent on the job each week decreased from roughly 46 in 1919 to about 44 by 1929. Most Americans lived better in the 1920s than ever before.

As beneficiaries of a rising standard of living, Americans spent more of their personal incomes on recreation and leisure activities. During the 1920s, spending on amusements and recreation increased 300 percent. Spectator sports and entertainment drew huge audiences and became big businesses. On September 22, 1927, a crowd estimated to be near 145,000 paid $2.5 million to watch heavyweight boxing champion Gene Tunney successfully defend his title against challenger Jack Dempsey at Soldier Field in Chicago. Almost 50 million fans listened to announcer Graham McNamee call the fight on the radio. One year earlier, moviegoers spent ten times that amount at box offices across the country to watch one movie—*The Big Parade*. And with more money to spend, Americans went on a buying spree purchasing radios, refrigerators, and automobiles at an unprecedented rate. The growth of install-ment buying made these consumer goods available to many with small cash resources. Whereas the annual sale of durable goods to consumers had averaged $4.65 billion between 1909 and 1918, they averaged $7.06 billion between 1919 and 1929, a 52 percent increase.

Manufacturing industries increased their output by almost two-thirds during the decade, but because of a tremendous increase in labor productivity due to technological advances, the number of workers engaged in manufacturing grew by less than 1 percent between 1920 and 1930. The growth of the automobile industry was especially impressive. By 1929 the industry accounted for more than 12.5 percent of the dollar value of all manufacturing and employed more than 7 percent of all wage earners engaged in manufacturing. The impact of auto manufacturing on related industries like steel, rubber, oil, gasoline, and glass was such that it provided jobs for roughly 3.7 million workers. However, the often-celebrated prosperity of the 1920s did not reward all Americans evenly and actually failed to touch the lives of millions. Statistical averages often tend to even out glaring discrepancies. Although the data varies, it does appear that wages did move "gently upward" during the 1920s. Contrary to some textbook generaliza-tions, there was no sharp rise in wages, and that was certainly true in the manufacturing sector. In fact, according to one noted labor historian, earnings from wages during the 1923–1929 period were "characteristically stable, reflecting the surplus of labor and weak unions" (Bernstein 2010, 66). Another problem suggested by the available data was that so-called skill differentials (the difference in earnings between skilled and unskilled workers) widened dur-ing the 1920s.

This growing wage gap was indicative of a tendency toward a maldistribution of income in the United States in general, which grew progressively worse each year during the decade. According to a 1929 Bureau of Labor Statistics report, it required an income of $2,500 a year to maintain a decent standard of living for a family of four. But nearly 20 million families earned less than that. At the same time, 12 million families showed earnings of $1,500 or less, while 6 million families fell below $1,000—which meant that nearly half of the nation's families were struggling to make ends meet in an era of vaunted prosperity. Yet the number of Americans with incomes ranging from $3,000 to $5,000 nearly tripled between 1927 and 1928, while those with incomes over $1 million almost doubled. In 1929 the "combined incomes of 0.1 per cent of the families at the top of the scale were as great as those of the 42 per cent at the bottom" (Bernstein 2010, 63). Just as striking were the statistics on savings, with more than 21.5 million families at the low end of the economic scale recording no aggregate savings at all.

Although economic life was modernizing at a rapid rate and technological advances were impressive, many would have to wait much longer to realize the benefits. Looking at the glass as half-empty from the vantage point of 1930, 49 percent of households still did not have inside flush toilets, 70 percent did not own a vacuum cleaner, 76 percent were without a washing machine, 92 percent did not own a mechanized refrigerator, and almost one-third still did not have electricity. Those who suffered the most were those who worked in so-called sick industries—coal mining, textiles, railroads, shipping and shipbuilding, shoe and leather production, and farming. Coal mining was especially hard-hit as overproduction drove down prices. Compounding problems, other fuels like gas, oil, and hydroelectricity became more competitive, while automobiles and trucks began to replace railroads (while railroads themselves became more fuel efficient). New mining technology also reduced the need for workers. As a result, the number of miners still at work in the pits in 1929 was about one-fourth of what it had been in 1923. Similarly, the eight-hour day, which had been the standard after the war, began to collapse, and the number of miners working nine- and ten-hour days increased. Safety standards eroded as well. In fact, the period 1925–1929 was the only five-year span between 1910 and 1940 in which mine fatalities actually rose. According to the Bureau of Labor Statistics, average hourly earnings in bituminous coal fell by 23 percent between 1922 and 1929. And because most miners lived in isolated communities with almost no other alternative employment opportunities, economic hardship intensified for families in mining towns.

AGRICULTURAL WORKERS

The Prewar Boom

The segment of the population most noticeably passed over by the surge in affluence during the 1920s was the nation's staple-crop farmers, those who produced grains and cultivated cotton. But that had not always been the case. The first two decades of the century had been prosperous times for the American farmer, so much so that the period is often referred to as the golden age of agriculture. During that twenty-year period real farm income increased by 40 percent and the value of the average farm more than tripled. Swept up in the excitement, farmers eagerly embraced the market economy and intensified the production of commercial crops. With profits up, many farmers purchased machinery, land, fertilizer, and purebred livestock. They spruced up their homes with new carpets, draperies, and furniture, while many installed pumps in their kitchens to eliminate the burdensome task of carrying buckets of water from a well to the house (even though they were unlikely to have either indoor plumbing or a water heater), put in telephones, and purchased automobiles.

It was the automobile more than modern conveniences for the home that captured the imagination of those living in the countryside. By 1920 there were nearly two-and-a-half million cars in rural America, and more than 30 percent of farmers owned at least one. Even a decade of economic depression on the farm failed to slow purchases, and the number of cars in the countryside nearly doubled between 1920 and 1930. In 1930 a farmer was nearly twice as likely to own a car as a phone, four times as likely to have one as to have water in his house, and five times more likely to have a car than to have electric light. The popular choice of farmers was Henry Ford's Model T. It was affordable, costing about $240 in the early 1920s, and simple to repair. With its tight turning radius, high center of gravity, and light weight, the Model T was ideal for unpaved rural roads that were often rutted and muddy. The Model T made work easier and facilitated the marketing of crops. But it also increased mobility and was most important to farm families as a mechanism for leisure and an antidote for isolation. Sunday drives became commonplace, allowing families to visit friends; participate more easily in community social life; and move beyond local towns for recreation, cultural enrichment, and shopping. As young people quickly realized, the car also revolutionized dating on levels of privacy and social mobility. But even

The decade of the 1920s was one of booming industrial productivity, symbolized by Henry Ford's use of mechanization and innovative management to produce utilitarian vehicles at a fantastic rate. Costing about $240 in the early 1920s, the affordable Model T, as pictured in this 1923 image, was lightweight and simple to repair, while its high center of gravity made it ideal for unpaved roads that were often rutted and muddy. Sunday drives became commonplace. (Library of Congress)

these signs of rural prosperity were misleading. Urban material standards were still much higher, and urban life was perceived to be much richer. As a result, despite the material improvements in the countryside, young people continued to leave the farm for the city.

The paradox of rural-to-urban migration amid unprecedented agricultural prosperity continued during the 1916–1920 period as good economic times simply got better. Farm incomes continued to rise as did crop prices, and for one of the few times in history, farm incomes surpassed average urban incomes. Feeling flush, many farmers moved to modernize their farming operations. One important item of "new" investment was the gasoline-powered tractor. A tractor could make up for the scarcity of labor experienced during wartime, free up land that had been used to feed draft animals, and allow for the production of more income-producing crops. Tractors, however, were expensive, and although fewer than

4 percent of farmers owned one at the end of the war, almost everyone agreed that they were the future on the farm.

The Postwar Bust

The agricultural boom continued for a brief period after the war, but the correction eventually came. Commodity prices dropped sharply in the summer of 1920 and remained stagnant for the remainder of the decade. In 1919 wheat had sold for $2.19 per bushel, potatoes for $2.20 a hundredweight, and cotton for $.35 per pound. Ten years later those same three commodities could fetch prices of only $1.05, $1.29, and $0.17. In addition, agricultural exports shrank as European countries recovered from the war and, on the domestic front, changes in the national diet and styles affected commodity prices. The trend among consumers was toward more fruits, vegetables, and dairy products and away from fats, starches, and carbohydrates. The new emphasis on slimness meant fewer potatoes and loaves of bread. With the onset of Prohibition in 1919, the demand for barley and other grains fell off. Shorter skirts and new synthetic fabrics like rayon curbed the demand for cotton and wool. It took less than one-half the amount of material to make a dress in 1928 than it had in 1918. Although some experts have argued that commodity prices only fell to their prewar levels and that the "artificial" spike in prices during the 1916–1920 period makes the decline in commodity prices look worse than it really was, there was another factor to consider. Simply put, the prices farmers paid for goods as consumers did not decline to the same extent as the prices they received as producers. Real incomes were less. By 1925 the average rural income was only 70 percent of that in the city. Producers of basic farm commodities demanded that the government come to their assistance but, for the most part (see Chapter 5), such help was not forthcoming during the 1920s. As a result, farmers were left to cope with their economic problems on their own.

A good many progressive-minded farmers thought that the most effective way to deal with their economic plight was to make their farms more productive. Urged on by many farm management specialists, they were encouraged to increase productivity through mechanization, specifically by purchasing a tractor. As a result of this campaign, the number of tractors on farms increased from 246,000 in 1920 to 920,000 in 1930 and agricultural productivity jumped by 18 percent during the decade. But tractors were expensive, and only a minority of farmers could use them cost effectively. In 1920 the U.S. Department of Agriculture estimated that a minimum of 130 acres was necessary to make a tractor pay, but three-fifths of American farms were under 100 acres. Ironically, although tractors increased the productivity of some, they intensified economic pressures on others. Especially pinched were middle-sized farmers whose farms were simply not large enough for them to capture the economies of mechanization. Some tried to increase the size of their farms, but many had to take out new mortgages to do so. Others simply gave up and sold out. In the end, although the average farm increased in size from 145 acres to 157 acres during the 1920s, there were 160,000 fewer farms at the end of the decade than at the start. While the numbers of farmers working fewer than 50 acres and the number tilling 175 acres or more rose, the number of farms 50–175 acres decreased by 206,000. It was the middle range that was being squeezed out in what would become the pattern in rural America for decades to come.

Rural Out-Migration

Farm failures and mechanization, coupled with the overall attractiveness of cities, served to increase the pace of rural out-migration, causing an absolute rural population decline of 1.2 million people between 1920 and 1930. Those most likely to leave were the young. As a result, 52.6 percent of farm operators were over the age of forty-five in 1930 in contrast to 48.1 percent ten years earlier. And out-migration had social consequences. As young couples with children left, attendance in churches declined, as did the number of students in schools, while the youthful vitality of rural society suffered as well. Out-migration also put added pressure on small-town businesses that were already under assault from the mail-order catalogue business and "automobility." In addition, community ties weakened as mechanization rendered traditional neighborhood work-sharing practices obsolete and depopulation eroded old social networks. Just as significant, out-migration undermined rural morale, instilling a sense of abandonment in those who remained. As historian David Danbom has poignantly noted, "The old forms of neighborhood life held on, but they lost effective meaning and local people became less reticent about letting them go" (Danbom 1979, 128).

Farm Tenancy and Sharecropping

The agricultural depression of the 1920s forced many farmers off the land, but it also intensified economic hardship and deprivation for many who stayed. In an effort to hold on to their land, many farm men took second jobs. But even these desperate efforts were often not enough to forestall bankruptcy. Many who lost their farms tried to keep going as tenants. As a result, the rate of farm tenancy, the new symbol of rural failure, pushed relentlessly upward as the number of white tenants increased by 200,000 during the 1920s. "Tenancy" was a term that was commonly used to describe anyone, excluding wage laborers, who worked someone else's land. Most commonly, a tenant was someone who paid cash rent and provided his own tools and work stock (a mule perhaps), feed for his animals, and seed. In most cases, he lived in a house on the farm as part of the arrangement. He kept what he, his wife, and his children produced for sale or to feed the family. A sharecropper, in contrast, was someone whose tools, feed, and seed were supplied by the landlord (costs deducted after harvest) to whom he turned over his crop for a share (from a third to a half) of what he produced. In a region blighted with poverty-stricken farmers, the average annual gross agricultural income in ten southern states in 1927 was only $609 in contrast to $1,611 in the rest of the nation.

One aspect of this backward and exploitative economic system was that there was no free market for labor. In theory, farmworkers could move from county to county or from one landowner to another and seek better terms, but, in reality, sharecroppers and tenants were most often so heavily indebted to the landlord that they were trapped until they could pay off their debts. In most cases, farmworkers were forced to purchase supplies at inflated prices either from the landlord's company store or from a local store owner or "furnishing" merchant who required the farmer to put up his future crop as collateral for the supplies he agreed to take on credit. A holdover from the nineteenth century, this "crop-lien" system was essentially a form of debt peonage. Sharecroppers and tenants were totally at the mercy of the landlord. Sharecroppers could be evicted at any time without cause, while tenants could have their rent contracts changed from season to season. Because this type of labor was so cheap, few landlords bothered to mechanize. In 1930, there were approximately 1,000 tractors in the entire South in contrast to 11,000 in the state of California. The productive capacity of an Iowa farmer was seven to eight times that of a southern farmer. In the words of one observer, "The field tools used by the typical tenant farmer would not seem strange to Moses and Hammurabi" (Gordon 2009, 266).

MEXICAN LABORERS: MIGRANT WORKERS

Another often overlooked form of farm labor involved migrant workers. During the 1920s much of this work was done by Hispanics in the Southwest. The development of agriculture in the Phoenix, Arizona, area in the 1910s and 1920s was closely linked to the labor and migration of Mexican workers. Central to the farming economy in the Salt River valley was alfalfa production followed by grain production (corn, barley, and sorghum), the dairy industry, and fruit and vegetable cultivation. Because of the favorable climate, Arizona's growing season was more or less a year-round operation and the need for sufficient farm labor a constant concern. Farming in the Salt River valley was still largely based on subsistence and the regional marketing of crops, and, as such, it favored having a large population of year-round farmworkers on hand. Mexican farmhands comprised a large part of the year-round resident labor that supported these local farming operations (the migratory farm labor that became more popular in the later 1920s and 1930s had yet to gain a foothold).

The completion of the Roosevelt Dam in 1911 changed the agricultural equation in the Salt River valley, in that the new water supply allowed for the irrigation of large-scale production of cash crops like cotton, citrus, and lettuce, which tremendously increased the demand for migrant labor by the 1920s. The great cotton boom of the late 1910s (farmers planted 72,000 acres across the valley in 1918) generated the first large-scale exodus of Mexican laborers to the Salt River valley. To meet the seasonal labor requirements for this crop, cotton farmers turned to the Arizona Cotton Growers Association (ACGA) for help in raising the number of laborers needed for the cotton harvest season. With the high wartime demand for cotton and a shortage of young men to pick it, the ACGA sent labor recruiters into Mexico. But there was a problem. The Alien Contract Labor Law of 1885 and Section 3 of the Immigration Act of 1917 made it all but impossible to import contract labor from outside the United States. To get around this problem, agricultural and railroad interests, along with large landowners, successfully lobbied for an exception that would allow for the importation of contract workers in the event of a labor shortage. Beginning with the 1918–1919 growing season, special trains brought thousands of migrant cotton pickers and their families into the United States from towns along the Mexican border. From 1918 until the end of the 1920–1921 growing season, growers hired 35,000 Mexican laborers to harvest cotton. The growers spent an estimated $325,000 on recruitment efforts, while they rushed ahead to plant a record number of 180,000 acres of cotton in 1920.

Despite predictions that 1920 would be a good year for cotton, the 1920–1921 season was a disaster. The price of cotton dropped from a high of $1.25 per pound to a low of 17 cents per pound. The end of the war and a change in the method of manufacturing tires (in which cotton had been a key component) caused the bottom to drop out of the market. Because of the low prices, many growers did not even bother to harvest their crop. Without a sustainable price for their commodity, growers simply let their cotton workers go, despite the fact that these Mexican migrant workers had been hired under contract. The Mexican Consulate in Phoenix estimated that 15,000–20,000 migrant workers were left stranded in the valley with no income, food, or shelter and no way to get home. Appeals to the ACGA fell on deaf ears as the association looked to abandon responsibility for returning these workers to Mexico. Mexican officials and the ACGA eventually arrived at an agreement whereby the association would provide free train transportation and reimbursement for unpaid wages, but the ACGA reneged on its promises. Left with no choice, Mexican President Álvaro Obregón released funds to allow for the return of the stranded workers.

An interesting situation soon followed that was to become a pattern in the employment of migrant workers. During the economic recession of 1921, Americans in the Southwest, in particular, began to blame Mexicans for a spike in the crime rate and raised demands that all Mexicans be repatriated (deported). At the same time, local politicians and patriotic groups called for economic and racial restrictions. But as soon as the 1921 recession eased and the 1920s boom began to pick up steam, the demand for Mexican labor quickly returned. Hiring agencies began doing a brisk business placing Mexican immigrants in jobs. It was estimated that Mexican workers made up 85 percent of all railroad track workers; 50 percent of the cotton pickers; and 75 percent of the sugar beet, fruit, and vegetable laborers. It was only with the onset of the economic depression at the end of the decade that growers again switched gears and began hiring American migratory workers (primarily from Oklahoma, Texas, and Arkansas) to meet their needs for the annual cotton harvest (the cotton economy had rebounded after the earlier recession and remained the primary moneymaking crop for area farmers). In 1930 official prohibitions basically stopped the entry of Mexican nationals into the United States for any sort of work.

Living Conditions

Mexican migrant workers in Arizona and elsewhere often lived in growers' camps. In the Phoenix area, these might often be in cheap auto courts on the outskirts of town or in shanty towns thrown together along rural roads or canals. Some of the families working in the cotton fields lived in large tents with hand-swept, hardened dirt floors. One small ranch in the area that grew alfalfa and cotton offered modest services for its workers. Workers could obtain water from the ranch and purchase milk for 10 cents a quart from the owners. Local farmers would occasionally hire Mexican girls from the camps to work as domestics. Local owners also employed recruiters to bring Mexican families to live and work for longer periods on their farms. Unlike other migrant workers who moved on to other states with the next crop, they lived in small houses and raised their children. One family recruited in 1918 settled on a ranch with four other farmworker families. Their small home had no cooling or heating, no glass in the windows, and no running water or electricity. The family cooked on a wood-burning stove, used an outdoor privy, and showered in a canvas tent. Many migrants who came to the area for short- or long-term work often drifted into the growing barrios in Phoenix and became permanent residents.

In neighboring California, Mexicans comprised the majority of farmworkers in 1920. By the late 1920s there were 386,000 Mexicans, making up 84 percent of the farm labor workforce in Southern California and 56 percent in the San Joaquin Valley. Paul Taylor, an agricultural economist and one of the few individuals doing research on migrant labor in the 1920s and 1930s, found in 1928, a year of excellent harvests, that Mexican farmworkers earned on average 35 cents an hour. Almost every member of a Mexican migrant family worked in the fields and children rarely attended school. Families lived in shacks, tents, army-like barracks, or *jacales*—huts with thatched roofs and walls that consisted of stakes driven into the ground close together and plastered with mud. They obtained their water from streams or wells dug by the growers that were often located close to privies or garbage dumps. Infectious diseases were common. Workers were often paid in scrip, which could be exchanged for goods only at higher-priced company stores. At the mercy of recruiters and growers, they were often deceived— promised one wage but paid another, promised more days of work than were available, or simply cheated by having hours shaved from their time sheets. Workers might not know from one day to the next if work would actually be available.

NON-FARMWORKERS

Workers struggled along with farmers during the 1920s. During the early days of World War I, as American industry began to assume the role of supplier for the Allied war effort, American radicals, most of whom opposed the war, came under increased attack for being unpatriotic. As the United States became directly involved in the war, those attacks intensified creating an environment where patriotism (defined as being prowar) and Americanism (increasingly defined as being antiradical) had become contested ideals. The main targets of the critics were the Industrial Workers of the World (IWW)—a radical labor union advocating an economic system in which workers would control the means of production—as well as antiwar socialists, and labor advocates who favored the idea of industrial unionism (organizing workers by industry rather than by craft or skill). In a war-related effort to mute the radical voice, the government passed a series of laws that limited free speech and dissent.

The "Red Scare" and Labor

Just as unsettling for many in government and industry was the Bolshevik Revolution that occurred in October 1917, overthrowing the Russian Tsar and establishing the world's first socialist state. Although U.S. leaders talked a good deal in public about the potential for revolution in this country, their rhetoric often masked their real fear, which was the threat of industrial unionization. The current climate provided American businessmen with a convenient justification to crush any uprising of American workers. If labor organizers became overly aggressive, they could be easily discredited in the eyes of a nervous American public by simply being labeled as Communists or, more commonly, Bolsheviks. This time of antiradical paranoia is known as the "Red Scare."

1919: The "Year of Unrest"

Shortly after the armistice, frustrated American workers began to make what they saw as deferred demands for pay raises (to keep up with the soaring rate of inflation), shorter hours, and improved working conditions. This led to an outbreak of strikes that has made 1919 the "Year of Unrest." During the course of that year almost eight-and-one-half million workers took part in 3,600 strikes. Sixty thousand clothing workers, 35,000 shipyard workers, 450,000 coal miners, and even three-fourths of Boston's 1,500 policemen who were forbidden to form a union, all went out on strike. It was in the steel industry, however, that the battle lines between capital and labor were most firmly drawn and there that the pattern of industrial relations for the next decade was set.

During the war steel workers saw themselves as patriotic producers and expected to be rewarded for their efforts. Instead, they found themselves forced to work twelve-hour days and six-day workweeks. Increases in the cost of living during the war intensified dissatisfaction as it minimized the effect of prior wage gains and pushed many workers below the minimal level of subsistence. In the late summer of 1919 an organizing committee led by William Z. Foster presented U.S. Steel Company president Elbert Gary with a list of demands that included the right of collective bargaining, the eight-hour day, and wage increases. Gary rejected all their demands. When pleas to President Woodrow Wilson to intervene in their behalf failed, 350,000 steel workers voted to go out on strike.

Strike leaders were on the defensive from the start. Negative public reaction to the Red Scare and the high level of strike activity allowed steel plant owners to link the organizing drive to "bolshevism" and to paint Foster, a former member of the IWW, a "red." Exaggerated newspaper accounts portrayed the steel districts as seedbeds of revolution. Owners soon joined in with their own propaganda campaign, which alleged that steel workers were predominantly immigrant radicals. Excerpts from Foster's own writings from when he was a member of the IWW were reprinted and the charge made that he was really a syndicalist advocating the destruction of the capitalist system.

The antiunion campaign quickly became increasingly repressive. Mounted police rode into crowds of workers at outdoor rallies and clubbed participants. Police arrested organizers and charged them with disorderly conduct, denied strikers the right to picket, and broke up meetings. When strike leaders complained to the Department of Justice that their civil liberties were being suppressed, Attorney General A. Mitchell Palmer, busily on the hunt for alien radicals to deport, refused to get involved. After months of organized intimidation, violation of basic human rights, and the steadfast refusal of steel owners to accept any sort of compromise, organizers acknowledged defeat and called off the strike on January 8, 1920.

The "American Plan"

The antiunion campaign of 1919 had done a masterful job of linking union activities with foreign subversion and portraying labor unrest as a threat to the American way of life. During the 1920s this general tactic reappeared in a slightly more sophisticated form as the "American Plan." Utilizing the techniques of public relations and advertising, business groups like the National Association of Manufacturers and the Chamber of Commerce built a public case that collective bargaining and the closed shop (where the employer agrees to hire only union members) were un-American because they limited the right of an individual to contract independently for the sale of his or her labor and because they impinged on the rights of private property. Making use of the same type of propaganda that had worked so well before, probusiness publications often referred to the closed shop as "sovietism" in disguise. They labeled unionism as a form of Soviet "collectivism" and all strike activity as "un-American." Conversely, the open shop (where employers would have the freedom to hire any worker they chose and no employee would be under any compulsion to join a union) became linked with patriotism, while antiunionism became synonymous with the American virtue of individualism. This antiunion campaign argued that one got ahead by one's own merit, not through collective action.

During the 1920s industrialists showed little reluctance in using strong-arm tactics when necessary. They cultivated antiunion shops, employed labor spies, hired professional strikebreakers, mandated that employees sign "yellow-dog" contracts (which required that they pledge not to become members of a labor union), blacklisted union activists, and gave financial assistance to struck companies. Yet another tactic that gained in popularity during the 1920s was the creation of Employee Representation Plans or, as organized labor referred to them, company unions. Company unions had no independence. Their bylaws usually prohibited them from bargaining for higher wages or improved working conditions, while grievance procedures failed to provide for any impartial arbitration. Organized labor regarded them as a sham in which management still retained final authority. In 1926 there were about 400 company unions in the United States with a combined membership of 1,370,000.

Welfare Capitalism

A small number of employers, however, adopted a different approach known as welfare capitalism. Although the concept had made its appearance during the prewar period, it really hit its stride during the following decade. Aimed at conciliation, welfare capitalism was essentially a paternalistic attempt to co-opt the growth of trade unionism through kindness. If employers could diffuse labor animosity through concessions, then perhaps strikes could be averted. Industrial peace would mean uninterrupted productivity and possibly an environment in which programs for industrial efficiency might be more easily implemented (enhancing production per worker and yielding greater profits). Satisfied workers might also reduce the rate of labor turnover and the need for costly retraining. To win employee allegiance (and a promise not to join a union), corporations set up profit-sharing schemes; paid bonuses in company stock; created pension and retirement programs that rewarded workers who stayed with the company; provided group insurance policies that would be voided if an employee switched jobs; and offered various health, safety, and recreational programs. The assumption was that workers might be induced to give up the advantages of collective bargaining and meaningful representation and identify with their employer and not a union, if the company was seen as doing more for their welfare. Although welfare capitalism never covered more than a minority of the workforce, a survey done in 1926 found that half of the 1,500 largest corporations in America were operating some type of "welfare" program.

One other basic element of welfare capitalism was the so-called Doctrine of High Wages. Prior to World War I, employers tended to believe that wages should rise only high enough to allow them to attract a supply of labor. Henry Ford broke ranks with this philosophy when he offered his workers the famous "Five Dollar Day" (more than doubling the pay of most industrial workers) in 1914. Ford, looking to bring about some stability in his workforce (he had to hire 53,000 workers every year to keep 15,000 workers on the assembly line every day) and to blunt union organizing, took a great deal of criticism from his fellow industrialists for doing so. By 1926, however, the rhetoric had shifted to the extent that it appeared as if employers had now come to accept the idea that higher wages enabled greater purchasing power, which allowed for a greater volume and variety of goods to be produced and sold. But between 1925 and 1929, when employers were most vocal in their public support of this philosophy, wages increased hardly at all. This was true for Henry Ford as well. Still riding his reputation as the prophet of high wages, Ford published a book, *Today and Tomorrow*, in 1926 in which he expounded on the "Doctrine of High Wages" in some detail. But rhetoric masked reality as Ford granted no general increase in wages between 1919 and the stock market crash in 1929. Moreover, in changing over to the Model A in 1927–1928, Ford laid off 60,000 men for more than a year in Detroit alone. According to one labor historian, for many of these workers, reemployment actually came at a reduced rate of pay.

Legal Setbacks

Organized labor saw union membership decline from roughly five million in 1920 to about three-and-one-half million by 1929. By 1930 union membership comprised only 10.2 percent of more than 30 million nonagricultural employees, a marked decline from 19.4 percent in 1920. Organized labor also lost ground on the legal front during the 1920s. The Clayton Antitrust Act of 1914 had attempted to protect unions from the threat of antitrust violations (being charged with forming conspiracies in restraint of trade) and court injunctions. This legislation also permitted practices such as peaceful picketing and the use of secondary boycotts. However, unfavorable decisions by the U.S. Supreme Court undermined all of those earlier assurances. The labor injunction, which had first appeared in the 1880s, achieved its widest use during the 1920s, a period when employers actually faced very few strikes. Also overturned was a 1918 federal law that had established a minimum wage for women in the District of Columbia. In its 1923 reversal, the court stated that such a wage could not be mandated by law because it violated "freedom of contract" protected by the Fifth Amendment.

AFRICAN AMERICAN WORKERS: SLEEPING CAR PORTERS

In a decade that witnessed a flood of union reversals, there was one notable story of labor union advance that involved A. Philip Randolph and the creation of the Brotherhood of Sleeping Car Porters (BSCP). Randolph was born in Crescent City, Florida, in 1889, the son of a self-taught minister of the African Methodist Episcopal Church. In 1911, looking for broader opportunities outside the racially restrictive South, Randolph migrated to Harlem in New York City. Twenty-two years old when he arrived, Randolph accepted whatever menial jobs he could find, began attending classes at the City College of New York and the socialist Rand School of Economics, started reading the writings of Karl Marx, and became a socialist. In 1917, Randolph started a monthly magazine, *The Messenger*, with coeditor Chandler Owen. Approaching events from a socialist perspective, the new periodical denounced American involvement in World War I; condemned segregation, racial violence, and capitalist exploitation of workers; and favored interracial working-class solidarity and trade unionism (although it sharply criticized the American Federation of Labor [AFL] for its racist policies).

In 1925 Roy Lancaster, Ashley Totten, and William Des Verney, three veteran Pullman porters, approached Randolph with an offer to head a new railroad porters' union. Randolph's prolabor background and the fact that he had never been a porter or ever worked in the railroad industry made him an appealing choice. As an outsider, his independence would provide him with some protection from company retaliation or pressure. It did not, however, protect him from charges that he was a meddling labor radical and a tool of the Communist Party. By the early summer *The Messenger* had taken up the porters' cause, and in mid-August Randolph formerly announced that he would lead the organizing effort to form a trade union. The first meeting of the new BSCP took place in the auditorium of the Imperial Lodge of Elks in Harlem on August 25, 1925.

The Pullman System

During Reconstruction, George Pullman, operating on the assumption that prosperous white passengers were accustomed to be waited on by black servants, recruited recently freed slaves to perform valet services on his new railroad sleeping cars. Fifty years later the Pullman Company, not the railroads, still staffed and operated the sleeping cars. By the end of World War I, the company was the largest single employer of African Americans in the United States with roughly 12,000 men on its payroll. Most of Pullman's employees worked as porters, but another 1,700 worked in its shops in Chicago, St. Louis, and Buffalo. The jobs performed by the porters—arranging sleeping compartments, carrying luggage, cleaning bathrooms, shining shoes (they had to buy their own polish and cleaning supplies), and attending to every passenger's needs—were ones that whites did not want. But for many black men it was an opportunity to rise economically. Pullman porters saw themselves as middle class and regarded their clean, crisp uniforms as status symbols and marks of accomplishment.

Working Conditions

The job of being a sleeping car porter, however, had its drawbacks. Porters had to constantly project the image, at least publicly, that they were docile servants. In fact, the company liked to tout the porter's efficient, subservient, and ever-polite nature in its advertising campaigns. To add to the indignity, white passengers invariably referred to black porters as "George," regardless of what their actual name was. Workers also resented the company's welfare workers who investigated their family life and habits and who organized baseball teams, picnics, singing quartets and choruses to keep them "contented." The encouragement of singing especially aroused the ire of Randolph, who felt it made porters the *"monkeys of the service"* and was a "disgrace to the porters. . . [and] an insult to the race" (Arnesen 2001, 90).

There were other issues as well. Porters worked upward of 400 hours each month for an average monthly wage of $67.50, with no time for family or for recreation and no avenue for promotion. Better-compensated positions such as conductor were reserved for whites. Porters were expected to arrive five hours before their shift to prepare the train for departure and to service the train after it arrived at its destination, although they were only paid for the duration of the trip. Generally, porters rarely had time to rest as management expected them to work around the clock. As a result, they frequently had to work back-to-back shifts on what was called the "double-out" without a rest period and sometimes for lower pay. As a final insult, porters were under constant observation by company "spotters," who, under the guise of being regular passengers, meticulously monitored their work. In disputes concerning work quality, managers always accepted the spotter's word without question and docked the porter's pay without hesitation. As one historian concluded: "That porters tended to be better off than most black workers did not change the fact that company managers had created and institutionalized a system of employment bias that gouged and grated African Americans. Pullman's white managers . . . constantly implied to the company's black workers that they were inferior and deserved no more than they received" (Kersten 2007, 28, 30).

The Organizing Drive

With a $10,000 grant from the philanthropic Garland Fund and the assistance of Milton Webster, the porter's unofficial leader in the

At the end of World War I, the Pullman Company employed roughly 10,000 African American men as porters on its railway sleeping cars. The jobs performed, along with the 400 hours worked per month and average monthly wage of $67.50, were ones that whites did not want. Despite the exploitation and the obvious need for a union, many black porters regarded themselves as middle class and considered their clean, crisp uniforms as status symbols and marks of accomplishment. This 1924 photograph offers a hint of that feeling. (Hulton Archive/Getty Images)

city of Chicago, the BSCP started recruiting members. Adopting the slogan "Service not servitude," the Randolph-led BSCP managed to organize 53 percent of the sleeping car porters by 1926, but Pullman executives ignored all requests for union recognition. Instead, they fought back. The company fired porters who joined the union, hired company agents to infiltrate union meetings, and organized its own Employee Representation Plan (company union) to compete with the BSCP. Considerable opposition also came from the black community where black churches and black-owned newspapers, especially in Chicago, thought that black workers should be grateful for the employment that Pullman offered and often talked up the company's charitable contributions to hospitals and YMCAs located in black neighborhoods. As a result, they advised against supporting union activity. To this opposition, the BSCP responded in kind. The union organized boycotts against pro-Pullman newspapers like the *Chicago Defender*, sponsored numerous mass meetings and conferences on black labor, and created a Citizen's Committee of prominent African American leaders to promote black unionism.

Although both the National Association for the Advancement of Colored People and the Urban League supported the BSCP, and black public opinion began to shift in its favor, progress was torturously slow. Randolph had hoped to gain a full-fledged charter from the AFL, which would have given the union prestige, political clout, and access to strike funds, but AFL president William Green repeatedly deferred any decision on formal affiliation. The onset of the Great Depression brought layoffs on the trains and mass resignations from the brotherhood. By 1932 its membership had dropped to fewer than 1,000. Unable to raise sufficient rent money, the BSCP found itself evicted from its New York headquarters in 1933. But New Deal labor legislation brought renewed hope. In 1934 Congress amended the 1926 Railway Labor Act to include sleeping car porters. The new law made it illegal for the Pullman Company to fire workers for joining the union and created a new National Mediation Board (NMB) to oversee union representation elections. The following year, the NMB administered an election in which the BSCP won the right to bargain for Pullman porters. But it was only after its constitutional challenge to the Railway Labor Act was rejected by the U.S. Supreme Court that the Pullman Company finally relented. On August 25, 1937, the twelfth anniversary of the founding of the BSCP, the company and the union reached an agreement. The new contract reduced the work month from 400 to 240 hours, provided time and a half for overtime work, raised wages by $12 a month to a minimum of $89.50, and established a new grievance procedure. It was the first major contract between a black union and an American corporation.

SOCIAL TENSIONS AND CULTURAL CONFLICTS DURING THE 1920s

The ethnic and racial bias shown against Mexican migrant farmworkers and African American sleeping car porters was symptomatic of a deep-seated nativism and racism that fueled many of the social tensions and a number of the cultural conflicts that characterized the 1920s. The battle over immigration restriction was one of the decade's cultural wars. Millions of Americans, many of whom might be classed as native-stock Protestants living along the densely populated East or West Coast, in small towns or the rural countryside (or recent migrants from there), seemed to have increased difficulty dealing with the scope and pace of social change. With a backward-looking vision of the nation and a traditional set of values rooted in religion or region, they often found themselves at odds with the manners, mores, religious and philosophical beliefs, and sheer numbers of a variety of ethnic groups entering the country in the late nineteenth- and early twentieth centuries.

Ethnic and Racial Bias

Asians had historically been targets of nativistic sentiments. Congress passed the Chinese Exclusion Act in 1882 to curtail Chinese immigration, while in the early twentieth century the state of California decided that it was time to place restrictions on those who had come to the United States from Japan. Many Japanese immigrants started out as store owners and restaurant operators, but soon others began to make their mark as an economic force in the produce business, which they soon came to dominate. By the 1910s Japanese producers operating out of the City Market in Los Angeles were supplying the city with 75 percent of its fresh vegetables. The more they prospered as successful small-business people, the more they became objects of discrimination. Finally, in 1913, after years of heavy lobbying by the Asiatic Exclusion League of California, the California legislature passed a law that effectively prevented about 45,000 Japanese noncitizen immigrants (*Issei*) from owning land in the state. This same lobbying group was eventually successful in persuading Congress to curtail Japanese immigration to the United States altogether in 1924.

As heavy concentrations of new immigrants from eastern and southern Europe began to arrive toward the end of the nineteenth century, many in this country became alarmed and increasingly called for some type of restriction. Some of these demands rested on notions of racial inferiority or what might be termed hereditary determinism. The new "science" of eugenics fostered the argument that humans possessed inbred traits of racial superiority and inferiority that could be measured. The result was the notion that humans fit neatly into fixed hereditary types with people from southern and eastern Europe, Asia, and Africa most often ranked at the bottom of the scale. Intellectuals like Madison Grant, a Nordic or Anglo-Saxon racialist who published the widely read *The Passing of the Great Race* in 1916, were very concerned about immigration and thought that the flood of recent immigrants from southern and eastern Europe was eroding racial purity and pushing the country toward a racial abyss. To Grant, preservation of the race required the exclusion of all inferior racial and ethnic groups.

Two months before the United States entered World War I, Congress overrode President Woodrow Wilson's veto and passed the Immigration Act of 1917, essentially a literacy test that denied entry to aliens who could not read English or some other language. The purpose of the law was to discriminate against immigrants from southern and eastern Europe, who were understood to be less literate than those from the northwestern part of the continent. America's entry into the war unleashed a torrent of antiforeign sentiment against "hyphenated Americans," especially Germans. Immediately after the war, a wave of strikes, many in industries like coal and steel with a large number of eastern and southern Europeans; race riots in Chicago, Illinois, Longview, Texas, Knoxville, Tennessee, and Omaha, Nebraska; and the increasing association of "aliens" with political radicalism (bolshevism, communism, or anarchism) during the Red Scare intensified the campaign to keep out all foreigners during 1919–1920.

The Trial of Sacco and Vanzetti

The growing hostility toward immigrants also played a significant role in the celebrated trial of Nicola Sacco and Bartolomeo Vanzetti, two Italians arrested in 1920 for the robbery and murder of a company paymaster and payroll guard at a shoe factory in South Braintree, Massachusetts. Their case generated a national debate over patriotism, judicial fairness, civil rights, radical ideologies, and immigration policy. After a trial that involved disputed ballistics evidence, conflicting eyewitness testimony, judicial prejudice, legal misconduct (jury tampering), and defense ineptitude, a jury convicted Sacco and Vanzetti in 1921. After years of failed death-row judicial appeals, the two were finally executed in August 1927. Riots and protests followed the execution as many still believed that Sacco and Vanzetti had not been given a fair trial grounded in solid evidence but instead had been convicted because of who they were and their political beliefs. They were both Italian immigrants and antistatist radicals who subscribed to the doctrinaire philosophy of anarchist Luigi Galleani and the belief that the elimination of the state was necessary to protect individual liberty.

The National Origins Act of 1924

Responding to an anti-immigrant sentiment that had been building in society for decades, Congress finally passed an emergency immigration statute in 1921 that set quotas on immigrants from any European country at 3 percent of each nationality living in the United States based on the 1910 census. Three years later Congress passed an even more restrictive law, the National Origins Act, that reduced quotas to 2 percent and shifted the database from the census of 1910 to that of 1890 (before the great bulk of eastern and southern Europeans arrived). That change had the effect of giving northern Europeans and Scandinavians an even greater advantage. Under the new law, Asians were excluded entirely. Providing executive endorsement of the legislation, President Calvin Coolidge declared in 1924 that "America must be kept American," and millions of Americans seemed to concur. Both restrictive measures had the common racist objective of attempting to maintain an ethnic status quo that favored what eugenicists called the Nordic or Teutonic peoples. The legislation also reflected a waning confidence on the part of many in society about the nation's capacity to absorb a constant stream of people from increasingly diverse ethnic, cultural, and religious backgrounds.

Prohibition: "Wets" versus "Drys"

A second battle in the cultural wars involved the question of whether society should prohibit the manufacture and sale of alcoholic beverages. As a crusade, Prohibition involved a strange partnership in which a number of progressive reformers joined with social conservatives to, as they saw it, improve social conditions by controlling behavior and dictating moral standards. Many nativistic, evangelical Protestants, already concerned with the transformation of American society, objected to the presence of neighborhood saloons and to the drinking habits of many urban immigrants. Racism was also a factor with many southerners who identified themselves as progressives supporting the argument that abolishing the sale of liquor was yet one more way to control African Americans. Armed with the argument that alcohol was detrimental to one's health, corroded family life, and promoted an inefficient workforce and that liquor interests corrupted American politics, "drys" assumed the moral high ground. With strong support in the rural sections of the South and the West, Prohibition also seemed to reflect a growing agrarian antipathy to the dominance of the city in American life. Led by the militant Anti-Saloon League and an adept use of modern pressure-group politics on the two major political parties, and bolstered by enthusiastic support from the Methodist and Baptist churches, the drys made steady progress. Between 1906 and 1917 twenty-one states, mostly in the South and West, passed Prohibition laws. It was World War I, however, that finally tipped the balance in the national debate. Prohibitionists were now able to link temperance with national preparedness and winning the war and argue that wartime food rationing and the need to export grain to the Allies made it simply immoral to waste precious grains by converting them into alcohol.

In the end, Congress decided to seek a dry utopia. The Eighteenth Amendment, banning the manufacture, sale, or transportation of intoxicants throughout the United States and giving both the states and the federal government the authority to enact enforcement measures, swept through Congress in 1917 with fewer than three days of debate. By early 1919 the required thirty-six states had ratified the amendment, five states without a single dissenting vote. The law took effect in January 1920. As one historian summed it up, the Eighteenth Amendment "symbolized the political and cultural victory of the small towns over the big cities; of evangelical and pietistic Protestants over Roman Catholics, Lutherans, and Jews; of old-stock Anglo-Saxons over newer immigrants; and finally, of rich over poor" (Parrish 1992, 97). Prohibition would continue to divide the nation along political, geographic, religious, and ethnic boundaries for the remainder of the decade. And, as Frederick Lewis Allen noted, few could see what lay ahead—

> rum-ships rolling in the sea outside the twelve-mile limit and transferring their cargoes of whiskey by night to fast cabin cruisers, beer-running trucks being hijacked on the interurban boulevards by bandits with Thompson sub-machine guns, illicit stills turning out alcohol by the carload, the fashionable dinner party beginning with contraband cocktails as a matter of course, ladies and gentlemen undergoing scrutiny from behind the curtained grill of the speakeasy, and Alphonse Capone, multi-millionaire master of the Chicago bootleggers, driving through the streets in an armor-plated car with bulletproof windows. (Allen 2010, 212)

The debate between the "wets" and the "drys" continued throughout the 1920s. Die-hard supporters continued to see it as a "noble experiment" that would work. Many in the middle and upper classes adopted a more hypocritical stance. Although they disapproved of Prohibition for themselves, they regarded Prohibition as good for the working class. In a racist twist on such hypocrisy, historian David A. Shannon noted that in Mississippi, which at the time had a population that was more than half black, whites insisted on enforcing the law against blacks while they "winked" at violations by other whites. Critics, in turn, intensified their conviction that Prohibition had been a terrible mistake. As it became increasingly apparent that Prohibition was unenforceable, many feared that widespread violations only encouraged a disrespect for the law. Others, noting the manner in which magazines and movies suggested that drinking was still taking place among the upper class, suggested that there was a double standard in society. It was not long before opponents got organized. One group, the American Association against the Prohibition Amendment, based its campaign on an assertion that the law violated individual rights and liberties and was corroding the social fabric. In 1929 Pauline Morton Sabin led a repeal effort through the newly formed Women's Organization for National Prohibition Repeal (WONPR). The primary argument of this group was that Prohibition was corrupting America's youth by encouraging socially acceptable lawbreaking. By 1931 the WONPR claimed to have 300,000 members in thirty-three states.

In enumerating factors that doomed Prohibition—flagrant violations of the law, an increasingly well-organized opposition, and the onset of the Great Depression—one might add another reality. As many of the rural, Protestant traditionalists who supported the Eighteenth Amendment gravitated to other causes, such as warring against evolution, jazz music, and the erosion of Protestant moral values, Prohibition became, in the words of one historian, "tainted with priggish fanaticism" (Dumenil 1995, 245). As the decade progressed, social commentators increasingly viewed Prohibition, the activities of the Ku Klux Klan, and the crusade against Darwinism as all part of the same movement—a failed attempt "to sustain the 'old moral order' . . . in an increasingly urban, sophisticated, and pluralist society" (Brown 1987, 189). Many within the urban middle class had initially joined those in the small towns and countryside in clinging to the more traditional values of their past and supported Prohibition. By the end of the decade, however, more and more of that urban middle class had moved away from those values as they began to feel more comfortable within America's emerging modern, consumer-oriented culture. As a result, they felt less of a need for restraint and sobriety. Ironically, the cultural pluralism that many prohibitionists had hoped to contain eventually helped to erode support for the idea.

The Ku Klux Klan

For many native-born, white Protestants, immigration restriction and Prohibition were only partial responses to the anxieties and insecurities brought about by the growing ethnic and cultural diversity in American society. One of those tortured souls who yearned to recapture an earlier, less-troubled time was William J. Simmons. Simmons, a former Methodist circuit preacher, salesman, and promoter of fraternal orders, was deeply affected by events that took place in 1915. He had probably read Thomas Dixon's racial polemic *The Clansman* (1905) and was keenly aware of the popularity of D. W. Griffith's recently released motion picture *The Birth of a Nation* (based on the Dixon novel), a film that glorified the Ku Klux Klan and ridiculed Black Reconstruction and the notion that blacks should be guaranteed political rights. But there was another event that summer that also caught his attention: the brutal lynching of Leo M. Frank. Frank had moved to Atlanta from New York to become manager of the National Pencil Company and quickly became a respected member of the Jewish community. In 1915, Frank was tried and convicted of murdering a fourteen-year-old girl named Mary Phagan, an employee at his factory. Although Frank was given a death sentence, evidence strongly suggested that a worker at the factory, not Frank, had committed the crime. Deeply troubled by the biased and inconsistent evidence presented at the trial, Governor John Slaton decided to commute Frank's sentence from death to life in prison. His action triggered a reaction. On August 16, 1915, twenty-five men calling themselves the Knights of Mary Phagan took Frank from his prison cell and lynched him. Historian Joel Williamson has suggested that Frank was murdered at a time when southerners had come to fear new threats to their social order that he defined as "hidden blackness, the blackness within seeming whiteness." He argued that southerners "began to look with great suspicion upon mulattoes who looked white, white people who behaved as black, and a whole congeries of aliens [Jews, Catholics, labor organizers] insidious in their midst who would destroy their . . . moral universe" (Williamson 1984, 465, 471). Two months later, the same group of murderers climbed Stone Mountain outside Atlanta and burned a giant cross.

The potent combination of novel, movie, and cross-burning convinced Simmons that it was time to take action.

Eager to revive the Ku Klux Klan, Simmons gathered together thirty-four like-minded individuals, including members of the Knights of Mary Phagan, who, on October 26, 1915, signed an application to the state of Georgia to charter the Knights of the Ku Klux Klan as a fraternal order. Simmons appointed himself Imperial Wizard. Determined to repeat the ceremonial cross-burning on Stone Mountain, Simmons, accompanied by fifteen of the original thirty-four charter members, boarded a sightseeing bus on Thanksgiving Day and rode to the "sacred" site. They then set ablaze a sixteen-foot, wooden cross and swore allegiance to the Invisible Empire, Knights of the Ku Klux Klan. The reborn Klan, like the first, emphasized white brotherhood and shrouded itself in regalia, rituals, and exotic titles to enhance its fraternal appeal. But the new, twentieth-century Klan was different, in that it was rabidly antiforeign, anti-Catholic, and anti-Semitic as well as antiblack. It was also quick to link nativism, racism, and anti-Catholicism with morality, Prohibition, and law and order by denouncing bootleggers, adulterers, and atheists, or anyone who offended its vision of a racially and morally pure America.

Looking for help in promoting the organization and placing it on sounder financial footing in the early 1920s, Simmons hired Edward Young Clark and Elizabeth Tyler of the Southern Publicity Association to apply modern marketing and advertising techniques to Klan recruitment. They did so with amazing results. In stressing the Klan's commitment to traditional moral values, Clark and Tyler smartly linked the Klan with Protestant fundamentalism. Speaking for the Klan, they defended the Bible as the literal truth and denounced evolution and any free interpretation of scripture. Sensing widespread fundamentalist support, the Klan began publishing books, magazines, and pamphlets that trumpeted the Christian message. In an attempt to win over the clergy, Clark and Tyler cleverly devised what they called the "church visitation." On any given Sunday, a group of gowned and hooded Klansmen would simply march down the aisle of a local church and interrupt the service to present the pastor with a substantial sum of money for the collection. Clark and Tyler also hired 1,000 salesmen denoted as Kleagles to conduct a door-to-door sales campaign where they hawked memberships at $10 apiece, keeping $4 for themselves. The remaining money was then funneled through the chain of command—$1 to the state boss, $0.50 to the regional director, $2.50

to Clark and Tyler, and the remaining $2.00 into the Imperial Treasury. By 1924, with membership hovering around four million, the Atlanta headquarters of the Klan was raking in $40,000 a month in initiation fees and dues.

Clark and Tyler instructed the Kleagles to play on whatever prejudice or fear was most pronounced in a given community. If a town was afraid of labor unions, Kleagles were told to push the Klan's position against foreign-born and radically led labor organizations. If they were working a dry community, they were to tout the Klan's tough stance against bootleggers. If a city was being inundated with immigrants, they were to inform anxious residents that the Klan stood for 100 percent Americanism. And when neighborhoods voiced fears of the postwar "new Negro," they were to remind them that the Klan had always known how to keep blacks in their place. There truly was "a scapegoat for every local tension" (Wade 1987, 156).

Key to the Klan's success was the way in which it drew on the culture of small-town America to become a part of ordinary white, Protestant life. It was patriotic, donated to local charities, and stressed its popular fraternal nature. In projecting itself into the daily lives of residents, the Klan attempted to create an exclusive sense of community united by race, religion, and moral consensus. A typical Klan gathering might bring the entire family to a barbeque with the singing of hymns, fireworks, and a giant cross-burning to climax the evening. Underscoring the emphasis on family values, the Klan changed its initial male-only policy and admitted women to its membership ranks in 1922. The following year, under the influence of Elizabeth Tyler, the Klan created the Women of the Ku Klux Klan. It was another brilliant strategy, drawing half a million white Protestant women to its ranks in the Midwest alone. Many of the women who joined had been participants in informal Klan auxiliaries and patriotic societies. In most instances, these female auxiliaries combined white supremacy with social service work. Some had been active in temperance and suffrage movements and saw the Klan as a way to further enable their moral natures. Working together they could protect their homes, families, and communities by helping rid the nation of liquor, prostitution, and gambling, while giving free rein to their strong anti-Catholic, anti-Semitic, and racist beliefs.

Those who flocked to the Klan seemed to come primarily from the unskilled, industrial working class comprising, in many instances, displaced farmers, tenants, and sharecroppers drawn by necessity to work in mills and factories. Cities experiencing rapid economic and population growth like Indianapolis, Denver, Portland, Dallas, Detroit, Tulsa, and Atlanta, where such development brought people of different social backgrounds into close proximity, served as fertile ground for Klan recruiters. The Klan also included in its ranks many small-business and professional people precariously clinging to a lower-middle-class perch on the status ladder only a rung or two above the working class. Those who advertised in Klan publications like the *Fiery Cross* included tailors, dry cleaners, grocers, druggists, dentists, and accountants. The Klan served as a refuge for many with little education or sophistication who felt marginalized and increasingly powerless in society. Increasingly burdened with the anxieties that often accompany rapid transformations in society, the Klan offered them status, security, and the promise of restoring an older America.

With membership soaring and revenues swelling, it was not surprising that a power struggle within the organization would eventually take place. First to go was Imperial Wizard William J. Simmons, ousted by Hiram Wesley Evans, a Texas dentist who had risen in the ranks to become head of the Dallas Klavern, and D. C. Stephenson, the Grand Dragon of Indiana. Simmons's greatest failing was that he had turned the everyday control of the organization over to Clark and Tyler and wished to maintain the Klan's identity as a religious movement. Evans, who became the new Imperial Wizard, wanted to move the Klan into politics. In that effort, he had the complete support of Stephenson. In 1924 after a lengthy, acrimonious, and highly publicized court fight, Simmons agreed to a cash buyout of $145,000 (he eventually received only $90,000) to drop his official connection to the Klan. With Simmons gone, Clark and Tyler soon followed.

The power struggle continued when Stephenson announced that he was going to split the Indiana Klan—the largest state organization where an estimated 10 percent of the state's population claimed membership—from the national body. But Stephenson, who once proclaimed to be the law in Indiana, then made a terrible mistake. In 1925 a jury convicted him of the rape and second-degree murder of Madge Oberholtzer, a twenty-eight-year-old director of the Young People's Reading Club operated by the office of the State Superintendent of Public Instruction. After Stephenson had kidnapped and then sexually assaulted her on an overnight train, Miss Oberholtzer took poison. When Stephenson denied her access to medical care, she died. When the judge sentenced the Grand Dragon of Indiana to twenty-five years to life in the state prison at Michigan City, he dealt the Klan, the vocal defender of the purity of white, Christian womanhood, a blow from which it never recovered. Within a year of the trial, Klan membership in Indiana fell from 350,000 to 15,000.

Feeling betrayed at not being granted a pardon by state officials who obviously wished to be free of his influence, Stephenson released his Klan files, which implicated a number of Klan-supported Hoosier politicians. The disclosures provided a field day for the press and led to a series of indictments. Other political scandals, including indictments for bribery and election fraud, removed corrupt Klan-supported politicians in a number of other states between 1925 and 1929. By 1930 the Ku Klux Klan was in deep decline nationwide, its membership having fallen to about 45,000. The unwillingness to respect differences of opinion, lifestyle, or belief and the refusal to accept people of different races or ethnic

After 1925, the formerly resurgent Ku Klux Klan, wracked by the criminal behavior of Grand Dragon D. C. Stephenson and further soiled by indictments for bribery and election fraud, went into decline. Although its membership dropped precipitously (from perhaps 4 million members in 1924 to about 45,000 by 1930), it still wielded enough national support to conduct a parade down Pennsylvania Avenue in 1928. (National Archives)

backgrounds heightened social tensions during the 1920s. Marked by the constant drumbeat of nativist and racist rhetoric, and often sullied by acts of intimidation, vigilantism, and violence, the quest for cultural conformity serves as a reminder that the Jazz Age was not all fun and frivolity.

Document: Samuel Hopkins Adams, "On Sale Everywhere" (1921) and Excerpts from Sinclair Lewis, *Babbitt* (1922)

The following two excerpts, one from a study of Prohibition by journalist Samuel Hopkins Adams and the other from the 1922 novel Babbitt *by Sinclair Lewis, view the state of the "noble experiment" from early in the decade and find it crippled by middle-class hypocrisy.*

"On Sale Everywhere"

From out the smoke screen of contentious generalizations [about prohibition] there stand forth . . . a few salient facts which may be summarized as follows:

There is a tremendous . . . decrease in the total consumption of alcoholic drinks.

The saloon, *as a public institution*, is almost extinct. . . .

But—anyone who wants a drink and can pay for a drink can still get a drink.

Most of those who drank when it was lawful continue to drink now that it is unlawful, and without any consciousness of moral or ethical deterioration.

Home brewing or purchase in bulk has succeeded to bar haunting as the source of steady supply, and the pocket flask to the punch bowl for social festivities.

For obvious reasons of convenience, the tendency under prohibition has been away from beer and wine and toward whisky and gin. Quick results are the desideratum, which may go far to explain such a phenomenon as the increased number of cases of alcoholism coming to the large city hospitals for treatment.

The rural districts, true to tradition, continue to imbibe strongly alcoholized hard cider, generally ignorant and universally indifferent as to whether or not it is illegal. . . .

The larger and licensed distillery is gone, but the small and illegal distillery flourishes sturdily alike in the remote mountain glen and the convenient tenement bathroom. . . .

Breweries continue to brew with diligence, and there is none too exigent an inquiry as to whether their output contains 4 per cent of alcohol or only the permissible one-eighth of that proportion.

Across the borders of the nation flows a constant, concealed stream of refreshment to be distributed through the agency of the immense bootlegging industry which has become the up-to-date exemplar of high profiteering. . . .

The bootlegging industry thrives because it is, to a great extent, ignored by the authorities and patronized by people generally regarded as "our best citizens." . . .

Laxity on the part of the officials charged with the enforcement of liquor laws is a symptom rather than a cause of the present reign of lawlessness. They simply reflect local conditions. . . .

On the question of prohibition enactment, the nation divided into two opposing sides, those who were for it and those who were against it. As to prohibition enforcement, there are three distinct divisions:

> Those who are for it.
> Those who are against it.
> Those who are for it for others and against it for themselves.

The latter are a numerous, influential, and highly important class, who have not been sufficiently reckoned with as a factor in the present situation. . . .

The prohibition law has never had a fair chance because it has never had the support of those elements of our populace which consider themselves the representative upholders of Americanism.

Babbitt

Now this was the manner of obtaining alcohol under the reign of righteousness and prohibition. . . .

[Babbitt] entered a place curiously like the saloons of ante-prohibition days, with a long greasy bar with sawdust in front and a streaky mirror behind, a pine table at which a dirty old man dreamed over a glass of something which resembled whisky, and with two men at the bar, drinking something which resembled beer. . . . The bartender, a tall pale Swede with a diamond in his lilac scarf, stared at Babbitt as he stalked plumply up to the bar and whispered, "I'd, uh—Friend of Hanson's sent me here. Like to get some gin." . . .

In growing meekness Babbitt went on waiting till Hanson casually reappeared with a quart of gin. . . .

"Twelve bucks," he snapped.

"Say, uh, but say, cap'n, Jake thought you'd be able to fix me up for eight or nine a bottle."

"Nup. Twelve. This is the real stuff, smuggled from Canada. This is none o' your neutral spirits with a drop of juniper extract," the honest merchant said virtuously. "Twelve bones—if you want it." . . .

"Sure! Sure! I understand!" Babbitt gratefully held out twelve dollars.

[Later, at Babbitt's party]

Through a froth of merriment he brought the shining promise, the mighty tray of glasses with the cloudy yellow cocktails in the glass pitcher in the center. The men babbled, "Oh, gosh, have a look!" . . .

Babbitt drank with the others; . . .

When, beyond hope, the pitcher was empty, [the guests] stood and talked about prohibition. . . .

"Now, I'll tell you," said Vergil Gunch; . . . "the way I see it is that it's a good thing to get rid of the saloon, but they ought to let a fellow have beer and light wines."

Howard Littlefield observed, "What isn't generally realized is that it's a dangerous prop'sition to invade the rights of personal liberty." . . .

"That's it—no one got a right to invade personal liberty," said Orville Jones.

"Just the same, you don't want to forget prohibition is a mighty good thing for the working-classes. Keeps 'em from wasting their money and lowering their productiveness," said Vergil Gunch.

"Yes, that's so. But the trouble is the manner of enforcement," insisted Howard Littlefield. "Congress didn't understand the right system. Now, if I'd been running the thing, I'd have arranged it so that the drinker himself was licensed, and then we could have taken care of the shiftless workman—kept him from drinking—and yet not 've interfered with the rights—with the personal liberty—of fellows like ourselves."

They bobbed their heads, looked admiringly at one another, and stated, "That's so, that would be the stunt."

Sources: Samuel Hopkins Adams. "On Sale Everywhere," *Collier's* 68 (July 16, 1921): 7–8, 22–25, and Sinclair Lewis. *Babbitt*. New York: Harcourt, Brace and Company, 1922, 106, 108, 113–15.

Document: T. Arnold Hill, "The Dilemma of Negro Workers" (1926)

The following selection by T. Arnold Hill is from the February 1926 issue of Opportunity: A Journal of Negro Life, *the publication of the National Urban League, and addresses the dilemma confronting black workers in the 1920s. Facing discrimination from both white employers and white-controlled labor unions, black workers are left not knowing whom to trust.*

Note: The terms "Negro" and "colored" that appear in the article were the accepted terms in use at the time.

"The Dilemma of Negro Workers"

Negroes are energetically seeking the proper course in the controversy between capital and labor. We say proper course because there has never been a concerted, enthusiastic opinion on this subject. . . .

Instead of prompting a healthy body of public opinion for or against unionism, the divergent views have led to confusion. The concern is not over intellectual issues, but with the practical application of trade unionism to the welfare of twelve million Negroes. . . .

Let us reason from the viewpoint of a skilled colored workman, earnestly seeking to support any measure that will benefit society, his family and himself. He knows that the Negro is permitted to do the casual and unskilled work and barred from trades and almost every type of white-collar job. He has inherited a conviction that the Caucasian, whether employee or employer, is opposed to his gaining economic security. . . .

. . . [H]e knows . . . that capital has denied him opportunities to work, often in public businesses that he is forced to support. He sees a friend serving a quarter of a century as a messenger for a large corporation, at odd times filling with credit the place of an absent clerk, but always the same messenger and never promoted. He knows of many who have passed civil service examinations, only to be denied the appointment when their color was discovered. He is familiar with the subterfuges practiced to block ascendancy in places where Negroes work. . . .

Just as he is ready to place the blame upon employers, he gets the frank admission from them that Negroes cannot be employed in certain places, but the blame is placed upon his white employees, who would leave him in the lurch if a single Negro were employed. He wonders to what extent organized labor is responsible for this intimidation. He is familiar with the resolutions of the American

Federation of Labor declaring the federation open to all working people regardless of race, or creed, or color, but he knows plumbers, machinists, boilermakers, railway mail clerks and electricians who have been denied membership. . . . He has had related to him the story of Sam Houston, who because he was the best bricklayer on the job was . . . promptly removed from his superior position by the business manager of his local, who reprimanded the foreman on the plea that it was "a white man's job."

Thus after much pondering, our colored worker is where he was when he began. Mindful of the discrimination of labor unions and employers, he distrusts them both and settles down to let the whole matter work itself out, content to take his chances on the future. He thinks of a third way out. . . . Would a national labor union of colored workers solve his dilemma? But colored workers are so few as to give no strength to a separate movement of them. But there are certain lines of employment in which Negroes predominate, so our inquirer wonders about this as a partial solution. He recalls that A. Philip Randolph is endeavoring to organize the Pullman porters. Here surely is a field in which there can be no opposition from white workers. His hopes are no sooner raised, however, than discouragement meets him again; for Mr. Randolph is having trouble . . . [gaining the support of] Negro leaders. . . . Editors are almost unanimously against the organization and many ministers have sided with the Pullman Company. The Pullman Porters, themselves, are divided—some want the union of the porters, others believe that the Pullman Porters Beneficial Association [the company union] will meet all requirements.

Apparently Negroes do not want organized labor, our friend conjectures. He despairs and wants to throw up the whole thing. Everything is chaotic and contradictory, but his faltering course is stiffened when he recalls that the Dining Car Employees are organized on twelve railroads and have been successful in raising their wages and improving their conditions of work. . .

. . . . And thus again our colored worker finds himself stumped. He has reached the limit of his information. There are contradictions, paradoxes, discrimination on both sides. Somehow he clings to the belief that the proper course is to ally himself with the forces that are opposed to organized labor, but instinctively he would like to be classed with the workers, and not the bosses. He knows nothing about the academic discussions. . . . He does not read industrial magazines or labor journals. He has made his own tests and they have failed to satisfy.

In an undertone, audible only to himself, he concludes that he will take a middle course. He will be on the fence, so to speak, as he thinks labor and capital are. He will join unions if he is convinced that labor will be fair with him or he will throw his strength to capital if capital will offer him work commensurate with his ability. And so he reads the papers, listens to speeches from both sides, agreeing at one time with capital and at another with labor, but at heart he is floundering in a sea of doubt.

Source: T. Arnold Hill. "The Dilemma of Negro Workers," *Opportunity* (February 1926). Archived at the Library of Congress.

3

INTELLECTUAL LIFE

EDUCATION

The One-Room School

Much has been said regarding the relative affluence of Americans during the Jazz Age, and one manifestation of that affluence can be seen in education. Affluence changed how people lived and the products they purchased, but it also allowed parents to provide a better education for their children than they ever had. Before the arrival of the car and the school bus, each rural township operated a grade school through grades six or eight. Most of these schools had only one room and one teacher. One student remembered the experience well:

> I went to an old country-style schoolhouse. . . . One building that had eight rows in it, one for each grade. Seven rows were quiet while the eighth one recited. . . . The woman teacher got the munificent sum of $30 a month . . . she taught every subject, all eight grades. This was 1929, '30, '31. . . . At the back corner was a great pot-bellied stove that kept the place warm. It had about an acre of ground, a playground with no equipment. (Green 1992, 126)

In 1920, nearly one in four students attended just such a school. Two hundred thousand of these schools were spread across the

In 1920 nearly one in four students attended a one-room school and 200,000 of them dotted the rural countryside, most notably in the South. Subjects were taught primarily through the recitation method, and while most students probably learned the basics, few were pushed beyond that. The rhythms of rural life—planting season and harvest—often interrupted the school year and reduced attendance. This 1921 rural schoolroom is typical. (Library of Congress)

rural countryside, most notably in the South. Although many rural residents developed a sentimental attachment to those schools and liked that they could maintain local control, the schools were substandard. Teachers were poorly trained (many had only a high school education), and students were ill-prepared for life beyond the farm.

School Consolidation

The school bus changed everything as it allowed for the consolidation of rural, one-room schools and the opportunity for students to extend their education beyond the eighth grade. Motor buses, made available by the school board, collected and carried school children to consolidated schools each morning and returned them home each evening. As an example of the new system in full form, the state of North Carolina proudly reported in 1927 that it operated 2,317 school buses, carrying an average of 87,000 students each day to 814 consolidated schools. School consolidation, which had started to become a popular panacea for the problems confronting rural education around 1910, enabled school districts to standardize curriculum and recruit better-trained teachers (a two-year course at a state teachers' college or normal school quickly became the new standard). Professionalization allowed teachers to concentrate on specific subjects or age groups, while high schools, in particular, were able to offer a wider range of courses. Many education reformers hoped that superior teachers and the expanded physical facilities of the consolidated school would make it a social center of the community. Optimists thought that such schools might open possibilities for adult education and facilitate the immediate adoption of more modernized agricultural practices. Children of more affluent white farmers often had the option of obtaining specialized instruction in agriculture and home economics outside the school through various local Granges and 4-H clubs. By 1929, 750,000 boys and girls were 4-H members. They attended monthly meetings where they were taught moral values and social skills, learned about scientific agriculture, and had the opportunity to participate in livestock competitions at county or state fairs. Although approximately 50,000 one-room schools had been absorbed into 10,500 consolidated schools by 1920, 212,000 one-room schools still remained. Progress was slow, but by the end of the decade, the number of one-room schools had declined by 25 percent.

School Attendance

During the 1920s more young people attended school. Average daily attendance in public schools increased from slightly more than 16 million grade-school-age children (about 75 percent) in 1920 to more than 21 million (about 90 percent) in 1930. But the expansion in public education did not come without its biases. Public schools in the South and in some border states like Missouri and Kentucky remained segregated, while students attending all-black schools received only one-third to one-half of the appropriations that students attending white schools received. Enrollments at secondary schools showed similar increases. In 1920, 2.2 million students were enrolled in high school. Ten years later that number had doubled to almost 4.5 million. Colleges and universities experienced the same exponential growth. By 1930, nearly 60 percent of the high-school-age population and almost 20 percent of the college-age population in the United States were enrolled in some type of educational institution.

Much emphasis has been placed on the Progressive Era drive to eliminate child labor and get children back in school. Compulsory school-attendance laws, which were on the books in some form in every state by 1918 (usually to age fourteen), helped with that goal, but these laws stood little chance of enforcement where public opinion opposed them. If employers wanted to hire, or if parents needed their children to work to supplement family income (a practice that was fairly common in the textile towns of the Appalachian South), then enforcement was weak. As historian David Shannon noted, "Affluence rather than law kept children in school and off the labor market" (Shannon 1965, 94).

During the 1920s students generally stayed in school longer than they had previously, a trend that was encouraged by the demands of business and industry for a well-educated workforce. For most students, the national average school year ranged from thirty-two to thirty-five weeks, but in the poorest rural districts, where funding was inadequate and families needed the income that children contributed in order to survive, the school year could be as short as twelve weeks. Increasingly though, more American families could afford to make ends meet without the wages of their children. And as they could do so, the value of education increased in importance. As the Lynds discovered in *Middletown*, priorities regarding education were changing. "Parents," they reported, "insist upon more and more education as part of their children's birthright; . . . . Education is a faith, a religion. . . . This thing, education, appears to be desired frequently not for its specific content but as a symbol—by the working class as an open sesame that will mysteriously admit their children to a world closed to them, and by the business class as a heavily sanctioned aid in getting on further economically or socially in the world" (Lynd and Lynd 1956, 219–20).

Standardized Testing

Educators increasingly focused their attention on designing programs that might better suit the needs of distinct groups of students. This often involved the categorization of students according to different levels of ability, a process that opened the door for standardized educational testing. World War I had shocked a number of educators regarding the inadequacy of the nation's schools.

When new recruits were given the Yerkes Alpha Aptitude Test to identify potential officers and to weed out those deemed unsuitable for service, two out of five tested below average. Similar tests were created after the war to attempt to measure the intelligence of students and thereby "track" them into classes designed to meet the needs of bright, average, slow, and special learners. The flaw in the design of these so-called intelligence tests, as was the case with the earlier military examinations, was that they did not measure innate intelligence but rather the extent of an individual's education, particularly the amount of one's training in English and mathematical reasoning. As criticism of these standardized tests mounted, school officials replaced "intelligence" tests with "achievement" tests that claimed to measure how well students learned and retained particular skills and knowledge components. According to one account, educators had nearly 1,300 different achievement tests that they could draw on by the early 1930s to evaluate student skills and development. Standardized educational testing had become institutionalized.

Colleges

As previously noted, enrollments at American colleges and universities recorded pronounced increases during the 1920s. Beginning in the 1890s, as a college education—once largely the preserve of the wealthy—increasingly came to be perceived as a necessary step on the way to a chosen profession, the numbers of young, middle-class men and women in attendance began to rise. During the decade, college enrollments nearly doubled from approximately 600,000 in 1920 to almost 1.2 million in 1930. And there was an expanding array of institutional choices: normal schools, state teachers' colleges, land-grant universities, and elite women's colleges, as well as Catholic and "Negro" colleges. As higher education became increasingly democratized, the college-educated son of a middle-class family was being followed by the daughter. As a result, there was a significant increase in the number of women attending college—from 85,000 in 1900 to 283,000 in 1920 to 481,000 a decade later. By 1930 approximately 40 percent of students attending college nationally were women. The surging numbers had a direct impact on undergraduate degree programs as colleges began to offer new majors in sociology, political science, engineering, business, marketing, advertising, art, drama, and physical education to complement the more traditional programs in history, literature, math, and the classics. Enrollment in graduate programs kept pace as well. Whereas colleges had awarded only 532 doctoral degrees in 1920, that number nearly quadrupled to 2,024 in 1930. But despite these increases, college was still an experience enjoyed by only a relative few. In 1928 a mere 12 percent of young people between the ages of eighteen and twenty-one were enrolled in higher education. The numbers for women were even lower, with only about 10 percent of the female population in that same age group attending college in 1930.

Nevertheless, the huge increase in school enrollments in the high schools and colleges influenced American life in a number of ways by raising literacy levels, cultivating expertise, expanding educational curriculums, and energizing the economy. "At the same time," noted historian Paula Fass, "the structure and mores of peer life on the campus helped to create the first modern American youth culture, a culture that was fed by the larger culture but that was also distinct and separate." A number of historians have commented on the youth centeredness of the culture during the 1920s, a dynamic that suggested "modernity, the impulse toward adjustment." According to Fass, "Throughout the twenties, America struggled with a torn conscience—with the fear of losing what was solid in its past and the excitement of what was new in its future, [F. Scott] Fitzgerald understood it well, just as he knew that youth had come to represent it all. The victory would, of course, belong to the young, and in attending to their styles, their fads, their music, and their lives, other Americans would accept it too" (Fass 1977, 122, 123, 128).

Attendance at college also provided students with the opportunity to experience "college life." In addition to time spent in lecture halls and studying in the library, students still found plenty of free time to attend college athletic events, rush fraternities or sororities, go to dances, or hang out with friends. Fueling the stereotype of F. Scott Fitzgerald's rebellious younger generation, dating, drinking, and sexual exploration remained at the top of most students' list of diversions. The decade also saw an increase in the popularity of Greek organizations and a dramatic jump in the number of new chapters and the construction of new houses on college campuses across the country. By 1930 approximately 35 percent of all college students could claim membership in a fraternity or sorority.

Expanding college enrollments had an impact on the campus profile in one other way as well. As student numbers rose dramatically during the decade, the popularity of college sports, especially football, increased accordingly. Universities that decided to create strong football programs, and had enthusiastic alumni willing to support them, built huge stadiums to promote their teams. Yale University built a new 75,000-seat stadium, while Stanford University surpassed that with an 86,000-seat venue. The University of Michigan, however, topped them all with a magnificent 102,000-seat coliseum for modern-day gladiatorial contests. As college football became a huge moneymaker for institutions, dozens of other universities quickly followed suit with their own 60,000- to 80,000-seat stadiums. Ticket receipts for college football games actually surpassed those for major league baseball for much of the 1920s. In 1927 more than 30 million spectators nationwide paid in excess of $50 million for college football tickets.

INTELLECTUAL INFLUENCES

The intellectual influences that this mushrooming college population might have encountered during the 1920s were essentially of two types—the elite culture and the emerging mass consumer culture. The artists and intellectuals that were representative of the less-popular first group tended to feel alienated from the dominant American culture for a variety of reasons and "rejected it as an acceptable framework for the human mind and spirit." As a result, "they either attacked it directly or fled from it" (Shannon 1965, 95). The more-popular second group, however, tended either to avoid the adversarial viewpoint or to embrace the dominant business-oriented culture with a fervor.

ELITE CULTURE

Most intellectuals of the more optimistic prewar era assumed that reason and good ideas could transform social institutions for the better. Intellectuals like Herbert Croly (*The Promise of American Life*) and Walter Lippmann (*Drift and Mastery*) took the position that intellectuals had "become indispensable to the efficient and enlightened management of the state, the economy, and the culture." Improvement would come, they believed, "once the nation's values and institutional arrangements caught up with the ideas of its most advanced and creative minds" (Parrish 1992, 186, 194). But this kind of intellectual optimism would disappear in the postwar decade.

One of the precursors of this change in mood was Henry Adams. Adams had died in 1918, but his celebrated autobiography *The Education of Henry Adams* (published as a small limited edition in 1907 but reprinted in 1918) struck a chord among the postwar generation of intellectuals. In a voice that was, as one historian put it, both "mordant and resigned," this descendant of one of the nation's founding political families reflected on the condition of Western civilization, in general, and the fate of the United States, in particular. Unlike other intellectuals of his generation, Adams believed that the exercise of political power in our democratic society had become wholly disconnected from intellectual and cultural "sensibilities." Critical thinking had lost its importance. Intellectuals had become irrelevant as voices of authority. In his pessimism, Adams questioned the dominant notions of social evolution and progress and worried about the human applications of science and technology going forward. For Adams, the social and physical world he knew seemed headed toward social decline and degeneration.

A good example of the dark mood of alienation running through the intellectual community in the early 1920s can also be found in a collection of essays edited by literary critic Harold Stearns. Stearns asked a group of about thirty intellectuals to contribute articles in their special areas of expertise to *Civilization in the United States* (1922). The theme running through all the contributions is their dismal assessment of the state of American culture and the common agreement among the writers that "the most amusing and pathetic fact in the social life of America today is its emotional and aesthetic starvation" (Allen 2010, 198). In the opinion of one historian, "The . . . writers agreed that the United States was an unlikely place for a renaissance, that it was disgustingly materialistic, that it was artistically and intellectually barren, and that its dominant mood was repressive" (Shannon 1965, 96). Seeing no way out of this dark age, Stearns did what many writers and intellectuals would do during the decade: he fled to Paris and became an expatriate. For those who chose to stay, many gathered in Greenwich Village or other urban bohemian enclaves where they could find solace while they continued to lash out at the deadening influence of the dominant business-driven culture.

For a number of the best writers during the 1920s, World War I proved to be a transformative event. When they wrote about the war—and many had experienced the carnage firsthand—they described it as a horrible and often psychologically destructive endeavor that left them totally disillusioned. In the words of expatriate poet Ezra Pound, men had died "For an old b**** gone in the teeth, / For a botched civilization" (Dumenil 1995, 152). One of the first writers to make an attempt to convey the experience of war was John Dos Passos with his novel *Three Soldiers* (1921). The novel, autobiographical in part as Dos Passos served as a volunteer ambulance driver for the American Expeditionary Forces in France, described the war through the eyes of three soldiers—a store clerk from San Francisco, a young Indiana farmer, and an aspiring composer from New York. They had all gone to war gaily but had quickly witnessed war's darker side. As the horrors became intolerable, and as the regimentation of military life and its dehumanizing servility became unendurable, the sensitive, introspective musician remarks: "I've got to a point where I don't give a damn what happens to me. I don't care if I'm shot, or if I live to be eighty . . . I'm sick of being ordered around" (Dos Passos 2003, 437).

The "Lost Generation": Hemingway and Fitzgerald

Of all the writers deeply affected by the war, the one who seemed to be able to sum up the experience with the most sensitivity and understanding was Ernest Hemingway. In *A Farewell to Arms* (1929), he based his characters on his own experience as an ambulance driver for the American Red Cross on the Italian front. At one point the main character comments, "I was always embarrassed by the words 'sacred,' 'glorious,' and 'sacrifice,' and the expression 'in vain.' " "I had seen nothing sacred, and the things that were glorious had no glory and the sacrifices were like the stockyards at Chicago if nothing was done with the meat except to bury it. There were many words that you could not stand to hear and finally only the names of places had dignity" (Hemingway 1995, 184–85). The characters that Hemingway represented were lost and in despair. They had come to find no meaning in life beyond simple hedonistic pleasures. They rejected the world as they saw it, but they had no real theory about what had gone wrong or how to fix it. "They reflected the feeling that the war had overturned Western civilization and left the world upside down" (Shannon 1965, 97). "With some Byronic self-consciousness and romantic self-pity, they [the writers] called themselves the 'lost generation.' " Credit for coining the term has been awarded to Gertrude Stein in conversation with Ernest Hemingway. Like Hemingway, they "believed in a world in which the only conceivable good is an intensification of stoicism, courage to endure rather than courage to do" (Sullivan 1996, 658, 659). And it was Hemingway in *The Sun Also Rises* (1925) that gave the "lost generation" fullest expression. In the novel, a group of expatriates in Paris and their friends, other artists and writers, feel that life is just too complicated to think about. Not knowing how to soothe their bored and rootless spirits, they drink constantly in an effort to avoid what to them is useless introspection.

Hemingway's spare, crisp writing style, his ability to compress emotion and meaning, his use of vigorous words, and his choice of themes offered a sharp break from the more genteel tradition that had characterized American literature before the war. And, as one historian has noted, "To a considerable extent, the intellectuals' revolt in the 1920's was a reaction against a style of life that had been honored before the war." And as for Hemingway, "his generation, which above all wanted not to be old-fashioned, lionized him as few American generations have lionized their authors" (Shannon 1965, 97).

The 1920s was a decade in which its youth set the tempo, and, as such, it should not be surprising that the literature of the period would reflect the contrast between the older and younger generations. If an argument can be made that there is an egotism that is reflected in every youth culture, then that of the 1920s was heightened by what one contemporary observer described as "the ease with which young folks could achieve economic, and therefore to a large extent moral and intellectual, independence." The writer who seemed to speak for this youthful, freedom-loving, anti-Puritanical demographic was F. Scott Fitzgerald, who first drew attention to the younger generation at the start of the decade with the publication of *This Side of Paradise* (1920). Written when its author was only twenty-four, most younger readers assumed that Fitzgerald understood their temper. Through Amory Blaine, the sensitive, world-weary central character, Fitzgerald undertakes an exploration of college life in the Jazz Age that made quite an impact. "Young people found in Amory's behavior a model for their conduct—and alarmed parents found their worst apprehensions realized" (Sullivan 1996, 661–62).

Fitzgerald's name then was, and still today is, commonly associated with the Jazz Age, a descriptive term that first appeared in *Tales of the Jazz Age* (1922). In writing about the hedonism of all-night parties and the exploits of self-indulgent, college-age, pleasure seekers, Fitzgerald managed to be "naughty, sophisticated, and shocking" and, in the process, won for himself celebrity status as the spokesperson for flaming youth. In fact, Scott and his wife, Zelda, became the couple who most personified the mood of the decade—"a fun-loving, irreverent, adventuresome pair who loved to party and to spend money recklessly" (Drowne and Huber 2004, 184). Fitzgerald's most acclaimed novel, *The Great Gatsby* (1925), tells the tragic story of a young man's obsessive quest to win back the love of his former sweetheart. But the novel is also a trenchant commentary on the decadent rich, "a powerful evocation of all that was rotten in the American dream in general and the dream decade of the 1920s in particular. The decay of the characters' souls is more tragic than the casual violence that snuffs out Jay Gatsby's life" (Cashman 1998, 204).

Often associated with the Jazz Age are the iconic drawings of John Held Jr. that were unique in their ability to capture "attitude" done as caricature. It was easy to recognize the Held man with slicked-down hair, wrinkled socks, and bell-bottom trousers, while the Held woman ("flapper") was just as familiar with her long, thin legs, rosy cheeks, knee-revealing dress, short or "bobbed" hair, and strand of pearls. This *Life* magazine cover from February 1926 captures the mood. (Library of Congress)

Complementing Fitzgerald's tales of the Jazz Age were the comical drawings of John Held Jr. His drawings, especially his sardonic sketches of "flappers," placed the older generation (portrayed as the Gibson girl and the Gibson man) in contrast with the younger and served as models for other illustrators seeking to capture the "type." It was easy to recognize a Held man. He was usually depicted sporting a raccoon coat with slicked-down black hair, wrinkled socks, and bell-bottom trousers. The Held woman (flapper) was just as recognizable with her incredibly long, thin legs, rouge-embossed cheeks, short, skimpy skirt, and tight-fitting little felt hat. Held truly captured "attitude" done as caricature.

Social Criticism: Lewis and Mencken

Other writers/intellectuals made their reputations criticizing the dominant culture. Sinclair Lewis was prominent in this group. Born in the small town of Sauk Center, Minnesota, in 1885, Lewis understood America from a provincial perspective. After attending Yale University where he was editor of the literary magazine, Lewis worked at a number of editorial jobs in different cities across the country. Nearing thirty, Lewis found himself having amassed a mental catalogue of keenly observed personality types that he poured into his early novels. In *Main Street* (1920), Lewis used a litany of character types to satirize small-town life. In the novel, Lewis pits Carol Kennicott, the somewhat sophisticated, recently married doctor's wife who arrives in mythical Gopher Prairie with lofty hopes of starting an experimental theater and organizing discussion groups and poetry readings, against the self-satisfied provincialism of everyone else in town. Complacency, tradition, and resistance to change defeat her at every step. In *Babbitt* (1922), Lewis attacks the values of the small businessman in the fictional city of Zenith and creates George Follansbee Babbitt as his middle-class foil. Babbitt is a booster, a joiner, a conniving real estate speculator, a social climber, and a nonthinker. He is crass, materialistic, complacent, chauvinistic, and bigoted. Most damning to Lewis, however, is that Babbitt is the ultimate conformist and, in a larger sense, a prototype for a society that has ceased to value individuality.

Lewis continued to criticize American culture in other novels written during the decade as well. In *Arrowsmith* (1925), he took a swipe at the American medical profession. Lewis uses the main character, research pathologist Martin Arrowsmith, to create a conflict between the ideal of pure scientific research and the crass pressures of commercial compromise. In *Elmer Gantry* (1927), Lewis lashes out at religious demagoguery. Through the main character, silver-tongued evangelist Elmer Gantry, Lewis portrays a self-indulgent hypocrite, whose career is marred by sensual desires he cannot control and the constant need to deceive his parishioners. In summing up Lewis's major novels, Mark Sullivan commented:

Of the types that Lewis satirized most fiercely, many were mainly in the world of business, the "go-getter," the smug success, the "human dynamo," the "mixer," the man who could "sell himself," the one who could "put his message across." As a consequence of the satires by Lewis and others—combined with several contemporary actualities, overemphasis on salesmanship, overrespect for business success—and also some contemporary scandals in business and politics, it resulted that some American types formerly treated with deference, even in some cases awe, found themselves, by the end of the 1920s, occupying pedestals lower than those to which they had been accustomed. (Sullivan 1996, 674–75)

Rivaling Lewis in the art of social criticism but having honed a style that was far more vitriolic was Henry Lewis Mencken. Mencken began his career as a newspaper columnist for the *Baltimore Sun* and then with the outbreak of World War I became coeditor, with George Jean Nathan, of a magazine called the *Smart Set*. Although the magazine promoted the naturalistic writing of Theodore Dreiser and Frank Norris and gave Americans their first opportunity to read James Joyce, it was never a commercial success. In late 1923 Mencken and Nathan began publishing a new monthly magazine, the *American Mercury*. Every month Mencken reserved several pages for his diatribes against some aspect of the "lowbrow" majority. The magazine featured writers such as Theodore Dreiser, Willa Cather, Sherwood Anderson, and Sinclair Lewis who had chosen to defy genteel traditions. The green-covered *American Mercury* "lambasted Babbitts, Rotarians, Methodists, and reformers, ridiculed both the religion of Coolidge Prosperity and what Mencken called the 'bilge of idealism,' and looked upon the American scene in general with raucous and profane laughter" (Allen 2010, 199).

The irreverent *American Mercury* was an immediate success, and by 1927 its circulation had climbed to 77,000. Mencken regarded himself as the enemy of hypocrisy, political cant, and greed and of religious, ethnic, and racial intolerance, all of which he found in plentiful supply during the era of Harding and Coolidge. He had utter disdain for politicians, rural countryfolk, members of the clergy, temperance reformers, Klansmen, religious fundamentalists, and fanatics of whatever stripe. Seconding the sentiments of Harold Stearns and his group, Mencken believed that America had proven itself an unfit place for the cultivation of serious artistic or intellectual endeavors. Capitalism, democracy, and religion had made that impossible. Capitalism valued only what would sell or make a profit; democracy compromised individualism and threatened to destroy it, while religion condoned repression and censorship under the banner of morality. Mencken dismissed the middle class, especially the members of that demographic who resided in the nation's small towns and hamlets, as either "boobs," "massed morons," or the "booboisie," and found most Americans to be "the most timorous, sniveling, poltroonish, ignominious mob of serfs and goose-steppers ever gathered under one flag in Christendom since the fall of the Eastern Empire" (Mencken 1921, 655).

Other writers and intellectuals admired Mencken's mastery of vocabulary and his humorous use of invective and idolized him as the champion of the "highbrow" crusade against the enemies of creativity and forward thinking. In 1927 Walter Lippmann called Mencken "the most powerful personal influence on this whole generation of educated people" (Allen 2010, 200). Attesting to his influence from another perspective was the conservative academic at the University of Chicago, who remarked, "The one thing that makes me fear for the future is the number of our students who read the *American Mercury*; on the campus you see it under every arm; they absorb everything in it" (Sullivan 1996, 675). But there was an area where Mencken was open to criticism. As one historian noted, "Mencken's cleverness and wit often masked the shallowness of his own social vision and analysis. He failed to grasp the shock of change that tormented millions of Americans" (Parrish 1992, 199–200).

The "Highbrow" Critique

Taken as a group, the "highbrow" intellectuals of the 1920s seemed to share a set of beliefs on current widely discussed topics. For the most part, they believed in a greater degree of sexual freedom and a more open discussion of sex. They objected to any enforcement of propriety through legislation. As a result, they detested censorship, deplored Prohibition, and regarded most reformers as meddlers. They tended to be religious skeptics and assigned to Mencken's great bourgeois majority and Lewis's "Babbitts" primary responsibility for most of society's repressions. They were frightened by the dehumanizing effects that they associated with the machine age and mass production and hated regimentation or anything that stifled creativity or individuality.

Until the appearance of the *American Mercury* and H. L. Mencken's wholesale attack on sacred icons, intellectuals had been on the defensive. But before long, other magazines joined in dissent. By mid-decade *Harper's* had reinvented itself with a bolder and more critical examination of American life and doubled its circulation in the process. *Harper's* was soon followed by the *Forum*, the *Atlantic*, and *Scribner's*. Meanwhile, more books reflecting the elite culture's view of the United States and of life, in general, found their way into print. As Frederick Lewis Allen noted, "Slowly the volume of protest grew, until by 1926 or 1927 anybody who uttered a good word for Rotary or [William Jennings] Bryan in any house upon whose . . . shelves stood *The Sun Also Rises* or *Notes on Democracy*, was likely to be set down as an incurable moron" (Allen 2010, 201–2).

The Southern Agrarians

In an interesting intellectual counterpunch to the Mencken-led attack on the "narrow-minded" defenders of traditional values, a group of southern intellectuals began to come together in defense of those values and to argue against the recent trends in modern society and art. Between 1922 and 1925 this group, led by Allen Tate, John Crowe Ransom, Robert Penn Warren, and Donald Davidson, shared their ideas in the journal *The Fugitive*. But the major statement from this expanding group of novelists, poets, and historians centered at Vanderbilt University in Nashville, Tennessee, came in a manifesto entitled *I'll Take My Stand: The South and the Agrarian Tradition* (1930). Often referred to as the "southern agrarians," these twelve individuals offered a spirited defense of agrarianism, regionalism, and tradition.

It has been suggested that their more formal response, in a sense a rebellion against modernity, had been prompted by the ridicule that had flowed from the national media during coverage of the famous 1925 Scopes Trial in Dayton, Tennessee (see Chapter 7). Much of the northern-based news coverage of the trial portrayed the event as a by-product of an ignorant southern mind. H. L. Mencken, who covered the trial for the *Baltimore Sun*, had referred to "Daytonians" as "yokels," "hillbillies," and "bigots." Harboring a long-standing bias against the northern disruption of the southern lifestyle, the agrarians harangued northern businessmen for continuing to dominate the South economically and for promoting an exploitative, consumer-driven, factory system that had made labor less satisfying, "brutal and hurried." It was modern, urban-industrial society that had left hard-working Americans feeling alienated and dispossessed. In their critique of the new economic order, the "agrarians" were not too far apart from the lost generation.

Where they diverged, however, was in the southern defense and even glorification of the rural folk culture of the American South. Lamenting the diminishment of tradition, stability, community, and religion rooted in the land, they could still proudly proclaim in the modern era that "the culture of the soil is the best and most sensitive of vocations" (Dumenil 1995, 160). But in trying to reclaim southern honor, they left themselves open to criticism. According to Lillian Smith, a southern-bred writer, they failed "to recognize the massive dehumanization which had resulted from slavery and its progeny, sharecropping and segregation" (Dawley 1991, 316).

THE EMERGING MASS CONSUMER CULTURE

While the rejection of the dominant business culture of the 1920s was the primary focus of the lost generation and had the greatest appeal to its more well-educated followers, the vast majority of Americans had their noses in reading matter of a different type. Popular literary tastes during the 1920s favored romance novels, Westerns, and crime stories. The appearance of subscription book clubs enabled millions of Americans to follow popular authors. In 1926, Harry Scherman started the Book-of-the-Month Club (BOMC) where its primarily middle-class members could receive a novel each month selected by a five-member panel of "distinguished" literary critics. By 1929 the BOMC had more than 110,000 members. Soon other organizations like the Literary Guild, started in 1927, moved to tap into a lucrative market. Book clubs, however, tended to follow a cautious policy of selecting safe and conventional titles for their readers. In 1922 DeWitt and Lila Wallace began publication of *Reader's Digest*, essentially a compilation of articles taken from other magazines and rewritten in condensed form. The magazine, cleverly marketed to readers as a convenient way to keep abreast of a wide sweep of American journalism, actually provided its readers with a carefully selected, constricted view of the world from a politically conservative perspective.

The decade also saw a number of women writers strike a popular chord. Writers like Anita Loos, Edna Ferber, Gene Stratton-Porter, and Mary Roberts Rinehart drew a large and loyal readership. Anita Loos's novel, *Gentlemen Prefer Blondes* (serialized in *Harper's Bazaar* in 1925), told the story of Lorelei Lee, a sexy gold-digger who has an obsession for fancy jewels and the cleverness to know how to obtain them. Although a number of writers dealt with the topic of immoderation and crass materialism and took a critical view of the decade's excesses, Loos employed her considerable comedic talents to lampoon those excesses as ridiculous and at odds with reason or common sense. The novel became the second-highest-selling book of 1926. Edna Ferber had a best seller in 1924 with *So Big*, an inspirational story about Selina DeJong, a young woman struggling to raise her son on a small truck farm near Chicago. Ferber's book won a Pulitzer Prize in 1925. Indicative of her story-telling talents were two other successful novels—*Show Boat* (1926) and *Cimarron* (1929). *Show Boat* told the story of three generations of the Hawks family, an acting troupe performing melodramas aboard the *Cotton Blossom Floating Palace Theatre* for small-town audiences along the Mississippi River. The book was somewhat provocative for the time as it touched on the racially sensitive issue of mixed marriage. The popular novel was adapted as a Broadway musical in 1927. Yet another success was *Cimarron*, a Western about the opening of the Oklahoma Territory in 1893, which became a popular film in 1931. Gene Stratton-Porter wrote two best sellers during the decade—*Her Father's Daughter* (1921) and *The Keeper of the Bees* (published posthumously in 1925). Critics often dealt harshly with her sentimental stories, but she had sold more than 10 million copies of her books by the time of her untimely death in a car accident in 1924. Mary Roberts Rinehart was a widely read mystery writer and for a time more popular than her British rival Agatha Christie. Although she shifted to romantic fiction during the 1920s, Rinehart continued to produce popular novels like *A Poor Wise Man* (1920), *The Breaking Point* (1922), and *Lost Ecstasy* (1927) although literary critics consistently gave her books unfavorable reviews.

Possibly the most popular writer during the post–World War I years was Zane Grey. A prolific writer of Westerns, Grey produced over sixty novels in which he portrayed life in the American West as a moral battleground where the struggle between good and evil was being waged. His novels had it all—settlers, wagon trains, cowboys, gunfighters, desperados, cattle drives, and Indians. Grey's big breakthrough as a writer came with *Riders of the Purple Sage* (1912), which sold more than two million copies and has been made into at least three movies. He continued his success into the 1920s with *The Man of the Forest* (1920), *The Mysterious Rider* (1921), *To the Last Man* (1922), *The Wanderer of the Wasteland* (1923), and *The Call of the Canyon* (1924). Grey sold more than 17 million copies of his short novels during his lifetime, and it has been suggested that more than one hundred films have been produced based on his stories.

Crime fiction and detective story magazines were also popular during the 1920s. In 1920, H. L. Mencken and George Jean Nathan, coeditors of the *Smart Set*, introduced *Black Mask* to the genre of mystery pulp fiction. Several of the more famous mystery writers like Dashiell Hammett, Raymond Chandler, and Erle Stanley Gardner got their start by publishing in *Black Mask* and other magazines of detective pulp fiction. Hard-boiled private eyes like Sam Spade first appeared in the pages of these magazines, and Dashiell Hammett's *The Maltese Falcon* first ran as a five-part serial novel in *Black Mask* beginning in September 1929. By the end of the decade, detective pulp fiction aficionados could choose from a number of crime story magazines such as *Real Detective Tales and Mystery Stories* (1925), *Clues* (1926), *Crime Mysteries* (1927), and *Detective Fiction Weekly* (1928).

Defenders of the Probusiness Culture

Some publications and authors did well during the 1920s offering a perspective that either accepted the dominant business civilization or celebrated it. During the decade, the *Saturday Evening Post* dominated the popular magazine market and did so by featuring the probusiness, mass consumer values of white, middle-class Americans. Although the *Post* occasionally published what one historian has called "the second-rate work of the first-rate authors," it generally tended to print "light stuff that was artistically trite, intellectually puerile, and socially conventional. The heroes of the stories were often little more than modernized versions of Horatio Alger's paragons of Social Darwinistic virtues. Optimism, boosterism, conformity, the hope of getting rich quick—in sum, the qualities of Sinclair Lewis's Babbitt—were the values expressed in these articles and stories" (Shannon 1965, 98). And, as it has been said, while thousands read Sinclair Lewis, millions read the *Post*.

Bruce Barton and *The Man Nobody Knows*

Perhaps the individual who is most remembered as a defender of America's business-oriented ethos during the 1920s was Bruce Barton. Barton, the son of a Congregationalist minister, has been described as a leader of "the new class of secular priests conveying the gospel of consumption to the nation's anxious flock of consumers" (Parrish 1992, 78). After graduating from college, Barton became a freelance writer and magazine editor. Shortly after the end of World War I, he joined Roy S. Durstine to create what would become one of the country's leading advertising firms—Batten, Barton, Durstine, and Osborne. Although he wrote advertising copy for some of the country's leading corporations, his real claim to notoriety came with his attempt to reconcile Christianity with consumption. In a series of articles and books written over the span of a decade—*A Young Man's Jesus* (1914), *The Man Nobody Knows* (1925), *The Book Nobody Knows* (1926), and *What Can a Man Believe?* (1927)—Barton fundamentally challenged old beliefs. Where orthodox Protestantism placed an emphasis on hard work and denounced idleness and self-indulgence, Barton argued that leisure activities and even conspicuous consumption were acceptable in modern society. To Barton, consumerism was a form of Christian devotion. The greatest sin was repression, the failure to enjoy life and seek self-fulfillment in one's everyday life.

To drive his point across, Barton offered an interpretation of a secularized Jesus that was consistent with the business values of the 1920s. In *The Man Nobody Knows: A Biography of Jesus* (1925), which made the nonfiction best-seller list for two years in a row, Barton described Jesus as the founder of modern business. He was an advertising genius, a supersalesman, a dynamic leader, a forceful executive, and a master of public relations and business organization. His simple parables were the most powerful advertisements of all time, while the manner in which he gathered his disciples showed that he was an excellent personnel manager as well. It is easy for critics, as historian Lynn Dumenil has suggested, to dismiss Barton's book "as a crass attempt to appropriate religion in the service of commercial success," but, as she noted, its immense popularity suggested "a continued need for idealized purpose rooted in religious tradition." Frederick Lewis Allen agreed. "Under the beneficent influence of Coolidge Prosperity, business had become almost the national religion of America. Millions of people wanted to be reassured that this religion was altogether right and proper, and that in the rules for making big money lay all the law and the prophets" (Dumenil 1995, 196; Allen 2010, 156).

THE HARLEM RENAISSANCE

The Emergence of a New Racial Consciousness

A number of factors came together in American society around the time of World War I to enable the black cultural flowering that occurred in New York City during the 1920s known as the Harlem Renaissance. One of these factors was the emergence of a new racial consciousness and pride that came to be identified as the "new Negro." The overseas experience gained by African American soldiers during the war greatly broadened their horizons. Although badly treated in the American army, black soldiers had been warmly received by the French. That experience taught them that there were limits to American racism. Encountering people of African descent who were either serving in colonial armies or living as private citizens in France and Great Britain also contributed to an emerging Pan-African view of the world. Like other American soldiers, they believed that they were participating in a great moral crusade to advance political justice and democracy around the world. They also believed that their participation in the war had earned "Negroes" some legitimacy in American society. In a sense, the war had enlightened black soldiers, broadened their horizons, and given them an enhanced sense of self-worth. But on their return, those same soldiers encountered only a revival of racism in place of hoped-for racial progress.

New York City had been the primary destination for many who took part in the Great Migration, and it was that migration that swelled the numbers of African Americans living in Harlem. The city was also the center of the nation's publishing industry that included a number of prominent black journals. *The Crisis*, the publication of the NAACP (National Association for the Advancement of Colored People) edited by W.E.B. Du Bois; the socialist *Messenger*, edited by A. Philip Randolph and Chandler Owen; the *Negro World*, the voice of Marcus Garvey's Universal Negro Improvement Association; and *Opportunity*, the publication of the National Urban League edited by Charles S. Johnson, were all based in New York City and became increasingly outspoken that a "new style" of more self-assertive black Americans was emerging. As generally perceived, they were more conscious of their rights and fully determined to preserve them. Helping to further develop this new race consciousness were a string of black newspapers—the New York *Age*, the Pittsburgh *Courier*, the Cleveland *Gazette*, the Chicago *Defender*, the Washington *Colored American*, the Indianapolis *Freeman*, and the Boston *Guardian*—that had become beacons to the black populations in the major northern cities. Providing further context to the awakening that was about to unfold was the fact that New York City was also the center for visual art, theater, and music as well as the home of many wealthy patrons of the arts.

The Cultural "Facilitators"

Historian Nell Irvin Painter has suggested that the literature, art, and scholarship of the Harlem Renaissance became well known because of the "careful networking" efforts of seven "visionary and well-connected" African Americans in Harlem and their white "allies" (Painter 2006, 193). Members of this influential group included W.E.B. Du Bois and Jesse Fauset at *The Crisis* and Charles S. Johnson at *Opportunity*. Both publications regularly published the short stories, poems, drama, and essays of black authors, and both regularly offered literary prizes during the 1920s. Also in the group were James Weldon Johnson and Walter White of the NAACP, philosopher Alain Locke at Howard University, and Casper Holstein, Harlem's numbers-racket kingpin who provided financial support. The group had a common aim—to overcome traditional black stereotypes and promote racial advancement through the arts. In working toward their goal, the seven formed a close cooperation with sympathetic whites such as Carl Van Vechten, the Harmon Foundation, and a number of white writers such as Eugene O'Neill, Sherwood Anderson, Sinclair Lewis, and Van Wyck Brooks. Major publishing houses like Alfred A. Knopf also provided outlets for the works of Harlem writers.

A number of other individuals also played special roles in encouraging black artists. One of those was Carl Van Vechten, a photographer and writer as well as an art, music, drama, and literary critic. Van Vechten, a transplanted Iowan, maintained a downtown salon where black artists were welcome guests and, as much as anyone, promoted black artists and performers professionally. He knew all the "important" people and had access to publishers and producers. He also became something of an authority on Harlem's nightlife and was often asked by his white friends to give them guided tours of all the "authentic" places. In 1926, however, Van Vechten caused an uproar with his sensational and highly commercial novel, *N****r Heaven*. Many were offended by the title of his work, which was actually a reference to the balcony where black patrons had to sit in segregated theaters and auditoriums. Just as provocative was his focus on the coarser aspects of life in Harlem that irritated the likes of Du Bois and Fauset who were not looking for a more "honest" depiction of the black urban experience. Despite their differences, black and white literary figures would often gather at Van Vechten's roomy apartment on West 55th Street for literary soirees. Another meeting place for Harlem artists was the unpretentious rooming house at 267 West 136th Street where notables Wallace Thurman, Zora Neale Hurston, and Langston Hughes resided in the late 1920s.

Another supporter of Harlem's cultural renaissance was Regina Anderson Andrews. The comfortable, middle-class African American daughter of a Chicago lawyer, Andrews came to Harlem to "find" herself amid the excitement generated by young black men and women who were writing, singing, dancing, and painting, all while working as a librarian at the 135th Street branch of the New York Public Library (NYPL). Her job placed her in touch with young artists, and she soon made the library a cultural center for black intellectuals. She also turned her apartment (which was described in Carl Van Vechten's *N****r Heaven*) into an uptown salon where all the intellectuals gathered. In 1926 the NYPL purchased (with the help of a grant from the Carnegie Foundation) the private collection of Arthur A. Schomburg. Schomburg, a Puerto Rican of African and German descent who had emigrated to Harlem in the early 1890s, was an ardent student of Caribbean and African American history and an avid collector of literature, art, slave narratives, and other materials. The collection, which included roughly 5,000 books, 3,000 manuscripts, and 2,000 works of art, formed the basis of the NYPL's Division of Negro History at the 135th Street branch in Harlem and later provided the foundation for the Schomburg Center for Research in Black History and Culture.

Equally influential to the Harlem Renaissance was wealthy white philanthropist William Elmer Harmon, who tried to rectify the problem of the lack of financial support available to African American artists by creating the Harmon Foundation in 1922. The foundation gave out annual awards and cash prizes for African American achievement in seven categories: literature, fine arts, science, education, industry, religion, and music. Toward the end of the decade, the Harmon Foundation began to sponsor all-black art exhibitions to showcase the stunning work of black artists and attract public attention. Taken as a group, the "seven" and their "allies" served as "facilitators," committed to finding talented black artists and then guiding their work toward publication, presentation, or performance. Folklorist and novelist Zora Neale Hurston "laughingly called the artists the 'N****rati' and their publishers and patrons 'Negrotarians'" (Painter 2006, 193).

The Cultural Integrationists

There were, however, divergent views within the Harlem Renaissance. One group, headed by Du Bois, Fauset, and Locke, favored cultural integration. They argued that artists had a moral obligation to convey certain positive, "refined" representations of African Americans to society. Black art had to convey a certain respectability that whites would accept willingly. It was believed that such positive images would do much to counter long-standing, negative racist stereotypes and help resolve racial conflict in America. Popular art forms like jazz and the blues, although eagerly embraced by many whites, sent the wrong message about black people. To integrationists, such musical forms were "unrespectable" because they represented a low-brow culture that was associated with Harlem's unseemly nightlife. To a mind-set guided by racial uplift, jazz was not "useful." Art and politics were seen as being inseparable, and art was the means by which African Americans could gain recognition as cultural equals. Long-sought-after political and social equality would follow.

The Opponents of Cultural Integration

Conversely, opponents of cultural integration argued that African Americans had a unique voice that could be expressed only through a distinctly black art. To capture black experiences truthfully, black artists needed to focus on the everyday lives and heritage of black people. Authentic self-expression, not contrived inspirational literature, was the correct path to follow. Art should be created for art's sake and not used as political propaganda. Leading this countergroup were Claude McKay, Langston Hughes, and Zora Neale Hurston. In *The Ways of White Folks* (1934), Hughes dismissed the notion that writers could promote racial harmony. One of his characters derisively expressed that sentiment by saying, "Art would break down color lines, art would save the race and prevent lynchings! Bunk!" (Hine et al. 2000, 407). In an often-quoted defense of the authenticity of black art and literature taken from his famous 1926 essay "The Negro Artist and the Racial Mountain," Hughes, speaking for a younger generation of black artists, argued that constraints placed on black artists to avoid certain depictions of black life only stifled creativity.

> We younger Negro artists who create now intend to express our individual dark-skinned selves without fear or shame. If white people are pleased, we are glad. If they are not, it doesn't matter. We know we are beautiful. And ugly too. The tom-tom cries and the tom-tom laughs. If colored people are pleased we are glad. If they are not, their displeasure doesn't matter either. We build our temples for tomorrow, strong as we know how, and we stand on top of the mountain, free within ourselves. (Hughes 1926, 694)

The Harlem Renaissance at Its Peak

The year 1925 saw the Harlem Renaissance achieve full flower. A number of very notable books had already appeared in print. James Weldon Johnson's *Book of American Negro Poetry* (1922) and Claude McKay's *Harlem Shadows* (1922), Jean Toomer's *Cane* (1923), Jessie Fauset's *There Is Confusion* (1924), Walter White's *Fire in the Flint* (1924), and Countee Cullen's *Color* (1924) all made favorable impressions. The publication of Alain Locke's *The New Negro* (1925), however, with its poetry, short stories, and essays on black art and culture, marked a new level of sophisticated discourse about African Americans written by African Americans. The book actually had its origins as a collection of articles by thirty-nine authors entitled "Harlem: Mecca of the New Negro" that appeared in *Survey Graphic* in March 1925. Approached by the editors to pull together contributions for a special issue on African Americans, Locke included a broad discussion of the nature of black art that was then in vogue. When the *Survey* issue sold 30,000 copies, Locke decided to bring the collection out as a book. His own essay "The Legacy of the Ancestral Arts" has often been misinterpreted to suggest that he wanted African American artists to emulate African art. What he really wanted was for black artists to seek inspiration from and take cultural pride in their rich African heritage. He regarded African art as a classic art form on par with the masterworks of Greece and Rome. What black artists could learn from African art was the discipline that African artists brought to their work, their "originality of expression," their mastery over material, and the "powerful simplicity of conception, design and effect" (Locke 1925, 673). To illustrate his edited anthology, Locke included stark black-and-white silhouette drawings with Egyptian motifs by African American artist Aaron Douglas.

No African American artist during the Harlem Renaissance was more influenced by Africa than Aaron Douglas. Born in Topeka, Kansas, educated in the public schools, and eventually graduated from the University of Nebraska's School of Fine Arts, Douglas came to New York City in 1925. There, under the tutelage of German folk artist Winold Reiss, Douglas began to work with African themes to gain a sense of the folk roots of African American people. In offering an interpretation of his technique, Nathan Huggins has suggested that, to Douglas, "music, the dance, that spirit beneath the substance—soul—were a connective tissue between the African and the Afro-American. In his art, he attempted to achieve that metaphor which would make that subliminal unity explicit." In pursuit of that goal, Douglas produced drawings that were stylized designs comprising stark black-and-white silhouettes. Human forms appeared as flat outlines, angular and elongated in shape, bending as if in motion, long-headed, and often with mere slits for eyes. "The effect was always savage: feline human figures crouched or moving as in dance" (Huggins 1973, 169).

For many black artists, however, Africa was an abstraction, and establishing a spiritual link was difficult. As a result, a number of writers chose to focus on "the spiritual, creative character which was commonly believed to be the essence of black culture" (Dumenil 1995, 162). In pursuit of that ideal, writers like Zora Neale Hurston and Jean Toomer turned their attention to the folk culture of the rural South. Hurston celebrated the common folk and freely employed the idioms and rhythms of black speech in her writing, while Toomer gained critical acclaim for *Cane*, a collection of stories and poetry about southern black life. But in describing the "primitive" black life of the region, such authors risked being censured by the cultural integrationists for coming perilously close to reinforcing long-standing pejorative stereotypes.

In 1926 Langston Hughes, Zora Neale Hurston, Wallace Thurman, and Helene Johnson started the journal *Fire* to feature the voices of a younger generation of writers and to call for a more innovative, modern approach in creating African American art. But in celebrating the themes of the urban masses that featured street life, drugs, prostitutes, urban slang, and stories that illustrated that blacks, too, could be guilty of color prejudice, they met with so much criticism from older black intellectuals who found their contributions vulgar that they shut down *Fire* after only one issue. The episode underscored just how uncomfortable some upper-class black intellectuals were with any probing of the new urban culture that was central to the lives of the larger black majority. They were unwilling to tolerate any shifting of the cultural focus away from the idea that only by demonstrating mastery of high culture could blacks achieve parity with whites.

This dilemma was certainly an issue to the few black writers who, in their search for distinctive black contributions to the arts, chose to explore jazz and the blues as examples of an indigenous urban black culture. In *The Weary Blues* (1926), Langston Hughes tried to

convey a bluesy tone in describing the artistry of a Lenox Avenue
piano player in Harlem:

> *He made that poor piano moan with melody.*
> *O Blues!*

(Dumenil 1995, 164)

Historian Nathan Huggins found it curious that except for Hughes
none of the other Harlem intellectuals took jazz, the new music,
seriously. "Of course, they all mentioned it as background, as
descriptive of Harlem life. All said it was important in the definition of the New Negro. But none thought enough about it to try and
figure out what was happening. . . . It is very ironic that a generation that was searching for a new Negro and his distinctive cultural
expression would have passed up the only really creative thing that
was going on" (Huggins 1973, 10–11). One talented artist who took
up the jazz theme late in the decade was Archibald Motley. After
winning a Guggenheim Fellowship that funded a year of study in
France, Motley created *Blues* in 1929, a colorful, rhythmical painting of Jazz Age Paris.

The Decline of the Harlem Renaissance

It has been suggested that there were actually two Harlems in the
1920s: the first, a by-product of the enthusiasm for black nightlife
and art "that bordered on being a cult"; and the second, a community of high unemployment, overcrowding, high rents, and crime.
In the 1920s Harlem became a symbol of the Jazz Age—"the antith-
esis of Main Street, Zenith, and Gopher Prairie." "Whatever seemed
thrilling, bizarre or sensuous about Harlem life was made a part of
the community's image; whatever was tragic about it, ignored." The
Great Depression brought an abrupt end to both the dream of the
new Negro and the image of Harlem as America's answer to Paris.
Black artists and writers of the Harlem Renaissance remained active
into the 1930s, but the cultural climate changed dramatically. Hard
times took their toll on the sales of books and literary magazines.
Subscriptions to *The Crisis* and *Opportunity* declined, and both journals published fewer works by creative black writers. Most black
artists, who had never been able to support themselves on proceeds
from art sales, found it nearly impossible to find buyers for their
work. Many black intellectuals, watching the cultural effervescence
of Harlem wane, left for more staid positions in academia. But the

toll on the community was worse. As Alain Locke sadly concluded in 1936, the Great Depression revealed the second Harlem, "a Harlem that the social worker knew all along but had not been able to dramatize. . . . There is no cure or saving magic in poetry and art for . . . precarious marginal employment, high mortality rates, civic neglect." "The depression brought everybody down a peg or two," stated Langston Hughes. "And the Negroes had but few pegs to fall" (Osofsky 1965, 234, 235, 238).

Document: John F. Carter Jr., " 'These Wild Young People': By One of Them" (1920)

The following selection offers a defense of the younger generation from one member of that demographic. Written in 1920, the same year that saw the publication of F. Scott Fitzgerald's This Side of Paradise, *the author tries to shift the blame for his generation's excesses back to the "oldsters" who seem to be so critical.*

" 'These Wild Young People': By One of Them"

For some months past the pages of our more conservative magazines have been crowded with pessimistic descriptions of the younger generation, as seen by their elders and, no doubt, their betters. Hardly a week goes by that I do not read some indignant treatise depicting our extravagance, the corruption of our manners, the futility of our existence, poured out in stiff, scared, shocked sentences before a sympathetic and horrified audience of fathers, mothers, and maiden aunts—but particularly maiden aunts. . . .

I would like to say a few things about my generation.

In the first place, I would like to observe that the older generation had certainly pretty well ruined this world before passing it on to us. They give us the Thing, knocked to pieces, leaky, red-hot, threatening to blow up; and then they are surprised that we don't accept it with the same attitude of pretty, decorous enthusiasm with which they received it, way back in the eighteen-nineties, nicely painted, smoothly running, practically fool-proof. "So simple that a child can run it!" But the child couldn't steer it. He hit every possible telegraph-pole, some of them twice, and ended with a head-on collision for which *we* shall have to pay the fines and damages. Now, with loving pride, they turn over their wreck to us; and, since we are not properly overwhelmed with loving gratitude, shake their heads and sigh. "Dear! dear! We were so much better-mannered than these wild young people. But then we had the advantages of a good, strict, old-fashioned bringing-up!" How intensely *human* these oldsters are, after all, and how fallible! How they always blame us for not following precisely in their eminently correct footsteps!

Then again there is the matter of outlook. When these sentimental old world-wreckers were young, the world was such a different place. . . . Life for them was bright and pleasant. . . . Christianity had emerged from the blow dealt by Darwin, emerged rather in the shape of social dogma. Man was a noble and perfectible creature. Women were angels (whom they smugly sweated in their industries and prostituted in their slums). Right was downing might. The nobility and the divine mission of the race were factors that led our fathers to work wholeheartedly for a millennium, which they caught a glimpse of just around the turn of the century. . . .

Now my generation is disillusioned, and, I think, to a certain extent, brutalized, by the cataclysm which *their* complacent folly engendered. The acceleration of life for us has been so great that into the last few years have been crowded the experiences and the ideas of a normal lifetime. We have in our unregenerate youth learned the practicality and the cynicism that is safe only in unregenerate old age. We have been forced to become realists overnight, instead of idealists, as was our birthright. We have seen man at his lowest, woman at her lightest, in the terrible moral chaos of Europe. We have been forced to question, and in many cases to discard, the religion of our fathers. We have seen hideous peculation, greed, anger, hatred, malice, and all uncharitableness, unmasked and rampant and unashamed. We have been forced to live in an atmosphere of "to-morrow we die," and so, naturally, we drank and were merry. We have seen the rottenness and shortcomings of all governments, even the best and most stable. We have seen entire social systems overthrown, and our own called in question. In short, we have seen the inherent beastliness of the human race revealed in an infernal apocalypse. . . .

Now I think that this is the aspect of our generation that annoys the uncritical and deceives the unsuspecting oldsters who are now met in judgment upon us: our devastating and brutal frankness. And this is the quality in which we really differ from our predecessors. We are frank with each other, frank, or pretty nearly so, with our elders, frank in the way we feel toward life and this badly damaged world. It may be a disquieting . . . habit, but is it a bad one? We find some few things in the world that we like, and a whole lot that we don't, and we are not afraid to say so or to give our reasons. In earlier generations this was not the case. The young men yearned to be glittering generalities, the young women to act like shy, sweet, innocent fawns—toward one another. And now, when grown up, they have come to believe that they actually were figures of pristine excellence, knightly chivalry, adorable modesty, and impeccable propriety. But I really doubt if they were so. . . .

Oh! I know that we are a pretty bad lot, but has not that been true of every preceding generation? At least we have the courage to act accordingly. Our music is distinctly barbaric, our girls are distinctly *not* a mixture of arbutus and barbed-wire. We drink when we can and what we can, we gamble, we are extravagant—but we work, and that's about all that we can be expected to do; for, after all, we have just discovered that we are still very near to the Stone Age.

Source: John F. Carter Jr. " 'These Wild Young People': By One of Them," *Atlantic Monthly* 126 (September 1920): 301–4.

Document: H. L. Mencken, "On Living in the United States" (1921)

H. L. Mencken, an accomplished linguist and one of the most skilled crafts-men of his time, gained notoriety as the editor of the American Mercury. *With a pen dipped in sarcasm and vitriol, he conducted a merciless assault against hypocrisy, greed, religious intolerance, stupidity, and political cant. Intellectuals found him entertaining. College students adored his irreverence. The masses, however, as the objects of his ridicule, only saw him as the devil. The following is a sample of one of his broadsides.*

"On Living in the United States"

It is one of my firmest and most sacred beliefs, reached after due prayer, that the Government of the United States, in both its legislative and its executive arms, is corrupt, ignorant, incompetent, and disgusting—and from this judgment I except no more than twenty lawmakers and no more than twenty executioners of their laws. It is a belief no less piously cherished that the administration of justice in the Republic is stupid, dishonest, and against all reason and equity—and from this judgment I except no more than twenty judges. It is another that the foreign policy of the United States—its habitual manner of dealing with other nations, whether friends or foes—is hypocritical, disingenuous, knavish, and dishonorable—and from this judgment I consent to no exceptions whatsoever.

And it is yet another that the American people, taking them by and large, are the most timorous, sniveling, poltroonish, ignominious mob of serfs and goose-steppers ever gathered under one flag in Christendom since the fall of the Eastern Empire. . . .

Well, why am I still here? In particular, why am I so complacent, . . . so free from indignation, so curiously happy? Why did I answer only with a few academic and polite *Hochs* when Henry James, Ezra Pound, and Harold Stearns issued their successive calls to the native intelligentsia to flee the shambles, escape to fairer lands, throw off the curse forever? The answer is to be sought in the nature of happiness. . . . To be happy one must be (a) well fed, unhounded by sordid cares, at ease in Zion, (b) full of a comfortable feeling of superiority to the masses of one's fellow men, and (c) delicately and unceasingly amused according to one's taste. It is my contention that, if this definition be accepted, there is no country in the world wherein a man constituted as I am—a man of my peculiar weakness, vanities, appetites, and aversions—can be so happy as he can be in the United States. Going further, I lay down the doctrine that it is a sheer physical impossibility for such a man to live in the United States and *not* be happy. If he says he isn't, then he either lies or is insane. Here the business of getting a living is enormously easier than it is anywhere else in Christendom—so easy, in fact, that an educated and unsqueamish man who fails at it must actually make deliberate efforts to that end. Here the general average of intelligence, of knowledge, of competence, of self-respect, of honor is so low that any man who knows his trade, does not fear ghosts, believes in nothing that is palpably idiotic, and practices the common decencies stands out as brilliantly as a wart on a bald head, and is thrown willy-nilly into a meager and exclusive aristocracy. And here, more than anywhere else in the world, the daily panorama of human existence—the unending procession of governmental extortions and chicaneries, of commercial brigandages and throat-slittings, of theological bufooneries, of aesthetic ribaldries, of legal swindles and harlotries—is so inordinately extravagant, so perfectly brought up to the highest conceivable amperage, that only the man who was born with a petrified diaphragm can fail to go to bed every night grinning from ear to ear, and awake every morning with the eager, unflagging expectations of a Sunday-school superintendent touring the Paris peep-shows.

Source: H. L. Mencken. "On Living in the United States," *The Nation* 113 (December 7, 1921): 655–56.

4

MATERIAL LIFE

The number of choices available to the average consumer during the 1920s seemed limitless. Advancements in technology and the development of new industries made automobiles, refrigerators, electric vacuum cleaners, and radios readily available. The advertising industry embellished the attractiveness of potential purchases, while the advent of installment buying made the purchase of those new wonders all that much easier. Although homeownership remained the number one priority for most Americans, the purchase of a car was not far behind. In fact, the two were most often inextricably linked as an automobile expanded the options for buying a home and provided the means by which to engage in the world of material culture that was rapidly emerging.

HOUSING

When the Lynds did their study *Middletown* (Muncie, Indiana), they found that the home was still the mainstay of the family and "a mark of independence, of respectability, of belonging" (Lynd and Lynd 1956, 103). In *Middletown*, 86 percent of the residents lived in single-family homes and 10 percent in two-family houses, while only 4 percent lived in apartments or over stores primarily in the downtown section of the city. The Lynds estimated that a family had to sacrifice well over its entire income for a single year to own a home or the income of one week each month to rent one. Although the federal census of 1920 revealed that most urbanites living in big cities were predominantly renters because of the high cost of living, in smaller cities like Zanesville, Ohio, where 70 percent of families had incomes below $2,000, 80 percent were still able to own their own homes. Homeownership was often a key statistic cited by chambers of commerce when trying to attract new businesses.

Neighborhoods: Housing Contrasts

Not surprisingly, the Lynds found that homes in *Middletown* differentiated by class and that there was a marked "unevenness in the diffusion of material culture." To make their point, the Lynds offered "snapshots" of typical dwellings sorted by class. The homes of the poorest working-class families remained essentially the same as they had been in the middle of the previous century— "bare little one-story oblong wooden boxes with a roof and with partitions inside making two to four rooms." Coming home from work after nine and a half hours on the job, the poorer working man "walks up a frequently unpaved street, turns in at a bare yard littered with a rusty velocipede [an early type of bicycle or tricycle] or worn-out automobile tires, opens a sagging door and enters the living room of his home." From this vantage point the entire house was visible—kitchen, living room, and bedrooms. "Worn green shades" hung down from the windows, and "ornate calendars" or "enlarged colored portraits of the children in heavy gilt frames" adorned the walls. "On the brown varnished shelf of the sideboard the wooden-backed family hair brush, with the baby bottle, a worn purse, and yesterday's newspaper, may be half stuffed out of sight behind a bright blue glass cake dish."

The working man with a little more money likely entered his property (which might be a two-floor home, a bungalow, or a cottage) through a "tidy" front yard with geraniums in the front windows "neat with their tan, tasseled shades and coarse lace curtains." A nameplate of "silvered glass" adorned the front door. The small living room was "light, with a rather hard brightness, from the blue- and pink-flowered rug, bought on installment, to the artificial flowers, elaborately embroidered pillows and many-colored 'center pieces.'" The furniture was commonly "straight-lined 'mission' of dark or golden oak" or, if the family was a bit more prosperous, "overstuffed." The sewing machine usually occupied a space in the living room or dining room, while the ironing board had its usual place in one corner of the kitchen. " 'Knickknacks' of all sorts" were plentiful: "easeled portraits on piano or phonograph, a paper knife brought by some traveled relative from Yellowstone Park, pictures that the small daughter has drawn in school, or if the family is of a religious bent, colored mottoes." A visitor might even have found a "standing lamp with a bright silk shade, another recent installment purchase and a mark of prestige. Some magazines may be lying about, but rarely any books."

Moving up a class or two, the distinctions were more pronounced. The homes of the less wealthy members of the business/professional class (bookkeepers, small retail store owners, and school teachers would fit in this group) revealed "an atmosphere of continual forced choices between things for the house and things for the children—between a hardwood floor for the front hall and living room or a much-needed rug and the same amount of money put into music lessons or the Y.M.C.A. summer camp." The house may have been an older one with very few adornments, with small rooms and "a miscellany of used furniture." Although the likelihood of seeing a radio was less than in a more prosperous working-class home, one might have "come upon a copy of Whistler's portrait of his mother or a water-color landscape and a set of Dickens or Irving in a worn binding." It was also common to find books from a missionary society or printed matter from the Woman's Club lying on the "mission library table."

The homes of the more prosperous members of this business/professional group displayed an even greater sense of pride. The street was most likely "neatly paved" and "tree-bordered," while the homes were "the last word in the up-to-date small house." These houses were shingled or stuccoed with well-maintained terraced yards, while "everything from the bittersweet in the flower-holder by the front door to the modern mahogany smoking table by the over-stuffed davenport bespeaks correctness." A long living room conjoined the dining room by a double doorway, while "colors in rugs, chair coverings, curtains, and the elaborate silk shades of the standing lamps" matched. Three or four pictures—"colored photographs or Maxfield Parrish prints"—hung at eye level from the walls, a pair of candlesticks sat on the bookcase, while a few bowls and trays completed the assortment of visible objects. The kitchen cabinet contained "every convenience" and rounded out the "complete small house."

For wealthier families, the contrast was even more marked. Some of these families inhabited older homes in the posh "East End" of town. Constructed of either heavy brick or stone, these large homes boasted "perhaps two stone lions guarding the driveway near the old hitching post and carriage block bearing the owner's name." Other wealthy families in this section of town lived in comfortable frame houses, while still others relocated to the newer college district. In this area the homes were of two types—single-story brick or field stone, or the white Dutch colonial style—and displayed "every convenience in the way of plumbing and lighting and with spacious glassed-in porches." When the homeowner returned from a day at the bank or office, he likely entered a large parlor or library in the older type of dwelling or a long living room in the new district. Either way, the atmosphere he encountered was one of "quiet and space." "The wide rooms, soft hangings, old mahogany, one-toned rugs or deep-colored Orientals, grand piano, fireplaces, cut flowers, open book-shelves with sets of Mark Twain and Eugene Field and standard modern novels, the walls hung with [Classical] prints . . . may be combined with certain individual touches, a piece of tapestry on the wall, a picture not seen elsewhere, a blue Chinese bowl" (Lynd and Lynd 1956, 95, 98–102).

Suburban Growth

Material life in the 1920s changed in many ways. One way was the growth of suburbia, which was anchored in the belief that single-family homeownership was still the number one priority for most Americans. The profits connected to real estate speculation, skillful marketing and financing, encouragement from urban transportation and utility companies, financial commitments from municipalities for road construction, and the popular craze for automobiles and the freedom of movement they made possible all converged to make the development of a new suburban landscape possible.

It has been said that the suburb fulfilled a unique social function: ideally located far enough from the city to offer the buyer a rural appeal—open space nearby, room for a garden in the back, and set away from the street by a front lawn—yet still close enough to the city for people to commute to work. Detached, single-family, suburban homes set on individual lots were seen "as images of sturdy independence in their apartness from their neighbors" (Gowans 1986, 30). One writer has termed this new home the "Comfortable House," and what made it comfortable was its emphasis on new labor-saving technology (electric vacuum cleaners, irons, toasters, laundry machines, electric or gas stoves, and refrigerators), innovative materials (porcelain tile on the inside and stucco on the outside), central heating, screens, and sleeping porches. Modern bathrooms served as shrines to hygiene, while kitchens increasingly resembled modern, culinary laboratories.

Real estate development expanded tremendously during the decade as homebuilders increasingly utilized the new technologies of mass production to meet a growing demand for middle-income housing as the middle class grew in number. This process was aided by the expansion of public transportation and the growing popularity of the automobile which opened up new housing sites, often some distance from the center of the city. Between 1920 and 1930 the suburbs grew twice as fast as the cities. For many, these new developments offered less congestion, more generous lot sizes, and varying degrees of middle-class exclusivity where restrictive covenants often excluded "undesirable" minorities.

The Southern California Real Estate Boom

One of the focal points for these new developments was Southern California. Between 1920 and 1930, 1.5 million people settled in the area, 1.2 million in Los Angeles County alone. By 1930, after tripling its population in just ten years, Los Angeles had grown to become the fifth-largest city in the nation. Real estate development fueled this rise, with approximately one-third of the population owning and occupying their own homes. This was in contrast to rental rates in 1920 of 87.3 percent in New York, 81.5 percent in Boston, and 72.6 percent in San Francisco. In the boom year of 1923 alone, some 25,000 new homes were built and sold to single-family buyers. A startling one million Americans found a new home during the 1920s in some two dozen or more new, suburban communities in greater Los Angeles.

As real estate developers bought and subdivided land for potential residential communities, they needed to sell those properties quickly to realize the tremendous profits that might result. It was a test of both salesmanship and promotion, and two of the best salesmen and promoters were Abbot Kinney and Harry Culver. Abbot Kinney actually predates the decade (he died in 1920), but his suburban vision lived on after his death. Kinney was well educated and well traveled and, along with his brother, the heir of the family's cigarette manufacturing business. Ultimately, the sale of that business left Kinney wealthy for life. Somewhere along the way, this man of many interests forged the idea of developing a

Mediterranean-style suburban development. He started his project in 1892 when he purchased a stretch of marshy tidelands on the site of the old Rancho La Ballona, about fifteen miles from downtown Los Angeles. Shortly after the turn of the century, Kinney began development of what would be called the Venice of America, part residential community and part fantasy resort. Alongside a winding Grand Canal (a half mile long, seventy feet wide, and four feet deep) Kinney laid out lots and began building residential cottages that were to be connected to the canal by fifteen miles of smaller tributaries and palm-planted lagoons. A series of gates would regulate the flow of seawater. Once completed, singing gondoliers would punt gondolas along the canal.

Kinney's suburban vision seemed to expand with the development. He spent an estimated $1.4 million to improve the harbor and waterfront (including construction of a 500-foot-long breakwater) and built several large piers. He also erected the Venetian-styled St. Mark's Hotel with elaborate columns and archways. To complete his vision of the new Venice as an upper-middle-class Italianate resort with cultural amenities that would serve greater Los Angeles, Kinney built a 2,500-seat auditorium for theatrical and orchestral performances that included a grand pipe organ and large windows that offered stunning views of the ocean. He also made sure that the spreading Pacific Electric streetcar system would connect Venice with the larger metropolis and, beginning in 1904, one could get on what was eventually called the Venice Short Line (VSL) in downtown Los Angeles and be dropped off at the beach fifty minutes later. Wednesdays were excursion days when the fare was only 25 cents. As a popular destination, the VSL carried 5.5 million passengers to Venice in 1920.

But Kinney's dream ran up against some harsh realities. When sales of the residential properties proved disappointing, and when visitors reacted with indifference to his cultural offerings, he reversed course and turned Venice into a West Coast version of Coney Island (the first of many themed parks in Southern California). The "Midway Plaisance" was pure carnival with circus acts, a giant Ferris wheel, amusement park rides, and a huge bathhouse with the world's largest saltwater plunge. Along the pier one could have fun at a skating rink, bowling alley, and shooting arcade. Everybody seemed to perform at the Venice Ballroom, so everybody danced there. The Ship Café, built on pilings alongside the pier, was a reproduction of the Spanish explorer Cabrillo's flagship, and a popular nightspot. And there were beauty contests, which seemed to be held constantly, and dance marathons, which were illegal in Los Angeles but legal in Venice.

Even the lowering of cultural expectations, however, could not save Kinney's Venetian dream. The water in the canals never circulated properly, and stagnation became a problem. In 1912 the State Board of Health intervened and declared the canals to be a menace to public health. Friction also developed between residents and some of the carny operators. Public debate followed over whether to end the city's independent status and incorporate with either Santa Monica or Los Angeles. When Venice became part of Los Angeles in 1925, the city decided to fill in most of the canals and pave them as public streets. The final blow to picturesque Venice came with the discovery of oil. Oil wells soon blighted the landscape and finally destroyed the visionary dream of Abbot Kinney.

More successful in realizing his suburban dream was Harry Culver. After arriving in Los Angeles from Omaha in 1910, Culver briefly apprenticed as a real estate agent before striking out on his own as a developer. In 1913 he formed the Culver City Investment Company and announced plans to build a subdivision named after his company on land that he had acquired between Los Angeles and Venice. To emphasize the community ideal, Culver set the stage by building two churches, a grocery store, a hardware store, and a real estate office, while at the same time putting in seven miles of sidewalks and setting up a local newspaper. He then proceeded to hire 150 salesmen (expanded to 250 by 1924) to start moving lots. Backed by the Pacific Electric Railway Company that was eager to help disperse the population outward toward the suburbs, and by a decision to locate the Metro-Goldwyn-Mayer film studios there in 1924, which added a good deal of cachet to the project, Culver was well on his way. To further promote his "city," Culver mounted a searchlight on top of his sales office (it was able to project a beam of light visible for thirty miles) and sponsored booster parades, baby beauty contests, soapbox races, and marathons. He even handed out honorary Culver City constable's badges to celebrities. Knowing that many of his potential buyers were, like himself, uprooted from the Midwest and unsure of their tastes, Culver fully outfitted many of his homes with furniture, dishes, silverware, linen and bedding, a Victrola, pictures to decorate the walls, a cuckoo clock, and a Ford in the garage. One could have it all for $500 down and $80 a month on a 7 percent loan compounded semiannually.

The Southern California Bungalow and Bungalow Court

The solution to the challenge of creating a moderately priced residential alternative for the hordes of new migrants to Southern California was the bungalow. A derivative of the Bengali cottage common in India, the bungalow took on its American characteristics in early twentieth-century California. By the 1920s the style could be found all over the country. In 1927 a survey, *Zanesville, Ohio and Thirty-Six Other American Communities*, described the typical midwestern bungalow as a four-room, one-story, working-class house. Offering a smaller form of residential space, the one- or one-and-one-half story wooden structure had a low-pitched, frequently shingled roof, wide eaves, and a signature front porch. The porch was usually supported by large pillars of stone or brick that accentuated the low profile of the house. In rethinking the interior arrangement of space, architects created an open floor plan that eliminated most of the dark hallways between rooms that had characterized older designs. With low ceilings, plain or gently curved stained oak or pine moldings, stained or clear-finished wooden floors, and built-in seats, the bungalow created the feel of open space and the look of simplicity to achieve what one writer called "a new level of tasteful functionalism in affordable housing" (Starr 1990, 188). Although the bungalows were smaller (usually around 1,500 square feet), they were popular because of their lower cost. Regarded by many as a "starter home," the bungalow enabled many younger members of the middle class and others with limited incomes to realize the suburban dream.

Joining the bungalow as a type of affordable housing in Southern California were hundreds of apartment house structures built during the 1920s in Los Angeles and Hollywood, as well as numerous bungalow courts and courtyard apartments. The latter two alternatives featured enclosed patios, walled gardens, and courtyards that provided owners with their own private spaces within an increasingly congested urban environment. As one author noted, "The landscaped court helped create community out of discreet dwellings, providing a spatial expression of common identity for residents recently arrived from elsewhere." The very first bungalow court (eleven units clustered around a central court) was the St. Francisco Court in Pasadena, designed by Sylvanus Marston in 1909. Originally intended to appeal to winter visitors from the East, each bungalow came fully furnished with Stickley furniture and assorted household utensils. Later courts, often done in the Spanish

Revival style that was popular on the West Coast in the 1920s, had common recreational facilities like a playground for the kids and tennis courts. Many added a common laundry room, while others incorporated a garage for the car to hide the symbol of congestion and maintain the illusion of tranquil privacy. Many of these bungalow courts were built in Hollywood near the film studios where they provided convenient housing for technicians, production assistants, and aspiring starlets who flocked to Hollywood during the film-crazy 1920s. Within a decade's time, the bungalow court would evolve into the motel, "which telescoped into an overnight stay the bungalow-court metaphor of instant community amidst rapidity of movement" (Starr 1990, 215–16).

One architect who attempted to create his own democratic vision of affordable housing for Southern Californians was Irving Gill. In 1910 Gill used a unique concrete construction (mixing concrete with warm earth tones or implanting it with colored tile to blend with the surrounding vegetation), the bungalow court design, and the idea of a garden environment to create Lewis Court in Sierra Madre, a small suburb near Pasadena, for a low-income, blue-collar clientele looking to rent. Three years later he completed another grouping of affordable garden cottages in Echo Park near downtown Los Angeles. His intention was to replicate this general idea toward the goal of creating an entire suburb of affordable garden apartments for working people. As luck would have it, he got his chance when an investment group retained him as chief architect for a proposed model community in the industrial city of Torrance in Los Angeles County. But as soon as Gill's project got under way, he ran into trouble from the same workers he was looking to benefit. Unions objected to his simplified designs and construction techniques because they reduced the number of workers required for the job. As a result of their protests, Gill was able to complete construction on only ten of his experimental garden cottages. As one chronicler has suggested, "Had the Torrance project not collapsed so ironically, . . . [Gill] might have accomplished a Levittown, Southern California-style, thirty years ahead of schedule" (Starr 1990, 222).

THE IMPACT OF THE AUTOMOBILE ON THE MATERIAL LANDSCAPE

In the early days in Los Angeles, the Big Red Cars of the interurban Pacific Electric system allowed Angelenos to live in forty-five communities scattered over a thirty-five-mile radius and commute to work in downtown Los Angeles or to nearby industrial districts. On reaching the downtown terminal at Sixth and Main, passengers could shift to the Yellow Cars of the Los Angeles Railway system, which operated within city limits. Travel was speedy and efficient and largely unaffected by competing automobile traffic. For tourists, the best and cheapest way to see Southern California was aboard a Big Red Car. Six thousand trains ran each day over 115 different routes, and the basic fare was just 5 cents. In 1924, a remarkable 109,185,650 passengers rode the rails.

Congestion

But things quickly changed. By 1927 Los Angeles County could claim one automobile for every 3.2 people. That was approximately 560,000 passenger cars and 76,000 trucks, being served by 450 gasoline stations. The new reliance on motorized transportation also brought about the idea of public transportation by motor bus, which was initially targeted at points in the outlying San Fernando Valley. In the ten years between 1917 and 1927, Los Angeles spent $24 million grading and paving 1,300 miles of roads. Experts had predicted that Los Angeles County would top out at 100,000 automobiles by 1919, but by 1924 there were at least four times that number, excluding the cars of tourists. Congestion was the result. Stalled in traffic jams that they could not control, streetcars lost their initial advantage. Running speeds slowed down on the Yellow Cars in the downtown area, and commercial and residential development between destination points on the interurban lines caused trips on the Big Red Cars to take longer as well. By 1933 streetcar usage was half of what it had been in 1924.

Gas Stations

Increased reliance on automobiles as the desired mode of transportation revolutionized gas stations and gave rise to a new form of popular art. Prior to World War I, filling stations were few in number and each looked like nothing more than a shed with a single gasoline pump in front. After the war, however, larger gas stations began to appear featuring multiple pumps and an indoor office. In the competition to sell gas and oil, station owners got creative and began to design their "filling stations" to resemble small houses. This new style fit in well with the homes in the surrounding residential areas and suggested a neighborly friendliness to local motorists. Eventually oil companies entered the fray and used architecture in an attempt to create a corporate identity that motorists might associate with that particular brand of gasoline. In pursuit of that idea, the Pure Oil Company built stations that resembled quaint English cottages, Socony-Vacuum chose the style of colonial houses, while Wadham's Oil Company opted for a design that looked like a Chinese pagoda. Others chose styles that reflected local tastes—suburban bungalows, Spanish haciendas, or mini-Tudor mansions. During the 1920s competition heated up in the area of service, with stations starting to offer engine repairs, tire changes, and headlight and battery replacements in addition to gasoline fill-ups and oil changes. In the process, stations expanded their service areas and storage facilities. By the late 1920s, the full-fledged "service station" had grown into an architectural style that resembled a big box-like structure that contained an office, the service area with multiple garage bays, a utility room, bathrooms, and any number of pumps located on islands in front.

Property Values and Urban Decentralization

The use of the automobile intensified the value of outlying real estate and gave further encouragement to suburban development. Over a twenty-year period between 1907 and 1927, land values in downtown Los Angeles increased by 800 percent, but property values in the outlying suburbs increased by twice that amount in just ten years (1917–1927). And while Los Angeles sprawled outward, banks, theaters, and department stores began the process of urban decentralization through the establishment of various branch offices. One section of Los Angeles that proved to be a model of this trend was the area along Wilshire Boulevard. In 1921 developer A. W. Ross concluded that the city was destined to grow westward toward Santa Monica and the Pacific Ocean. He also surmised that motorized consumers would be willing to drive up to four miles to shop. Finally deciding on a narrow east–west roadway called Wilshire, at a point halfway between downtown and the ocean, Ross decided to build his auto-retailing shopping district called the Wilshire Boulevard Center. When completed, shoppers from nearby areas got in their cars and came to shop just as Ross had predicted. To accommodate these motoring consumers, he built spacious parking lots. When the city widened Wilshire Boulevard in 1924, Ross ensured that the new road included synchronized traffic lights and landscaped traffic islands that today would be called "turn lanes." In 1928 the original plan was renamed the Miracle Mile.

The Wilshire district soon began to assume a special commercial aura with the construction of the Ambassador Hotel that opened for business in January 1922, the first important hotel of the 1920s' boom era in Los Angeles and famous for its Cocoanut Grove nightclub. As a destination for the affluent, dinner could be enjoyed for $2.50 ($37.50 in 2018 dollars), with a cover charge of 75 cents ($11.25 in 2018) for an evening of dancing to the music of Abe Lyman's Ambassador All-Star Orchestra or perhaps Duke Ellington's band jamming to the rhythms of the Jazz Age. The Cocoanut Grove featured an exotic North African Moorish decor, with an oasis waterfall and palm trees procured from the set of *The Sheik* (at the suggestion of Ambassador resident Rudolph Valentino, the star of that film). Outshining the Ambassador Hotel in grandeur was Bullock's Wilshire, a branch of a major downtown department store. The Bullock's Wilshire, an Art Deco masterpiece designed by John and Donald Parkinson, exuded the confidence and optimism of the city when it opened in 1929. Reflecting the architecture of the new City Hall downtown, a 464-foot tower atop a square colonnaded base that was completed in 1928, the structure rose ten floors from its five-story base and featured green copper siding against beige cast stone, with frosted glass and dark tropical wood in the interior along with disc and torch branch chandeliers. With its two main entrances facing the rear parking lot "where automobiles arrayed themselves in reverent formation like giant black mantises praying before a copper-green altar," historian Kevin Starr saw the building as a "temple to the automobile." To suggest what gods were being celebrated, Starr referred to Herbert Sachs's ceiling mural above the south entrance, which featured images of transportation from the god Mercury to the *Graf Zeppelin* which stopped in Los Angeles in August 1929. "Here and throughout the store," noted Starr, "like icons in an Orthodox cathedral, were repeated depictions of the automobiles which had created a new type of American city" (Starr 1990, 83).

FOOD

Adding another characteristic to the decade was a culinary revolution that contributed to the standardization of American cuisine and the emergence of modern eating habits tailored to a population increasingly on the go. Kitchens became modernized, foods became "freeze-dried," national brand-name products dominated grocery shelves, scientific nutrition and dieting increased in importance, while "fast-food" fare became popular nationwide. The contemporary American diet was beginning to take shape.

The Changing Diet

Well into the mid-nineteenth century Americans had relied on a heavy diet that included large quantities of meat, starches, fat, and sugar but very few fruits and vegetables. Cooks used a lot of salt but very few other spices or seasonings. Toward the end of the nineteenth century, however, things began to change. Middle-class consumers started to take advantage of commercially processed foods like condensed soups and canned fruits and vegetables, and diets became more varied and a bit more nutritious. But there were exceptions even to these modest improvements. In the South, a black or white tenant farmer's or sharecropper's diet might consist of little more than ground cornmeal mush or bread, fried salted pork, molasses, and some local vegetables. Most farmers in the Midwest fared better, but even their diets depended a great deal on what they could raise and what was in season. Although the so-called summer diet included fruits and vegetables, the winter diet usually did not, centering instead on pork, grains, potatoes, and beans.

World War I helped to bring about a change in thinking about diets. Because of shortages in foodstuffs and a reduced agricultural labor force, the government started a food conservation program. As part of that program, the Food Administration, whose staff included a number of home economists and reformers influenced by the ideas of an emerging group of nutritionists, told people that they could stay healthy even if they ate less as long as they consumed a proper amount of proteins, carbohydrates, minerals, and vitamins. Reducing one's caloric intake was also a good thing to do (campaigns for "meatless" and "wheatless" days encouraged this). If Americans could reduce their reliance on white wheat flour and meat along with sugar and butter, and consume more beans and lentils for their proteins, rely on cornmeal, oats, and grains other than wheat for their carbohydrates, use more vegetable oils to reduce fats, and eat more fruits and vegetables, a healthy "patriotic" diet could be achieved. In 1919, Dr. Harvey Wiley, a noted pure food crusader who became a health columnist for *Good Housekeeping* magazine during the 1920s, declared that he was optimistic about the future of the American diet because he believed the wartime lesson that "wholesome" foods, those which were "simple and as near to nature as possible," would usher in an era of simple cooking (Levenstein 2003, 159).

Immediately after the war, as middle-class families began to reduce the number of servants and many middle-class women began to work outside the home, the trend toward an increased reliance on convenient, commercially obtained foods and simpler, healthier meals continued. As part of this trend, sales of canned fruits and vegetables, condensed soups, canned pork and beans, and tomato sauce increased. Meanwhile, improvements in transportation—refrigerated railcars and over-the-road trucks—allowed a wider variety of fresh meats, fruits, and vegetables to reach dinner tables than ever before.

Although most food continued to be prepared and eaten in the home, and food preparation remained the responsibility of the married woman, less time and effort were being spent on cooking. Simple meals became the norm, and one-dish meals and casseroles became increasingly popular. Breakfasts consisted of dried cereal or eggs, toast, and citrus fruit. Students and employed members of the family often carried light lunches with them when they left home, while the more affluent might grab a hot lunch at a restaurant or lunch counter. Dinners remained the main meal and tended to center on roast or broiled meat or poultry, potatoes, and a vegetable. Salads also became increasingly popular. Two well-known salads created during the 1920s were the Cobb salad, developed in 1926 by Robert Cobb at his Brown Derby restaurant in Los Angeles, and the Caesar salad, named after Caesar Cardini, an Italian chef who created his special salad for a group of visiting Hollywood celebrities at his restaurant in Tijuana, Mexico, in 1924. By 1930 the average American consumed 5 percent fewer calories than before the war, ate much more fruit (especially citrus fruits) and green vegetables, drank and ate considerably more milk (pasteurization removed milk's previous unhealthy stigma) and cheese, while reducing the amount of flour and cornmeal, potatoes, and red meat.

The Self-Service Grocery Store

Another related innovation that revolutionized the retail food industry was the self-service grocery store. Prior to World War I most grocery items were located behind a counter and the selection process was left to store clerks, who would then box and often deliver the groceries to a customer's home. In 1916 Clarence Saunders changed that when he introduced a new self-service format at his Piggly Wiggly grocery store in Memphis, Tennessee. Shoppers could now choose items from open shelves, placing their personally inspected selections in baskets that were then carried to the front of the store for the "checker" to total up. The popular Piggly Wiggly, which operated primarily in the South and Midwest, grew from 515 stores in 1920 to 2,600 stores by 1929. In Los Angeles, Ralph's Grocery Company switched from clerk- to self-service in 1926. Before the end of the decade, Ralph's operated sixteen large stores that it called "supermarkets." Rather than delivery service, Ralph's provided automobile parking lots.

Dieting

As notions of diet and nutrition changed, the idea of a slim figure came to be regarded as more attractive than a plump one. As a result, people became more conscious about their weight and adopted a new approach to food consumption—dieting. Diet manuals and commercial diet programs were popular, while the leading women's magazines featured articles on the topic, published advice columns, and suggested weekly menu plans to readers who wanted to count calories and lose weight but still eat healthfully. As the notion of female beauty shifted from the curvaceous figure of the prewar Gibson girl to the thin, waistless figure of the flapper, younger women went on diets to conform to the slimmer images of women being presented in magazines and motion pictures. New clothing styles that featured shorter, leg-revealing dresses and sleeveless bodices that exposed bare arms only added to the rush to get slim. The most popular proponent of scientific dieting was Dr. Lulu Hunt Peters whose book, *Diet and Health, With Key to Calories* (1918), continued to be a national best seller throughout the 1920s. Gimmick diets gained popularity as well in which dieters were instructed to limit their meals to just a few items. One popular plan was the "Hollywood Eighteen Day Diet" that recommended a restrictive 585-calorie diet that was limited to eating only grapefruit, oranges, Melba Toast, green vegetables, and hard-boiled eggs. Food companies quickly picked up on the trend and assured consumers that their products provided "quick energy" without being "fattening." Even cigarette companies promoted their product as a way to avoid weight gain and improve digestion.

Commercial Food Processors

During the 1920s large food companies came to dominate food processing, and by the end of the decade, the food industry had become the largest sector of American manufacturing. Corporations such as General Mills, Standard Brands, and General Foods spent millions of dollars researching and developing improved methods of packaging and preserving food. General Mills also took the lead in marketing when it created a fictional housewife named Betty Crocker, who appeared in magazine and radio advertisements offering recipe recommendations and encouraging the use of General Mills products. Independent agricultural producers often formed trade associations and marketed their products under common labels such as Sun Maid raisins ("Had Your Iron Today?") or Sunkist oranges with the intention of getting consumers to identify with their brand. In 1924 Clarence Birdseye developed a process for quick-freezing fresh foods in cellophane packages, which prevented their deterioration in the thawing process. After purchasing his patents on the process, the General Foods Corporation began selling the first commercially packaged frozen fruits and vegetables under the Birds Eye Frosted Foods brand name in 1930 and launched the frozen food industry. A similar process occurred in the dairy

In 1924 Clarence Birdseye (shown here in a photo from 1943) developed a process for quick-freezing fresh foods in cellophane packages, which prevented their deterioration in the thawing process. Five years later, Birdseye sold his patents of the process to the Postum Cereal Company (soon to become General Foods), and the following year the company began selling the first commercially packaged frozen fruits and vegetables under the Birds Eye trademark. (Bettmann/Corbis)

industry, with giants like Sealtest and Borden gaining a dominant position. Starting with an advertising campaign that assured consumers of product purity, those corporations then shifted their marketing campaign to convince consumers that milk was not just for infants and small children but also a vitamin- and mineral-rich drink and recipe supplement that was nutritious for everyone. By 1925 Americans were consuming a record amount of milk and milk products.

Eating on the Go!

During the 1920s, Americans started taking their meals outside the home at a greater rate than had previous generations, and a growing number of commercial eating establishments began catering to a society that was increasingly on the go. The number of restaurants in the country actually tripled between 1919 and 1929. One major reason for this change was the passage of the Eighteenth Amendment. With alcohol sales now illegal, popular upper-class restaurants that featured French cuisine could no longer prepare their dishes with wine or serve wine to their customers. Deprived of the income from the sale of wine, many "fancy" restaurants could no longer operate profitably and were forced to close. At the opposite end of the culinary divide, Prohibition also closed the working-class saloons and thereby eliminated the "free lunches" (sausages, hard-boiled eggs, crackers, and cheese) that came with the order of a 5-cent glass of beer. At the same time, an expanding urban workforce of lower-middle-class male and female office, shop, and department store employees needed a place to grab a quick bite to eat on a short lunch hour. As a result, a whole range of new quick-service restaurants—lunchrooms, diners, tearooms, cafeterias, automats, and sandwich shops—sprang up to fill the void created by the closures of traditional eateries.

Lunchrooms and Diners

During the 1920s lunchrooms were very successful at attracting lunchtime crowds. Usually located on the ground floor of urban office buildings, lunchrooms provided counter service where a customer could get a grilled sandwich, a bowl of chili, a slice of meatloaf, or a salad. By 1920 most large cities could claim dozens of lunchrooms, and several chain operations established scores of outlets throughout the Midwest and East Coast. Diners were also

popular, especially among factory workers and taxi drivers looking for inexpensive, simple dishes. Diners were slightly different
from the lunchroom, in that they were commonly free-standing,
stainless steel structures that featured a grill, a counter, and a number of booths. Catering primarily to the breakfast and lunch crowd,
most diners remained open twenty-four hours a day. It has been
estimated that by 1932 there were 4,000 diners operating across the
country.

Tearooms

Tearooms were another popular option for Americans looking for
an affordably priced meal in a pleasing environment. Located primarily in urban downtown districts, the earliest tearooms tended
to be owned and operated by women for predominantly middle-
class female customers. Tearooms commonly served moderately
priced "light" meals (salads, sandwiches, chicken pies, and cakes)
and afternoon tea in a charming, respectable environment. Some
tearooms attempted to attract male customers by offering a heartier
fare like chopped beefsteak. One of the more famous tearooms of
this type was the Russian Tea Room in New York City that was
opened in 1926 by a group of exiled members of the Russian Imperial Ballet who had fled the Russian Revolution. Miss Ida L. Frese,
perhaps the most noted tearoom operator, established her business
on the ground floor of the huge former Vanderbilt mansion on Fifth
Avenue in New York City. At that site and her two other operations, Miss Frese was said to employ 100 women who served 1,800
customers a day.

Cafeterias

The tearoom, however, could not keep pace with other establishments offering faster service at lower prices. Chief among these
was the self-service cafeteria. As a fad, cafeterias had been popular in California even before the war. The genius behind the idea
in that state was Horace Boos, who, along with his three brothers,
opened his first cafeteria in downtown Los Angeles in 1906. With
locally employed shop girls in mind, Boos designed an operation
that allowed customers to assemble meals from a wide selection of
inexpensive entrées and side dishes that were kept warm in metal
containers on steel steam tables. One merely had to slide a tray
down a tiled counter and make one's selections. Open for lunch and

dinner, the cost-effective operation eliminated the need for waiters (busboys were hired to collect and return the dishes) and tipping (the Boos brothers liked to say that the money saved from the tip could be used to buy a piece of pie). Although some critics called the operation a "grabeteria," the general public loved the concept. By the mid-1920s, there were six Boos Cafeterias in the city and another serving the vacationing crowd on Catalina Island. Picking up on the restaurant theme idea, the Boos brothers designed their cafeterias to resemble quaint English inns with half-timbered ceilings, wrought iron lanterns, and subdued lighting. As writer Carey McWilliams noted, the cafeteria was like an "indoor picnic," and picnics were popular in Southern California (Henstell 1984, 110). Several major cafeteria chains operated during the 1920s, some adopting Mesopotamian, Egyptian, or other exotic indoor decor to enliven the experience. A year after the death of Horace Boos in 1926, the surviving brothers sold their interests to the Childs Corporation, which operated a chain of 110 restaurants nationally. Chain-operated cafeterias were also very popular in the Midwest and South and tended to feature regional cuisine. In the South, a typical menu might include fried chicken, biscuits and gravy, corn bread, collard greens, Jell-O salad, and sweet potato pie.

"Automats" and Sandwich Shops

Two other types of fast-food eateries were the "automat" and the "luncheonette" or sandwich shop. Automats had been around since 1902, and the idea, of Swedish origin, reached its peak in popularity in Philadelphia under the name Horn and Hardardt. The ultimate in fast-food design, the automat featured rows of coin-operated vending machines offering hurried customers a variety of hot and cold prepared food that was visible behind little glass windows. At the cost of only a nickel for each selection, a hungry customer could have a ham sandwich, a bowl of soup, or a slice of pie. In a luncheonette or sandwich shop, almost all meals were prepared in front of the customer. With a limited menu that offered instantly prepared sandwiches, beverages, and maybe dessert, the sandwich shop found its niche. A close cousin to the sandwich shop was the fast-food hamburger stand made famous by Walter Anderson and Edgar Waldo "Billy" Ingram, who opened a hamburger restaurant in Wichita, Kansas, under the name White Castle in 1921. Claiming that they offered only select cuts of ground meat delivered fresh to their restaurant each day, customers could watch their lunch being

prepared right in front of them on a hot grill. Tasty burgers (smoth-
ered with cooked onions and selling for 5 cents) and innovative
marketing quickly made the venture a success. Customers could
even enjoy the convenience of "carryout," and the chain encouraged customers to "Buy 'em by the sack." By 1931, the White Castle
System of Eating Houses (all built to resemble tiny white, medieval
castles) operated 115 restaurants in the Midwest and along the East
Coast. Imitators soon followed. By the end of the decade, the hamburger had eclipsed the hot dog as America's favorite fast food.

CLOTHING

Clothing styles, like much of the popular culture during the 1920s,
changed rapidly. Skirts became shorter, bathing suits briefer, while
more pliable fabrics offered more freedom of movement. Taking
their cues from fashion designers and fashion magazines, the glamour of motion picture stars, and sophisticated advertising, the fashion conscious followed the trends as they sought social acceptance,
professional success, or pleasure. Mail-order catalogues and the
availability of ready-to-wear clothing allowed ordinary Americans
to join in the fun as well.

Women's Fashion and Dress

The most enduring prewar, Progressive Era image of the ideal
woman was the Gibson girl. Wearing her long hair "up" above her
high forehead, she presented a "busty" figure with a very narrow
waist, broad hips, and well-concealed legs. Conversely, the image of
the ideal woman of the postwar decade was the flapper. She bobbed
her hair, covered her forehead, flattened her chest, hid her waist and
hips, and showed her legs. Although the two were ideal types, they
were emulated to varying degrees by many women. These popular images also suggested different conceptions of a woman's role
in society. For the former, that was maternal and "wifely," while
for the latter, that was boyish and single. The Gibson girl embod-
ied stability, while the flapper represented "motion," "intensity,"
"energy," and "volatility." As one historian noted, while "the Gibson girl seems incapable of an immodest thought or deed, the flapper strikes us as brazen and at least capable of sin if not actually
guilty of it. She refused to recognize the traditional moral code of
American civilization, while the Gibson girl had been its guardian." For those who were concerned about the shifting social mores
of the 1920s, what Frederick Lewis Allen called the "revolution

in morals and manners," what most seemed to upset them was the flapper's modernity and with it the repudiation of traditional morality and femininity. Although always a youthful minority, the flapper came to be an "extreme manifestation of changes in the life styles of American women" (see Chapter 1), many of which were made evident in fashion and dress (Yellis 1969, 44–45).

The Flapper "Look"

The flapper wore her hair in a "Ponjola" bob, a style that was first introduced by dancer Irene Castle during the war. She usually covered her head and forehead with a tight-fitting cloche hat; plucked and redrew her eyebrows; and used a range of cosmetics that included heavy face powder, rouge, deep red lipstick, and dark kohl eyeliner to give herself a provocative feminine look. Her dresses were snug, straight-lined, low-waisted, short (just below the knee by 1925 was the shortest), and rather plain. For evenings out on the town, she often wore sleeveless gowns with low necks and deep-sculpted backs. Adding to the overall effect were flesh-colored silk or rayon stockings that she very often rolled below the knee, or went without during the summer, and high-heeled shoes (firmly attached for dancing) with t-straps across the top of the foot. Women often accessorized their new fashions with long strings of beads or faux pearls. During the 1920s, the major department stores commonly presented their merchandise in attractive combinations to tempt shoppers into purchasing an entire matching ensemble. After archaeologists discovered King Tutankhamen's tomb in 1922, Egyptian-themed scarves, earrings, necklaces, and brooches (the scarab, a sacred beetle in ancient Egypt, was a very "in" motif) were very popular along with new fashion shades with exotic names like Coptic, blue lotus, sakkara (saqqara), mummy brown, and carnelian. For undergarments, the flapper replaced the corset with a girdle or nothing at all and wore a brassiere-like garment to minimize her breasts. As Kenneth Yellis has noted, this "abandonment of the traditional female aesthetic paralleled the rejection by many women of the passive sexual, social and economic role from which it had derived its force and relevance" (Yellis 1969, 49).

Clothes Designed to Meet One's Needs

Women in the 1920s also moved in the stylish direction of adopting clothing that better met their needs. Women's clothing tended to be lighter and more comfortable, with fewer undergarments and more pliable fabrics that offered more freedom of movement. A greater variety of fabrics, colors, types of clothing, and designs were available than ever before. Women's fashions occasionally took their cues from the men's side of the aisle as men's fashions offered suggestions for jackets that resembled blazers, blouses that looked like men's shirts, and even pants that were modeled after men's trousers. Economy, simplicity, and ease of care were in vogue, and as the demand for these new clothes increased, manufacturers made them available. The most popular colors were beige and black, and wardrobes could be easily accessorized with stockings, shoes, gloves, handbags, and costume jewelry. French designer Gabrielle "Coco" Chanel introduced the classic "little black dress," a fashion staple to this day, in 1926.

Then as now, the time of day dictated what women might be wearing in the 1920s. At night, lavish evening gowns made of velvet, satin, crepe de Chine, or silver and gold lamé might be seen adorned with metallic embroidery, beads, or rhinestones. In the afternoon, a stylish woman might sport a more casual "frock" with a knee-length skirt and short or fitted sleeves. Colors would be bright, and the patterns varied. Such dresses were often adorned with narrow belts, sashes, bows, or artificial flowers attached to the dress at the dropped waist. Women's suits tended to be practical but still elegant with straight, hip-length jackets (single- or double-breasted, or "edge to edge") worn over straight matching skirts, usually in navy, brown, tan, black, or perhaps a daring white pinstripe. Casual attire might include what was known as a morning dress or housedress. These informal dresses, shorter and slimmer than they had been before, were usually made of cotton fabric and featured in various patterns. Not surprisingly, women usually wore them in the home while doing household work. The attention paid to these housedresses in the various mail-order catalogues suggests that they were a popular and essential part of a middle-class woman's wardrobe.

Clothing as a Marker of Social Respectability

It has been remarked that even working girls could dress comfortably and attractively on a more limited budget. But as fashion became more important, especially to the younger set, peer pressure and the need to gain social acceptance intensified as well. As one writer noted, "More than anything else, fashionable clothes served as the principal marker of social respectability." "Being considered old-fashioned, out-of-date, or—worse yet—unable to afford stylish new products was a fate many Americans went to great lengths to avoid during this decade of unprecedented consumerism" (Drowne and Huber 2004, 95). The Lynds underscored this dynamic in their study *Middletown*. Cotton stockings and high black shoes were no longer tolerated. As one working-class mother commented, "No girl can wear cotton stockings to high school. Even in winter my children wear silk stockings with lisle or imitations underneath." The same could be said for the dark flannel "waists" and wool skirts with a silk waist for "dress up" that were popular at the turn of the century. These items had given way to "an insistence upon a varied repertory in everything from sweaters to matching hose." As one business-class mother commented, "My daughter would consider herself terribly abused if she had to wear the same dress to school two successive days." Another business-class mother started her daughter off to high school wearing fine gingham dresses and lisle hose and thought she was suitably outfitted. But after only a few days at school, the daughter confided to her mother that she was "just an object of mercy!" After that, the mother provided silk dresses and silk stockings rather than see her daughter socially ostracized. One of the major criteria for eligibility into one of the exclusive high school girls' clubs was the "ability to attract boys," so a poorly dressed girl certainly felt social pressure and ridicule. As one girl who had finally been asked to join one of the "better" clubs stated, "I've known these girls always, but I've never been asked to join before; it's just clothes and money that make the difference" (Lynd and Lynd 1956, 162–63).

The Standardization of Fashion

Although the flapper received most of the attention, other women were impacted by changes in fashion as well. A peek inside any Sears, Roebuck and Company catalogue during the decade shows that merchandisers deliberately targeted women in Middle America and took their fashion leads from New York society and magazines like *Vogue*. In fact, it has been said that the styles in these catalogues, of not only dresses but also hats, coats, shoes, lingerie, cosmetics, and accessories, were only three months behind what was actually available in New York department stores. Novelist F. Scott Fitzgerald, who certainly knew something about the younger generation, commented that the flapper was actually passé by 1923 and that "though the Jazz Age continued, it became less and less an affair

The Season's
NEW STYLES
are FASCINATING
so Different
so undeniably Chic

Fur
Collar

17N10690
Fox
$8⁹⁸

Beaverette
Fur Collar
and Cuffs

17N1225
All Wool
Velour
$17⁴⁸

17N1353
Winter Weight
Polo Cloth
Woman's Coat
$9⁹⁸
Junior Sizes
$8⁹⁸

17N1260
Silk Seal Plush
$15⁹⁵
Karakul FurCloth
$15⁹⁵

Sears, Roebuck and Co.
Dallas, Texas   5

During the 1920s, mail-order catalogs encouraged the mass consumption of ready-to-wear clothing. With the development of free rural mail delivery, consumers who lived far from urban centers could keep up with current style trends. It has generally been assumed that the fashions available through the Sears, Roebuck and Company catalog often fell short of haute couture, but, as this 1923 advertisement for fur-trimmed coats shows, that was not always the case. (Sears, Roebuck and Company, Dallas, Texas, 1923)

of youth" (Fitzgerald 1931, 460). It was obvious by then that women in other age groups had begun to copy her style. With designs that were quite modish, and with prices that were affordable, most women could be well dressed just by shopping through the mail-order catalogue or by purchasing inexpensive sewing patterns (costing about 20 cents each) for up-to-date styles. Mass production of garments was made easier by the "tubular" cut of women's wear. The new loose, modern fit meant that dresses could be manufactured in a standard range of sizes that required little in the way of adjustment for the individual figure. At the Bullock's department store in Los Angeles, female customers could even choose their selections from six different personality categories— romantic, statuesque, artistic, picturesque, modern, and conventional. The artistic type, for example, was described as "a bit enigmatic. Usually with a suggestion of the foreign. Usually dark-haired, dark-eyed. A type that may accept vivid colors, bizarre embroideries, eccentric jewellery. The artistic type welcomes the revivals of Egyptian, Russian and Chinese motifs and colorings. Peasant necklines. Berets. Hand-loomed fabrics" (Herald 1991, 16). In a way, the diffusion of stylish, mass-produced, ready-to-wear clothing had the effect of breaking down distinctions based on class. One contemporary commented, "Only a connoisseur can distinguish Miss Astorbilt on Fifth Avenue from her father's stenographer or secretary" (Yellis 1969, 57).

As mass production pushed fashion toward even greater standardization, it also gave consumers a wider range of choices in fabrics, textures, colors, and styles, as well as a selection of clothing suited to specific occasions or needs. And as women increasingly engaged in outdoor sports such as hiking, horseback riding, golf, tennis, boating, and swimming, designers worked to create suitable attire. A hiking outfit might include serge or tweed knickers (knee-length pants), while horseback riding might feature flared jodhpurs. Women golfers often wore pleated, knee-length skirts along with patterned sweaters, while tennis players donned short, slim dresses made of white rayon, cotton, or silk and white hose. Female boaters might be seen in loose, bell-bottomed pants made of silk, cotton, or crepe de Chine. Wide-legged versions of these pants, called "beach pajamas," were also worn over bathing suits at the beach. If the weather turned cooler, an "outdoor" woman might don a Fair Isle sweater or a coat sweater, which was essentially a cardigan-style sweater with a high shawl collar, pockets, and cloth belt.

The One-Piece Bathing Suit

In interviewing people for their study of clothing worn by residents of *Middletown*, the Lynds came across one young high school boy who remarked: "The most important contribution of our generation is the one-piece bathing suit for women" (Lynd and Lynd 1956, 160). Debatable as that statement might be, women's swimwear changed radically during the 1920s. Prior to World War I, women wore "bathing costumes," garments of itchy wool fabric that covered most of the female form. In 1908, Annette Kellerman, a champion swimmer, wore a one-piece body stocking into the surf at a beach near Boston and was promptly arrested. That date, however, marked the beginning of a change. By the 1920s, bathing suit manufacturers had invented a machine that could knit a stretchy, elastic fabric that could be made into a swimsuit that clung to every curve of the body. In 1921, the Jantzen Company came out with a one-piece suit that featured a scoop-neck, sleeveless top that was sewn at the waist to a pair of trunks. Four years later, Fred Cole, a Jantzen rival, created a popular suit for sunbathing. Called the "Prohibition Suit," it had a low-cut neckline and a tiny skirt that was most revealing for the time. Catalina Swimwear, a third competitor, then created a swimsuit that had more sex appeal than the Jantzen but was not as daring as Cole's. The "Rib Stitch 5" model featured a nearly backless, form-fitting suit that became extremely popular with women in the late 1920s. Not surprisingly, the trend toward body-hugging swimwear caused a stir, and a number of public beaches tried to enforce dress codes in which violators could be fined for indecent exposure.

The Impact of the Popular Media on Fashion

Changes in the popular media had its impact on fashion as well. Movies, and new fashion magazines, allowed women to see what other women were wearing, while an outfit worn by a popular screen idol could set off a short-lived fad. In 1927 Sears, Roebuck and Company advertised boots that were endorsed by Gloria Swanson and hats modeled by Clara Bow and Joan Crawford. Historian Lynn Dumenil has made an interesting argument regarding women's sexuality during the 1920s as it relates to film. Conceding that "most women identified the new sexuality as a form of freedom and equality," she noted that the new sexuality was often expressed through consumption. "Indeed, most heroines attracted the opposite sex not through the body but through the clothes, jewelry, and cosmetics that adorned it." As a result, most movies utilized some version of the "make-over" plot, in which a restrained female character trades in her dowdy attire for the clothes of the flapper to gain or regain her husband. The emphasis on physical attractiveness fueled the growth in the number of beauty shops (5,000 in 1920 but 40,000 by 1930) and the sale of cosmetics ($17 million in 1914 but $141 million by 1925). And these products promoted the youthful appearance. Fashion shows and beauty contests (the first Miss America Pageant was held in Atlantic City in 1921) gained widespread coverage in the media and kept potential consumers abreast of current fashion trends. "Women," said Dumenil, "were encouraged to identify their youth, and thus their sexual attractiveness, with the goods that adorned their bodies."

The new sexuality that drew women to embrace the cult of beauty and consumption also "entailed a sexual objectification of women, an emphasis on their sexuality to the exclusion of other qualities." Early feminists had championed sexual freedom for women and saw it as part of a broader process of liberation that would subvert a hierarchy based on gender and lead to advancement in politics and the workplace. But, as Dumenil suggests, "the mass media of movies, advertising, and periodicals, co-opted this emphasis on sexuality, with little of its egalitarian content." Having blunted the feminist point of view, the "new woman's sexuality thus lost much of its radical potential." Enhanced freedom was "accompanied by sexual objectification and linked to consumerism, which ushered in the modern trend of defining women in terms of their sexual allure and adornment" (Dumenil 1995, 140–43).

Men's Fashions

If American women turned to French designers for the latest fashion ideas, well-dressed American men looked to London designers for the latest in men's wear. If a man wanted to wear something appropriate for a formal dinner, an evening wedding, or a performance at the opera, he would have donned his "formal" suit. This fancy outfit would include a swallow-tailed coat ("tails"), trimmed with satin, and a pair of matching trousers, trimmed down the sides with a strip of satin ribbon. These formal black or midnight-blue suits would usually be worn with a white, waist-length linen vest over a starched white dress shirt that featured a detachable collar, French-style cuffs, and cufflinks. A white bow tie, black silk top hat, white gloves, patent leather Oxford shoes, spats, and a white flower boutonniere would top off the look. The dress for a slightly less formal occasion like the theater, a small dinner party, or dinner at a nice restaurant would be the semiformal suit or "tuxedo." Made of a worsted material in black or blue, the jacket dropped the tails and featured pants that might not be trimmed at all. The tuxedo vest could be black or white, but the tie was always black ("black tie" affair). The accompanying accessories were similar to the formal attire except that a dome-shaped bowler would be worn in place of the top hat.

A more standard attire for fashionable men was the standard business suit (jacket, trousers, and vest) that came in a variety of colors. Early in the decade, suits fit rather snuggly and suit jackets were often tapered at the waist. Later in the decade, however, suit jackets became longer, roomier, and less defined at the waist. Trousers had cuffs and front creases. The business suit could be worn to the office but also to a daytime event like a movie matinee or a church service. Most men's dress shirts featured detachable collars that came in varying degrees of stiffness, but men shifted to shirts with attached collars that were softer and more comfortable by the middle of the decade. Affluent, stylish men might also be seen wearing colorful printed silk shirts like those described by F. Scott Fitzgerald in his novel, *The Great Gatsby*: "He [Gatsby] took out a pile of shirts and began throwing them, one by one, before us, shirts of sheer linen and thick silk and fine flannel, . . . shirts with stripes and scrolls and plaids in coral and apple-green and lavender and faint orange, with monograms of Indian blue" (Fitzgerald 1980, 93). Like women, men wore hats. One casual chapeau was the fedora, which was commonly made of soft felt. This popular hat usually sported a decorative ribbon around its base and featured a formal crease that ran across the top. One other popular hat for men was the peaked cap, which featured a flat design with a short front brim. The hat could be found in plaid, tweed, or herringbone woolen material, in corduroy, or in a solid-color poplin.

Trendsetters in Men's Fashion

As movies and sports became increasingly popular during the decade, silent film stars like Rudolph Valentino, celebrities like Charles Lindbergh, and sports stars like golfer Bobby Jones and tennis player Bill Tilden became fashion icons. When Valentino appeared in *The Sheik* in 1921, he set the standard for masculine sex appeal. Young women swooned in their seats, and young men rushed to copy his look by shaving their beards and moustaches (the inexpensive, mass-produced safety razor now made that chore possible at home) and parting their slicked-down hair down the middle. After Lindbergh completed his historic transatlantic flight in 1927, young men purchased leather aviator jackets and helmets to wear when touring in their open automobiles. Meanwhile, a well-dressed man on the links might be seen wearing golfing knickers and a sweater, while a tennis enthusiast might sport white flannel trousers and a V-necked sweater vest over a white-collared shirt. One of the major trendsetters in men's fashion during the decade was Edward, Prince of Wales, who looked impeccable on the golf course in his stylish tweed "plus-fours," knee socks, and colorful Fair Isle knitted, pullover sweater that became tremendously popular in this country.

The College "Look"

Another type of venue in which to find fashion-conscious men during the 1920s was colleges and universities. On the more elite,

Ivy League campuses, a young man might be seen wearing some type of sports jacket or blazer, flannel trousers, and ascots rather than ties. At other less prestigious colleges, male students still might be seen adopting their own unique style of attire. Some of the popular choices were sharp-brimmed hats, racoon fur coats, and two-toned saddle shoes. Loose-fitting, baggy pants were also popular on some college campuses. These pants resembled the wide-leg trousers known as "Oxford bags" that were worn by young undergrads at the University of Oxford in England and became a fad in the summer of 1925. On cold winter days or football Saturdays, a trendy collegiate man, if he could afford it, might don a bulky, knee-length raccoon fur overcoat. Other fashionable outerwear included the belted trench coat and the more formal knee-length Chesterfield coat that featured a rather distinctive black velvet collar. Men did accessorize, if it could be called that. Wallets were customarily made of leather, pigskin, or occasionally ostrich skin. Most men also wore some type of timepiece—either a pocket watch on a chain or a more convenient wristwatch, a style introduced in the 1920s. Decorative cigarette cases and lighters were popular as well. And, despite Prohibition, a number of men (and some women) carried either a chrome-plated or monogrammed pocket flask (easily hidden under a long raccoon coat), which was quite the "in" thing to do.

Document: Elizabeth Robins Pennell, "Eats" (1922)

Although the trend in the 1920s was toward an increased reliance on convenient, commercially obtained foods; simpler, healthier meals; and commercial eating establishments catering to a society increasingly on the go, at least one writer thought that something was being sacrificed in the process.

"Eats"

It is astonishing how lightly we take the serious things of life. We eat our three meals a day regularly, and any number of nondescript meals between, and it never occurs to us to stop to consider their influence not only on our daily life but upon the fate of humanity. And yet, what we are is the result of the way we have eaten, just as surely as what we shall be depends on the way we eat now. . . .

. . . . We prostitute our meat, our poultry, our game, our fish, our eggs, our vegetables, our anything and everything that is fresh and fair and flawless, to the monster of cold storage. We have looked upon the fruits of our land, tasted them, known them to be good, and then stored them away until their flavor is frozen out of them, and the cook must exercise his ingenuity to disguise their tasteless-ness. . . . Nourishment has gone; what is worse, taste has gone; and eating has become a mere mechanical stowing away of fuel to keep the machine working. We eat, we know not what. . . .

[The pace with which we consume our meals is also a problem].

Hurry to us as a nation is, of course, no grievance, for our pride is in what we think our hustling. The American business man would neglect a duty if he did not bolt a Quick Lunch, and, having accepted this Quick Lunch as our ideal, everything is arranged to quicken our already quick pace. Some *cafés* dispense with tables and set plates and cups and tumblers on the widened arm of a chair, an irresistible invitation to those who sit down to get promptly up again. Others retain the tables but crowd them too close to induce people, who do not enjoy being jostled like pigs at a trough, to stay longer than they can help. The Automat does better still, since, after you put your money in the slot, the sandwich or salad, the coffee or chocolate, that comes out may be swallowed as you stand—not one fraction of a second lost in a hunt for a seat. But it is the Cafeteria that does best. There, when at last you begin your lunch or dinner, you must be double quick in order to catch up the time you spent waiting in a long line as if you were at a railway ticket office; calculating how many knives, forks and spoons will see you through, not forget-ting the paper napkin; pouncing upon odd morsels from huge tubs of food; balancing a heavy tray as your accumulations increase, as you recklessly dive into your pocket for money at the desk, as you scuffle for a table or a chair. And if you venture to slacken your pace while you gobble down soup, meat, salad, with the ice cream melting before your eyes, more weary tray-balancers at your back, scowling reproach, would cure you of your slowness. And yet, in one I tried for economy's sake—and paid for by my extravagance in the reaction—I have seen parsons, professors, army and navy offi-cers, civil servants, museum directors, at the dinner hour, feeding, not dining, by this degrading method. I have seen children emerge triumphantly from the line with two portions of ice cream and two of pie, exulting in their emancipation from the solids. . . . Now, what can children brought up in this way, what can people willing to put up with the degradation, know of the art of dining or even of ordinary decency at table? As a result of our indifference, our own manners are going and our aliens are shedding the little courtesies they practiced in their native lands. Our health is going. We have become as a nation puffy-faced, sallow, fat, through our eating the wrong thing, in the wrong way, at the wrong hour. The man who first wrote "Eats" above his restaurant door, spoke the truth better than he knew, in one word pointing out to us the depths to which we have sunk.

The idea of dinner as something to be rushed through and escaped from, has become national. . . . Dinner, rightly understood, is a ceremony, the great event of the day, a work of art to linger over, to delight in. Man has evolved no higher form of pleasure, none that is such an eloquent incentive to the art of conversation. When people do not devour their food as if a taxi was ticking away a fortune at their door, but talk as they dine, they talk their best. . . . We do not take time to know that food is good and drink is great—to talk ourselves or to listen to others talk. . . . We tear at express speed through our "Eats" and exalt ourselves as a model for all the world.

Source: Elizabeth Robins Pennell. "Eats," *The North American Review* 215 (March 1922): 353–60.

Document: G. Stanley Hall, "Flapper Americana Novissima" (1922)

The following is an excerpt from an article by G. Stanley Hall, a pioneering American psychologist and an expert on adolescent psychology. Focusing on the "flapper" (considered here as a high school teen), he attempts to describe the traits of this new cultural phenomenon whom he sees as "more or less a product of movies, the auto, woman suffrage, and, especially, of the war" (775).

"Flapper Americana Novissima"

She wore a knitted hat, with hardly any brim, of a flame or bonfire hue; a henna scarf; two strings of Betty beads, of different colors, twisted together; an open short coat, with ample pockets; a skirt with vertical stripes so pleated that, at the waist, it seemed very dark, but the alternate stripes of white showed progressively downward, so that, as she walked, it gave something of what physiological psychologists call a flicker effect. On her right wrist were several bangles; on her left, of course, a wrist watch. Her shoes were oxfords, with a low broad heel. Her stockings were woolen and of brilliant hue. But most noticeable of all were her high overshoes, or galoshes. One seemed to be turned down at the top and entirely unbuckled, while the other was fastened below and flapped about her trim ankle in a way that compelled attention. This was in January, 1922, as should be particularly noted because, by the time this screed meets the reader's eye, flapperdom, to be really *chic* and up-to-date, will be quite different in some of these details. . . .

A good dance is as near to heaven as the flapper can get and live. She dances at noon and at recess in the school gymnasium; and, if not in the school, at the restaurants between courses, or in the recreation and rest-rooms in factories and stores. She knows all the latest variations of the perennial fox-trot, the ungainly contortions of the camel walk; yields with abandon to the fascination of the tango; and if the floor is crowded, there is always room for the languorous and infantile toddle; and the cheek-to-cheek . . . which necessitates the maximum of motion in the minimum of space [which] has a lure of its own, for partners must sometimes cling together in order to move at all. . . .

The flapper, too, has developed very decided musical tastes. If she more rarely "takes lessons" of any kind, she has many choice disks for the phonograph, and has a humming acquaintance with the most popular ditties; and if she rarely indulges in the cakewalk, she has a keen sense of ragtime and "syncopation to the thirty-second note," and her nerves are uniquely toned to jazz, with its shocks, discords, blariness, siren effects, animal and all other noises, and its heterogeneous tempos, in which every possible liberty is taken with rhythm. . . .

Girls whose dress indicates straitened resources often lavish money upon expensive perfumes which, curiously enough nowadays, they generally prefer not pure, but mixed; so that they sometimes radiate an aura of delicate odors on the street, the components of which it would puzzle an expert to identify. . . .

She dotes on jewelry, too, and her heart goes out to the rings, bracelets, bangles, beads, wrist watches, pendants, earrings, that she sees in shop-windows or on some friend or stranger. Her dream is of diamonds, rubies, sapphires, and gold; but imitations will go far to fill the aching void in her heart. . . .

The hair, which the Good Book calls a woman's "crown of glory," of which amorists in prose and poetry have had so much to say, and . . . has always been one of the chief marks of distinction between the sexes, is no longer always so. The old-fashioned, demure braids once so characteristic of the budding girl are gone.

Nor is the hair coiled, either high or low, at the back of the head. This medullary region long so protected is now exposed to wind and weather, either by puffs on either side, or, still more, by the Dutch cut which leaves the hair shortest here. . . . It is now more nearly immodest, I am told, to expose an ear than a knee, and special attention is given to the ear-lock. It is very *chic* to part the hair on one side to keep it very smooth . . . but on all sides of the head it must be kept tousled or combed backward . . . and the more disordered it is here, the better. In all such matters, as in so many others, the girl imitates, consciously or unconsciously, her favorite movie actresses. . . .

Her manners have grown a bit free-and-easy, and every vestige of certain old restraints is gone. In school, she treats her male classmates almost as if sex differences did not exist. Toward him she may sometimes even seem almost aggressive. She goes to shows and walks with him evenings, and in school corridors may pat him familiarly on the back, hold him by the lapel, and elbow him in a familiar . . . way. . . .

Never since civilization began has the. . . [young flapper] seemed so self-sufficient and sure of herself, or made such a break with the rigid traditions of propriety and convention which have hedged her in. From this, too, it follows that the tension which always exists between mothers and daughters has greatly increased, and there now sometimes seems to be almost a chasm between successive generations. If a note of loudness in dress or boisterousness in manner has crept in, and if she seems to know, or pretends to know, all that she needs, to become captain of her own soul, these are really only the gestures of shaking off old fetters. . . .

She has already set fashions in attire, and even in manners, some of which her elders have copied, and have found not only sensible, but rejuvenating. Underneath the mannish ways which she sometimes affects, she really vaunts her femininity, and her exuberance gives it a new charm. The new liberties she takes with life are contagious, and make us wonder anew whether we have not all been servile to precedent, and slaves to institutions that need to be refitted to human nature, and whether the flapper may not, after all, be the bud of a new and better womanhood.

Source: G. Stanley Hall. "Flapper Americana Novissima," *Atlantic Monthly* 129 (June 1922): 771–80.

5

POLITICAL LIFE

The stereotype that has emerged from the 1920s is that it was a period of both economic abundance and political conservatism coupled with voter apathy and a dearth of citizen activism. It was a time when individuals turned inward. Able to afford the pleasures and commodities of the "Jazz Age," Americans became increasingly self-indulgent, displaying either a cynical disregard or general indifference toward the well-being of the larger public sector. In this view, "privatized consumption" supplanted the "public-spirited citizenship" and political engagement that had characterized the Progressive Era. The disillusionment that came with the end of World War I, the atmosphere of intolerance generated by the "Red Scare," and the culmination of long-fought campaigns for women suffrage and Prohibition seemed to exhaust the reform spirit. Instead of political activism, the "lost generation" of the 1920s supplied a great deal of social criticism without offering any meaningful solutions, while the majority of Americans sought satisfaction in material and recreational pleasures. As one historian has noted, "Commentators often speak of the rise of 'consumer society' in the 1920s as a way to encapsulate these political and economic transformations. They frequently use the term to explain the economic vibrancy and political passivity that they take to characterize the decade, and to link the two" (Glickman 2007, 16).

"BEYOND SUFFRAGE"

Political Engagement

Like most simple generalizations, this one glosses over too much. Citizen activism, especially among women, remained vibrant throughout the decade, although with diminishing results. With the ratification of the Suffrage Amendment in 1920, the powerful coalition of women's groups and organizations that had come together behind that single goal fragmented. Settlement house workers, members of middle-class women's clubs, prohibitionists, pacifists, trade union organizers, and militant feminists demanding equal rights in addition to the vote all began to pursue their own separate agendas. Although a number of women chose a partisan course and sought an active role within one of the two major political parties, many others followed Maude Wood Park into the newly formed League of Women Voters (LWV), the successor organization to the National American Woman Suffrage Association. The league, founded in 1920, centered its efforts on nonpartisan political education that would help women become engaged in politics. Organized on both the state and local levels, the LWV set up citizenship schools, conducted educational campaigns on college campuses, invited political scientists to speak at its meetings, and sought to infuse potential voters with an interest in politics. Hopefully, such a program would improve on the disappointing results of the 1920 presidential election in which only one-third of eligible female voters chose to cast a ballot.

Women also joined the early twentieth-century trend toward interest group politics by forming the Women's Joint Congressional Committee (WJCC), a loose coalition of fourteen women's organizations, to conduct national lobbying efforts in Washington, D.C. Looking to educate voters, democratize politics, and push for federal legislation supported by its member organizations, the WJCC publicly set a political agenda in 1921 that included Prohibition, establishing a federal prison for women, protection of infants, physical education in public schools, peace through international arms reduction, and protection of women in industry. Bold action quickly got the attention of politicians. Confronted with what appeared to be the mobilization of women voters as well as an emerging organizational sophistication on the part of women, male politicians hurried to address their demands. Responding to WJCC pressure, Congress established a Women's Bureau in the Department of Labor to monitor working conditions. The WJCC also won

With the ratification of the Suffrage Amendment in 1920, the powerful coalition of women's groups and organizations that had come together behind that singular goal fragmented. Disappointingly for many, the potential power of the "woman's vote" did not materialize. As it became apparent that women were not going to vote as a bloc, male politicians reduced their attention to women's issues. Alice Paul, head of the National Woman's Party, is pictured on the right in this photo. (Library of Congress)

support for the inclusion of physical education in public schools and saw its lobbying efforts for peace bear fruit with the convening of the Washington Conference on Naval Disarmament. Congress also passed the Cable Act in 1922 that protected the citizenship status of women who married foreign nationals and also sent a Child Labor Amendment (the Supreme Court had invalidated a second national child labor law in 1921) to the states for ratification in 1924 (a ratification process that ultimately ended in defeat). Led by Mable Walker Willebrandt, assistant attorney general in charge of Prohibition, income taxes, and prisons, as well as intense lobbying from women's groups, Congress passed legislation that created the first federal prison for women in 1924.

Legislative campaigns were successful at the state level as well. By mid-decade, twenty states had approved laws admitting women to jury duty. Responding to women's demands for additional protective labor legislation, all but four states set limits on working women's hours; eighteen states required rest periods and meal hours; and sixteen states enacted prohibitions on night work in certain occupations. In addition, fifteen states and the District of Columbia had passed minimum wage regulations for women. In an effort to prevent the enforcement of the law in the Washington, D.C., area, the Children's Hospital brought suit, alleging that it was being forced to pay higher wages. Hearing the case on appeal, the U.S. Supreme Court, in *Adkins v. Children's Hospital* (1923), struck down the minimum wage law on the grounds that such laws violated the Fourteenth Amendment's protection of freedom of contract. The decision appeared to place all the protective labor legislation that politicians and citizens had fought for and won during the previous twenty years in jeopardy. Justice Sutherland, in writing for the majority of the court, made a special point of noting that the passage of the Nineteenth Amendment had eliminated all differences in the civil status of men and women. In other words, he seemed to be saying that women were legally as capable as men in contracting for their employment. Although much of the earlier legislative success in the area of women's work had merely extended protections won earlier in the century, progress emboldened women to move in new directions.

The Sheppard-Towner Act

By the end of World War I many women had become alarmed by the exceptionally high rates of maternal and infant mortality. In 1918 the United States ranked eleventh among twenty nations in infant mortality and seventeenth in maternal mortality. Two hundred thousand infants under the age of one and 18,000 new mothers were dying each year. After winning the vote, various women's groups led by the WJCC began to push for legislation by which the federal government would commit matching funds to the states to create programs that would establish prenatal and child health-care centers and pay for nurses to visit new mothers at home. Responding to the vigorous lobbying effort, Congress passed the Sheppard-Towner Maternity and Infancy Protection Act, the nation's first major welfare measure, in July 1921. To win backing for the measure, however, supporters had to agree to accept the legislation on a temporary basis until June 1927. At that time, a fierce legislative battle over continuation of the program and the amount of funding for it was won by its supporters, who gained a short two-year extension but with a cut in appropriations. That victory proved to be a hollow one, however, as Congress decided to terminate the landmark program in 1929. The defeat of Sheppard-Towner was symbolic. Early in the decade the threat of a "woman's vote" had enabled women's organizations to get some special-interest legislation through Congress, but by mid-decade it was clear that women were not voting as a separate bloc. As one historian noted, based on data available after a decade of woman suffrage, "Observers concluded that sex had less to do with determining a vote than place of residence, wealth, occupation, race, nationality, or religion" (Goldman 2001, 292). As a result, women found it increasingly difficult to have male politicians take them seriously.

The Equal Rights Amendment

Women activists not only had to contend with the increasing indifference of male-dominated legislatures in furthering their political agenda but also had to deal with infighting among themselves. The primary point of contention was the proposal put forward by Alice Paul and the National Woman's Party (NWP) for an Equal Rights Amendment (ERA). For Paul, women needed to move beyond suffrage and establish true equality between the sexes by ending all legal barriers confronting women on account of gender. An NWP survey had shown that many states still denied women the right to equal pay for equal work, to serve on juries, to be employed at certain jobs, or to work under certain conditions. In many states wives were still not entitled to keep their own earnings without their husband's consent, make contracts, or exercise the right of equal guardianship. Paul and the NWP regarded any law that confirmed women's difference from men as an obstacle to women's freedom.

Where the debate became most contentious was in the area of protective labor legislation for women. To Paul and her supporters, such laws should be abolished because they disadvantaged women economically. Maximum hour laws, for example, might deny women employment, overtime pay, and promotion or block their access to higher-level, white-collar jobs that required extended hours. Other protections, such as limitations on night work, excluded women from certain occupations. Such statutes, they argued, defined women as weak and dependent, essentially made them wards of the state, restricted them to low-paying jobs, and prevented them from competing with men for jobs and advancement. Using language that hearkened back to the Seneca Falls Declaration of Sentiments of 1848, Paul proposed a simply worded amendment that stated: "Equality of rights under the law shall not be denied or abridged by the United States or by any state on account of sex." Dubbed the Lucretia Mott amendment by Paul to honor the nineteenth-century women's rights activist, the ERA bitterly divided the women's movement.

Almost all the other major women's organizations, including the LWV, the National Consumers League (NCL), and the Women's Trade Union League, opposed the ERA. Long-time reformers like Florence Kelley at the NCL saw the amendment as a threat to the entire body of protective labor legislation for women that had been painstakingly established during the Progressive Era. Such legislation had been premised on the idea that women had a right to a sustainable wage and to a workday and a work environment that did not threaten their health, safety, or morals and that the government (state and federal) should assume a greater responsibility for guaranteeing those rights. Opponents of the ERA argued that protective labor laws helped women because they worked primarily in "female" occupations for longer hours and lower pay than men. Protective laws narrowed the gender gap. Abolishing those laws, opponents argued, would not place women on an equal footing with men but, instead, allow employers to go back to exploiting women as they had in the past. As Mary Anderson, head of the Women's Bureau, noted: "Women who are wage earners, with one job in the factory and another in the home, have little time and energy left to carry on the fight to better their economic status. They need the help of other women and they need labor laws." Opponents of the ERA tended to see it not as an egalitarian proposal but as an elitist one, contrary to the needs of the average working woman. That position seemed to resonate with some in the NWP as well. As one NWP member wrote to a friend, the party was running the risk of "forsaking humanism in the quest for feminism" (Rosenberg 1992, 80). Although few Americans supported the ERA during the 1920s, and Congress gave it little serious consideration, the heated debate between social feminists and equal rights feminists over how best to promote human equality hampered efforts to focus legislative attention on issues concerning women and children.

The Political Activism of Black Women

Another division that hampered political progress for women during the 1920s was the racism and indifference that prevented cooperation between white and black women activists. Feeling empowered by passage of the Nineteenth Amendment, African

American women hoped that the newly won franchise would enable them to confront long-standing issues such as segregation, the disenfranchisement of black male voters, the sexual abuse of black women, economic discrimination, and lynching. Immediately after ratification, African American women's organizations such as the Colored Women Voter Leagues that had been formed in several southern states began voter registration drives. White southerners, however, resisted these efforts, using the same methods—poll taxes, literacy tests, grandfather clauses, and harassment—that had been used to deny the vote to black men. Through organizations like the National Association of Colored Women and some assistance from the National Association for the Advancement of Colored People (NAACP), African American women pushed back with a campaign to try and get Congress to reduce the congressional representation of states that hampered a woman's right to vote. When that tactic failed, they approached white women's organizations looking for support in enforcement of the Suffrage Amendment. Fearful that such cooperation would hinder their own political agendas, neither the LWV nor the NWP was willing to anger southern Democrats in Congress to support black women in the South.

Looking to mobilize their numbers as a political interest group within the Republican Party, black women organized Republican Clubs in states outside the South. Hoping to have a greater impact, they then created the National League of Republican Colored Women in 1924. Initially, the Republican Party curried the favor of black women and invited their leaders to the party's national leadership conference. But that feeling of inclusion did not last long. By 1929 African American women were beginning to feel disillusioned with President Herbert Hoover and the Republican Party's lack of concern for the economic problems facing black people as the Depression deepened. Although African American men and women continued to cast their ballots for the Republican Party in 1932, a shift of allegiance to the Democratic Party had started. Much of the political organizing that occurred as blacks transitioned away from the party of Lincoln to become part of a new Democratic political coalition during the 1930s had been established as a result of the networking of black women during the 1920s.

The Anti-Lynching Crusade

On June 24, 1922, a group of African Americans marched in Washington, D.C., to protest the federal government's failure to enact any anti-lynching legislation. Funds to support such marches were often raised by African American women's clubs. In fact, it was African American women such as journalist Ida Wells-Barnett and activist Mary Church Terrell who had worked for years to bring national attention to the problem. Yet it was not until economic pressure caused by the Great Migration of African Americans out of the South that southern leaders were forced to confront lynching as part of a system of racial intimidation. In an attempt to slow the exodus of black workers North, some moderate white businessmen and community leaders formed the Commission on Interracial Cooperation (CIC) in 1921. Initially, the commission was unwilling to share authority with any black leaders, but under pressure from the NAACP, the CIC eventually became more integrated. At its annual meeting in 1924, twenty-two African American men attended and black civil rights leader W.E.B. Du Bois acknowledged his support of the effort toward inclusion.

When limited interracial cooperation failed to move the issue forward in any meaningful way, however, middle-class black women used their own institutions—colored women's clubs, church groups, the NAACP, and the Young Women's Christian Association—to train themselves as political activists. Throughout the 1920s black women had been trying to tell white women of the South that lynchings would be stopped only when white women raised their voices against the lawlessness. In 1930, that discourse finally convinced one white woman to do something. This woman was Jessie Daniel Ames, a suffragist from Texas and a member of the woman's committee of the CIC. Having grown impatient with the slow progress of the CIC, she decided to lead other southern white women into the formation of the Association of Southern Women for the Prevention of Lynching (ASWPL). Drawing on knowledge gathered from their contact with African American women activists and their own experiences as southerners, members denounced a racial system that exploited sexual anxieties (the fear of black on white rape) to maintain white supremacy. "Public opinion has accepted too easily the claim of lynchers . . . that they were acting solely in the defense of womanhood. In the light of facts, we dare not longer permit this claim to pass unchallenged nor allow those bent upon personal revenge and savagery to commit acts of violence and lawlessness in the name of women" (Buhle 2009, 528). The spirited campaign waged by the ASWPL during its first eight years has been credited with having contributed to a 50 percent reduction in the incidence of lynching in the South.

POLITICS IN THE 1920s: A CONSERVATIVE AGENDA

In their domestic policies, Presidents Warren Harding, Calvin Coolidge, and Herbert Hoover advanced variations of the same conservative theme—low tax rates, low interest rates, high tariffs, government–business cooperation, minimal government regulation, and a balanced budget. Often presented in the abstract, each of these policies directly impacted the daily lives of every American.

Taxation—"Trickle-Down"

During the war, income taxes (allowed by the Sixteenth Amendment to the Constitution in 1913) rose sharply as did federal expenditures. After the war, Americans wanted relief. The sticking point was what type of taxpayer should receive the greatest share of any anticipated tax reductions. The task of deciding that thorny issue fell to Andrew Mellon, one of the richest men in America with controlling interest in a number of corporations, including the Pittsburgh National Bank, the Alcoa Aluminum Company, and Gulf Oil, and who served as Treasury secretary for all three Republican presidents during the Jazz Age. Philosophically, Mellon disliked progressive taxation (the more you make, the more you pay) if tax rates on the wealthy were allowed to reach excessively high levels. In his view, high tax rates penalized the rich, encouraged wealthier individuals to shift their investments from highly taxed private enterprises to tax-exempt government bonds, discouraged new investments, and retarded economic growth. If, however, the wealthy were allowed to keep a larger portion of their income through lower taxes, they would automatically reinvest that money in more profitable private enterprises and bring about higher productivity. The average American worker-consumer would eventually realize the benefits of that policy through job creation (and perhaps more hours and/or overtime pay) and lower prices. Critics called the theory "trickle-down."

In the Revenue Acts of 1921, 1924, 1926, and 1928 the Republican-controlled Congress passed a series of tax cuts that lightened the tax burden on almost everyone but gave substantial reductions to the wealthy. In the process, the top tax rate fell from its wartime high of 77 percent in 1918 to 73 percent in 1921 to 46 percent in 1924 to 25 percent between 1925 and 1928. In addition to the reductions in income taxes, Congress repealed the excess profits tax for corporations and cut the estate tax by 50 percent. The revisions to the tax code amounted to major tax savings for wealthy individuals and corporations. By 1926 a person who made a million dollars a year paid less than one-third in income taxes than he paid in 1920. Ironically, a large part of the money that wealthy individuals saved as a result of lower taxes did not actually go into new investments as Secretary Mellon anticipated; it went instead into speculation that failed to create more jobs or more real wealth. The failure to realize the anticipated benefits of trickle-down exacerbated the maldistribution of wealth. By 1929 the top 0.1 percent of Americans had a combined income equal to the bottom 42 percent. In 1929, that same top 0.1 percent controlled 34 percent of all savings, while 80 percent of Americans had no savings at all. While disposable income per capita increased by 9 percent from 1920 to 1929, it increased by 75 percent for those with income in the top 1 percent. This maldistribution of income, coupled with an increase in credit debt and an erosion of purchasing power, was a contributing factor to the stock market crash of 1929.

Tariff Revision

The tangled issue of tariff legislation also had an impact on the daily lives of many Americans. After the war, farmers followed the lead of other organizations with common economic interests and formed the Farm Bureau Federation, a pressure group comprising mostly prosperous, commercial producers. With a good deal of political influence exerted by the farm bloc (representatives and senators from agricultural states) and support from allied commercial interests like farm-equipment manufacturers and rural bankers, farmers were able to win several legislative concessions that expanded the monetary resources of the Federal Farm Loan Bank system and, through the Agricultural Credits Act of 1923, made low-interest loans available to cooperatives that marketed farm products. But these "victories" did nothing to address the critical issues of overproduction and low prices.

In desperation, the farm bloc abandoned its previous low tariff/free trade position and became united behind the idea of protectionism. With the end of World War I and the resumption of normal production in Europe, American manufacturers were apprehensive over a revival of foreign competition. As a result, they pushed to raise tariff duties. But to assure enough votes for passage of a protective tariff for manufacturers, they had to make concessions to the farm bloc. Through the Emergency Agricultural Tariff Act of

1921 and the Fordney-McCumber Tariff of 1922, Congress raised tariff duties on dozens of foreign agricultural products, including wool, wheat, corn, beef, and sugar, to prohibitive levels. But as it had always done, the new higher tariff raised the duties on manufactured goods that, in turn, burdened consumers (including farmers) with higher prices. By making it more difficult for foreign exporters to earn dollars in the American market, the new tariff also created a climate that lessened the demand for American agricultural products abroad.

Because the new tariff legislation had done nothing in a meaningful way to address the persistent problems of overproduction and low prices, farmers tried a second approach. The new plan, introduced in Congress by Senator Charles McNary of Oregon and Representative Gilbert Haugen of Iowa, authorized a new federal entity, the Agricultural Export Corporation, to purchase, on the American market, eight basic farm commodities—corn, wheat, flour, wool, cotton, sheep, cattle, and hogs—at a price that would restore a farmer's purchasing power to where it had been in 1914, a concept known as "parity." The Agricultural Export Corporation would be free to sell the exportable farm surplus on the world market at the prevailing price that would be much lower. The difference would be partially made up by assessing a "fee" on transportation and processing companies. The entire plan was essentially a way to subsidize farmers without creating any means to curb the resulting overproduction as artificially arranged higher prices encouraged farmers to produce more. Congress passed McNary-Haugen legislation twice, but President Coolidge vetoed the bills on both occasions stating that it was unconstitutional, fiscally unsound, and a bureaucratic horror. Many people saw it as a brazen attempt to raid the U.S. Treasury by a special-interest group. The plan also had another problem. In trying to provide even more incentives for increased production, McNary-Haugen sought to enrich bigger more efficient corporate farmers, while providing little assistance to hard-pressed family farmers. In the end, farmers got nothing.

A Probusiness Climate

Historians have been quick to recite examples by which the administrations of Harding and Coolidge (and later Hoover) adopted probusiness policies between 1921 and 1928. Starting with generous tax reductions for wealthy individuals and corporations and higher tariffs on imported products, the government continued to find ways to facilitate business. Federal regulatory agencies that had been set up during the Progressive Era to oversee big business were increasingly staffed with conservative appointees who were not expected to be tough on business. In sync with executive and congressional actions, the Supreme Court (Harding was able to make four appointments to the Supreme Court—including a new chief justice—between 1921 and 1923) and the Justice Department consistently took a hard line against strikes, boycotts, and protective labor laws, while refraining from rigid enforcement of antitrust statutes (choosing to settle many cases by consent decree). At the same time, a legion of new lobbyists employed by various special-interest groups intensified their efforts to gain a sympathetic ear from probusiness legislators. But it was actually at the Department of Commerce under the direction of Secretary Herbert Hoover between 1921 and 1928 that some of the most effective government–business cooperation was done.

Herbert Hoover and the Department of Commerce

Herbert Hoover, an engineer and business executive before opting for government service, was greatly impressed by the ways in which the War Industries Board had rationalized industries during the war to maximize production. As a result, Hoover believed that government could do more than just create a favorable climate for business: it could actively aid the business community. As Hoover later noted, it was "not the function of government to manage business," but it was proper for government "to recruit and distribute economic information; to investigate economic and scientific problems; to point out the remedy for economic failure or the road to progress; to inspire and assist in cooperative action" (Shannon 1965, 40–41). To do this, the government, through the Department of Commerce, would have to hire experts/specialists, gather economic information such as statistics on prices, costs, markets, and volume of production, and distribute that information to interested concerns. When firms in the same industry agreed to share information about the operation of their business, they would be better able to "rationalize" their entire industry rather than just their own company. There were elements in Hoover's thinking—competing firms cooperating with shared information and possibly dividing markets among themselves or agreeing to certain prices—that were in opposition to traditional laissez-faire economics, but Hoover did not care. Competition in the traditional sense was too disorganized and likely to become chaotic (irrational). In pursuit of his ideal, Hoover established the Bureau of Standards and the Bureau of Foreign and Domestic Commerce within his department and set his trained economists to work turning out studies that had utility to businessmen. Under Hoover's direction, the Bureau of Standards became a major scientific research center and a leader in engineering standardization, while the Bureau of Foreign and Domestic Commerce actively searched for foreign markets for American products and offered advice on foreign investment opportunities.

Business Cooperation and the Trade Association

Secretary Hoover believed strongly in the benefits that could result from businesses that engaged in "voluntary cooperation." In pursuit of that goal, Hoover encouraged manufacturers to form trade associations. Essentially organizations of relatively small businesses in a single industry, the firms involved would promote the standardization of products and share information relevant to their trade. Although trade associations had been around since the Civil War, under Hoover, the Department of Commerce promoted the formation of hundreds of new ones. Encouraged by the department to establish forums for the exchange of ideas, trade associations conducted periodic meetings and often published their own trade magazines. For its part, the Department of Commerce urged members of an association to take steps—such as adopting a uniform accounting system or establishing a uniform formula for figuring costs—that would minimize competition between firms. Critics contended that trade associations could not be relied on to act in the public interest because they shared information in a manner that smacked of collusion and contributed to a greater concentration of economic power. To them, trade groups were merely a means by which businesses could fix prices, allocate markets, and engage in other practices that were in violation of current antitrust laws. Hoover thought otherwise, firm in his belief that voluntary associations would bring about the elimination of waste and promote efficiency, reduce costs, and improve the competitiveness of American capitalism globally without running afoul of antitrust. In two cases heard before the Supreme Court in 1925, the Court supported Hoover, stating that it was legal for trade associations to publish critical information on cost and price as long as it was not the organizations' "explicit purpose" to standardize prices in the industry.

The Growth of Oligopoly

With the Department of Commerce encouraging business cooperation, and with the Supreme Court, the Department of Justice, and regulatory agencies like the Federal Trade Commission doing little to enforce competition, the government created a climate that encouraged economic concentration. The tendency toward the concentration of corporate wealth and power in the hands of a relatively few corporate entities, known as oligopoly, was not new to the 1920s, but government policies quickened its pace. By 1929 the 200 largest corporations in the United States controlled almost half of the corporate assets and about one-fifth of the total national wealth. Concentration could be found in most industries but was especially evident in manufacturing, banking, mining, and public utilities. Even retail, once the safe haven for the small entrepreneur, witnessed the rise of big corporations that established chains of retail outlets. Chain stores purchased their goods in volume from wholesalers and, as a result, offered customers lower prices and a wider range of selection than most independent retailers. The nation's leading grocery store chain during the 1920s was the Great Atlantic & Pacific Tea Company, or, as it was known to most consumers, A&P. By 1929, the A&P was operating more than 15,000 stores nationwide with combined sales of over $1 billion. Other grocery retailers like Kroger and Safeway sought to copy the A&P model. But with lower prices and a wider selection of goods, these chains soon drove many smaller independent stores out of business. But the smaller grocery retailers refused to go quietly and, in 1926, formed the Independent Grocers Alliance, a national trade association that enabled its members to coordinate marketing strategies and obtain the same wholesale discounts that the larger chains were getting.

POLITICS AND PROHIBITION

When Congress passed the legislation (Volstead Act) to enable the Eighteenth Amendment, it simply stated that all traffic in beverages that contained more than one-half of 1 percent alcohol by volume was illegal as of January 1, 1920. To Frederick Lewis Allen, looking back on the moment a decade later, it seemed that Congress had legislated "with a sublime disregard for elementary chemistry—which might have taught it how easily alcohol may be manufactured—and for elementary psychology—which might have suggested that common human impulses are not easily suppressed by fiat" (Allen 2010, 223).

The Problem of Enforcement

The task of enforcing the law was left to the Prohibition Bureau under the purview of the Department of the Treasury. By the end of the decade, the bureau had about 3,000 active agents who were paid an annual salary of roughly $2,500 to close down illegal smuggling and bootlegging operations that netted perhaps $2 billion a year. It was an impossible task. The country had 12,000 miles of coastline and borders. The Canadian border was relatively unguarded, while

In 1925, it was estimated that Treasury agents seized only about 5 percent of all illegal liquor smuggled into the United States that year. The illegal diversion and redistillation of commercial/industrial alcohol and the illegal production of homemade beer and wine further taxed enforcement efforts. There were, however, some successes. In 1925, federal agents smashed 172,000 illegal stills. This photo shows agents dumping confiscated booze after a raid. (Library of Congress)

the Mexican border proved to be another porous point of entry. The Caribbean also offered a nearby haven for offshore smugglers. Supply ships would linger near the Florida or New Jersey coast-line waiting for the opportunity to offload their lucrative cargoes. Speedy launches with enough horsepower to outrun Coast Guard boats would then bring the booze ashore. According to one estimate, about 2,000 cases of liquor landed at the coves and bays of Long Island Sound each day. In 1925, the assistant secretary of the Trea-sury in charge of enforcement estimated that his agents seized only about 5 percent of all the illegal liquor smuggled into the United States that year. Perhaps the greatest source of illegal liquor sold to Americans during the Jazz Age, however, came from the diversion and redistillation of alcohol that was intended for commercial and industrial use. Illegal distilling provided another source of supply as did home production of beer and wine. A home-brewing setup could be purchased at the local hardware store for less than $10. It was said that manufacturers of corn sugar saw a six-fold increase in sales during the 1920s to meet the demand from moonshiners and amateur home brewers.

Law enforcement was able to register a few victories along the way, but the task was difficult. During the first two years under Prohibition, the government filed 3,500 civil and 65,000 criminal actions against lawbreakers and won approximately 65 percent of those cases. During 1925 alone, federal agents smashed 172,000 illegal stills, while two agents, Izzy Einstein and Moe Smith, became national celebrities as crime-busters. But despite the suc-cesses, there was a great deal of resistance. A few states repealed local laws that supplemented the Volstead Act. Other states left the entire fiscal and administrative burden of enforcement to Wash-ington. Corruption was another problem. With so much money to be made from the illegal liquor business, the bribery of officials became common practice. It has been estimated that about 10 per-cent of those hired for enforcement were fired for corrupt activi-ties between 1920 and 1930, but it is impossible to estimate how many others took bribes and were not caught. Local juries often failed to convict popular bootleggers, and mayors, police chiefs, sheriffs, and county and district attorneys routinely accepted bribes to impede vigorous enforcement of the law. Chicago Mayor William Thompson, an avowed "wet," openly thumbed his nose at enforcement. Equally critical of what appeared to be a decline in respect for the law were civil libertarians who grew concerned that the police often followed questionable legal procedures and demonstrated little regard for basic constitutional rights. Acting on tips supplied by informants, local police and federal agents often broke into homes and places of business without valid search warrants. Two hundred alleged violators of the Volstead Act were shot by police between 1920 and 1929.

"Wets" versus "Drys"

The two political parties split on the issue. The Democrats, the party of the "wets," either wanted the law modified to allow for light wines and beer or favored outright repeal, while the Republicans, the party of the "drys," resisted any modification of the law. But by the middle of the 1920s, it was becoming increasingly apparent that dissatisfaction with Prohibition was on the rise. Politicians, especially many urban Democrats, began to speak out against the "noble experiment," which they probably would not have done if they thought it politically inexpedient to do so. As one historian put it, "The most relevant question to ask about prohibition after about 1927 was why did it last as long as it did rather than why was it not more rigidly enforced" (Shannon 1965, 70). One reason for the delay in repeal was that many Americans who disapproved of Prohibition for themselves still approved of it for others. The Republican Party, whose support was strongest among the middle class, simply refused to risk alienating their political base.

By 1928 the argument over Prohibition had reached such an intensity that it could not be kept out of the presidential political campaign. Democratic candidate Al Smith, a wet on the issue, adopted a conciliatory position that essentially left the question up to the states to decide. Herbert Hoover, in turn, publicly endorsed the motives behind the law and left it at that. Voters considered him to be "dry." When Hoover won the election by a wide margin, drys accepted his victory as a referendum on Prohibition.

Hoover actually had misgivings about the law and called for a postelection study of the enforcement problem by a governmental commission. Two months into his administration, a commission of eleven individuals headed by former attorney general George W. Wickersham began a study of the issue. Nineteen months later, and well after the stock market crash and the onset of the Great Depression, the commission turned in its final report. Looked at in its entirety, the document revealed that the commission considered enforcement a failure and that the social costs—the promotion of disrespect for the law on the part of ordinary citizens, gangland violence, overreach on the part of the police, and a demoralized federal judiciary—outweighed the benefits. Each of the eleven commissioners also submitted a personal summary of their views. Only five recommended moving forward without substantial changes; four favored modification of the amendment; and two were for outright repeal. But the commission as a whole agreed to further trial.

After reading the commission's report, President Hoover promised more efficient enforcement of the law, placed the Prohibition Bureau under the supervision of the Department of Justice, and raised the civil service requirements for federal agents. A year later, as economic conditions worsened, Hoover, an Iowa Quaker who detested alcohol and the saloon, came out in favor of repeal.

THE APATHETIC VOTER

Low Voter Turnout

One of the interesting characteristics of politics during the Jazz Age was the low degree of political participation as reflected in voter turnout for elections. It seemed like many voters had come to regard politics as simply irrelevant and showed their disinterest by staying away from the polls in droves. Actually, voter turnout had been declining ever since the election of 1896 when 79 percent of eligible voters cast a ballot in that year's presidential race. Four years later, turnout dropped to 73 percent and then to 65 percent in 1904 and 1908. In 1912 (an election in which there were actually four separate tickets in the field) only 59 percent voted. After recovering slightly to 62 percent in 1916 where entry into the war was an issue, voter turnout resumed its downward trajectory to a mere 49 percent in 1920 and 1924. Much of the overall decline occurred in the South where disenfranchisement of both black and poor white voters reduced turnout to just 20 percent in the elections of 1920 and 1924. At the same time, voter turnout in the North in 1924 was only 58 percent. It has been estimated that during the 1920s close to 25 percent of all eligible northern voters never cast a ballot.

The low turnout of 1920 triggered a public discussion. Many well-to-do voters began to worry whether sufficient numbers of the "right sort" of people were going to the polls. Ironically, they operated under the misassumption that workers and immigrants were voting in greater numbers than members of their class when, in actuality, nonvoters tended to come disproportionately from the ranks of recently enfranchised women, young people, immigrants, and the poor. Sufficiently alarmed, and hoping to preserve their influence and safeguard the nation, many middle- and upper-class voters decided that they should start a campaign to urge nonvoters to the polls.

The "Get-Out-the-Vote" Movement

In 1924 hundreds of thousands of Americans joined the "Get-Out-the-Vote" movement for the duration of that year's presidential election. Expressive of the fears of the middle- and upper classes, the effort became something of a conservative, patriotic crusade. In Washington, D.C., Simon Michelet, a staunch Republican, founded the National Get-Out-the-Vote Club and published statistical material on nonvoting. More significant were the actions of the National Association of Manufacturers (NAM), an influential organization that launched a massive publicity campaign centered on the slogan "Vote as you please, but vote." During the campaign, the NAM printed more than 20 million pamphlets and stickers urging voters to cast a ballot, and called on groups like the Elks, the Masons, the Rotary Club, the American Bankers Association, the Motion Picture Producers Association, and even the Boy Scouts of America for support.

The movement quickly gained momentum in the summer and fall of 1924. Party leaders got behind the effort as did the major presidential candidates. Ministers encouraged their parishioners to vote, while newspapers urged their readers to register and do likewise. The LWV organized conferences, visited voters in their homes, and came up with the idea of using an "auto caravan" to increase political interest. Meanwhile, the Boy Scouts did its part by distributing posters and literature provided by the NAM. Not to be outdone, radio stations ran commercial spots urging voters to register and vote, movie houses showed slides on voting, and restaurants clipped little reminders to their menus. In Cleveland, Ohio, a milk company created special bottle caps to remind voters to register, while the Kiwanis Club of Aurora, Illinois, adopted the extreme tactic of trying to shame nonvoters by publicly listing their names in much the same fashion that "patriots" had tried to "out" "slackers" during the war. Although the movement always claimed to be impartial, in matter of fact it reflected the values and fears of the middle and upper classes. As the *New York Times* stated, "Underlying the movement for getting out the vote is the common belief that precisely the intelligent man, or the man who should be intelligent by reason of economic opportunity and education, refuses to vote. The tenement districts turn out on election day, rain or shine. The residential districts play golf." As historian Michael McGerr noted, "In membership, language, and aspirations, the Get-Out-the-Vote movement betrayed its roots in conservative America" (McGerr 1986, 196, 197).

The Get-Out-the-Vote movement reflected party as well as class interests. Some White House correspondents assumed that the campaign would help defeat the liberal, third-party candidacy of Senator Robert La Follette, the nominee of the Progressive Party, and help elect Calvin Coolidge. Spearheading the third-party protest was the Conference for Progressive Political Action (CPPA) that had scored some victories in the 1922 elections. Partisans hoped to tap popular dissatisfaction with the two major parties and unite a variety of disaffected interest groups under one banner. At the national convention of the CPPA, held in Cleveland, Ohio, on July 4, 1924, nearly 1,000 delegates, comprising mainly labor unionists and representatives of various farmers' cooperative societies who had not experienced Republican prosperity, and a number of socialists, feminists, and intellectuals, rallied behind the nomination of La Follette in hopes of rekindling a progressive reform movement. La Follette selected Senator Burton K. Wheeler of Montana, who had helped expose corruption in the Justice Department, as his running mate.

The key issue raised in the Progressive Party's platform was the "control of government and industry by private monopoly." Supporters believed that big business exerted undue influence with the courts, Congress, and the executive departments, while, at the same time, it "crushed competition" and "stifled private initiative and independent enterprise." As remedies, the new party advocated more vigorous enforcement of antitrust laws, government ownership of private utilities (especially hydroelectric power and railroads), the elimination of injunctions against striking workers and the right of workers to collective bargaining, a lowering of the tariff, and tax reductions on moderate incomes along with a repeal of the Mellon tax cuts for the wealthy. Although the platform focused on the issue of inequality of property, most voters did not seem to care. On Election Day, with only one-half of the eligible voters going to the polls, Coolidge garnered 15.7 million votes to Democrat John W. Davis's 8.3 million and La Follette's 4.8 million. Although the La Follette–Wheeler ticket carried only one state, it ran ahead of the Democratic Party in eleven others. Working with a hastily assembled campaign staff and a meager campaign budget of little over $200,000, the protest was able to underscore considerable popular discontent with the conservative status quo.

Although Coolidge won the election by a wide margin, the Get-Out-the-Vote campaign was a flop. As historian Michael McGerr stated, "To most commentators, the electorate appeared as 'apathetic' as ever. On election day sirens blew, church bells rang, and Boy Scouts bugled the people to the polls," but across the nation voters continued to stay away from the polls at roughly the same rate as they had in 1920. Two years later only 42 percent bothered to vote in the off-year congressional contests. In an interesting liberal take on nonvoting, the *Nation* chose to blame the politicians who failed to serve the people rather than the voters. As the *Nation* saw it, leaders "who berate the absentee voters never question our institutions and our political methods." "The remedy lies elsewhere—in the restoration to the voter of faith in the two political parties and in our politics and government." According to the *Nation*, nonvoting should not be seen as political "laziness" but as a collective political statement:

> Multitudes . . . deliberately refuse to vote because they feel they have nothing to gain by doing so; that the choice lies between representatives of two parties which are both hopelessly corrupt and outworn, between whom there is no essential difference in principle or program. They feel that this is a rich man's country . . . that our institutions . . . are no longer adapted to a nation . . . under the conditions of extreme capitalism. (McGerr 1986, 197, 201)

The Impact of Social-Cultural Issues on Voter Turnout

To the surprise of everyone, voter turnout in the Election of 1928 suddenly rebounded to 57 percent, a level not seen since 1916. It appeared that in the contest between Yankee Protestant Herbert Hoover and Irish Catholic Al Smith, the emotional intensity that voters felt toward certain social-cultural issues had reinvigorated their interest in politics. Smith's Catholicism triggered alarms among millions of voters in the Bible Belt. From the vantage point of rural, small-town America, Smith, the four-term governor of New York, appeared to be the stereotypical big-city politician with connections (however tenuous) to the infamous Tammany political machine. His parents were Irish immigrants. He had grown up in New York City and had once lived in a tenement. He had a lower-class New York City accent, sported a derby hat, and had even chosen "The Sidewalks of New York" as his campaign song. On top of that, he opposed national Prohibition. Hoover suggested a different set of social-cultural values. Born in West Branch, Iowa, a small midwestern farming town, he had genuine roots in rural, middle America. His mother, a devout Quaker, taught him the principles of simplicity and sobriety, and he often referenced the Bible as a guidebook for life. His intense belief in individualism fit well with the cultural zeitgeist of the 1920s, and his leadership in the Commerce Department as the architect of a new economic order allowed him to bask in the glow of Republican prosperity. As one historian has commented, "In 1928, the public record of neither candidate mattered a great deal. If American politics is normally 60 percent emotion and 40 percent rational calculation, the ratios in 1928 leaped to 80–20" (Parrish 1992, 211). Hoover won overwhelmingly, garnering 58 percent of the popular vote and carrying forty of forty-eight states, including New York.

THE HARDING SCANDALS

It is difficult to pinpoint the origins or the depths of what might be termed "political malaise," but such a condition appeared to grip American society during the first half of the 1920s. In his contemporary account of the decade, Frederick Lewis Allen has described the nation after the war as "spiritually tired." "Wearied" by war and suffering from the "nervous tension" of the Red Scare, Americans hoped for a period of calm. Having turned away from the thought of more political idealism, "they hoped for a chance to pursue their private affairs without governmental interference and to forget about public affairs" (Allen 2010, 108). Sadly, what they got instead was political spectacle played out as the Harding scandals.

It is probably safe to say that few voters expected much in the way of action or innovation from Warren G. Harding when he was elected in 1920. After all, the former Ohio senator had promised only a return to "normalcy." And fewer still were aware that Harding had one fatal weakness—he simply lacked the ability to be discriminating when it came to the choice of friends and advisors, "to distinguish between honesty and rascality." As Frederick Lewis Allen has noted, "He had been trained in the sordid school of practical Ohio politics. He had served for years as the majestic Doric false front behind which Ohio lobbyists and fixers and purchasers of privilege had discussed their 'business propositions' and put over their 'little deals'—and they, too, followed him to Washington" (Allen 2010, 110). Much of the corruption that took place in the Harding administration was the work of this so-called Ohio Gang.

Four years after Harding's death in office in 1923, half a dozen members of his administration, including two cabinet-level officials, had been forced to resign and were then indicted for crimes defined as defrauding the government, bribery, and conspiracy. One of the first to run afoul of the law was Charles R. Forbes, head of the Veterans Bureau. During his two years in Washington, it was estimated that his department squandered over $200 million in graft and waste. Disregarding the federal bidding process on construction projects, Forbes regularly demanded bribes before letting new hospital contracts. He also sold hospital equipment and medical supplies to friends at fire-sale prices and then arranged for his own cash "kickback" by having the bureau buy those supplies back at higher prices. When Harding discovered the irregularities in Forbes's office early in 1923, he allowed him to resign. After Harding's death, Forbes was tried and sentenced to prison for fraud.

Similar malfeasance occurred in the Justice Department. Harry M. Daugherty, Harding's close friend and chief political advisor, won appointment as attorney general. A friend of Daugherty's by the name of Jess Smith was given an office in the Department of Justice where he arranged bribes for Thomas W. Miller, the Alien Property Custodian. The bribes were paid by one Richard Morton who represented the American Metal Company, an internationally owned concern whose stock had been confiscated by the Alien Property Custodian during the war on the grounds that it belonged to Germans. Morton's claim was that the stockholders were not German but Swiss and that they should be reimbursed. Morton was willing to pay to have Smith arrange for expediting their dubious claims. After his part in the scheme became known, Smith committed suicide. Miller eventually served a year in prison. Daugherty was tried twice for his role in the affair but was found not guilty on both occasions. Coolidge removed him from office after Harding's death.

The most spectacular fraud that occurred on Harding's watch involved naval oil leases. On entering office, Harding's secretary of the Interior, Albert B. Fall, persuaded Edwin Denby, the secretary of the navy, to transfer control of two naval oil reserves into his department. It was later discovered that Fall had received a $100,000 "loan" from one Edward L. Doheny for the lease of the

Elk Hills reserve in California to his Pan American Petroleum Company. A similar deal was arranged with Harry F. Sinclair of the Mammoth Oil Company for a lease of the Teapot Dome oil reserve in Wyoming. For this privilege Sinclair allegedly gave Fall $200,000 in bonds and $85,000 in cash. Convicted of accepting a bribe, Fall was fined $100,000 and sentenced to a year in jail. Denby was later forced to resign. As for the oil leases, they were later voided in a civil case. Motivation for all the crimes seemed to be nothing more than simple greed.

When the oil scandals started to appear on the front pages of newspapers early in 1924, there was a sufficient outcry to provoke President Coolidge to appoint a special government counsel to investigate the fraudulent dealings. But the popular mood quickly shifted, and the public soon began to direct their criticism at Senator Thomas Walsh, selected to lead the investigation of the oil scandals, and Senator Burton K. Wheeler, appointed to examine the crooked dealings within the Department of Justice. In the eyes of many, their investigations were too relentless and exhibited signs of partisanship, had gone on far too long, and were further upsetting the status quo. Walsh and Wheeler had become, in the public's mind, something akin to political mudslingers (the *New York Tribune* called them scandalmongers). Besides, Harding had died in office in 1923. Coolidge had now taken over and appeared to be a pillar of rectitude (journalist William Allen White called him a "Puritan in Babylon"). Why dwell unnecessarily on the past? It was time to move on. But politics and government had been discredited. As Frederick Lewis Allen remembered from the vantage point of 1931, "Resentment at the scandals and resentment at the scandalmongers both gave way to a profound and untroubled apathy" (Allen 2010, 136). And to journalist Mark Sullivan writing in 1926, "The effect on the country's morale was definite, visible, and most damaging" (Sullivan 1996, 653).

HOOVER'S RESPONSE TO THE DEPRESSION

One of the thorniest problems facing Herbert Hoover when he took office in 1929 was the farm problem. In responding to the farm crisis, Hoover sought a solution that would follow the general guidelines that he had set down as secretary of commerce: voluntary cooperation and limited government involvement. The result was the Agricultural Marketing Act, passed in June 1929, and the creation of the Federal Farm Board. With a $500 million budget, the Federal Farm Board looked to help farmers help themselves. It would make loans to farm cooperatives so that they might use their greater buying power to purchase farm equipment, fertilizers, and pesticides more cheaply and pass those savings on to farmers. The cooperatives could also become more directly involved in marketing and thereby reduce the charges imposed by middlemen. In addition, the Federal Farm Board would loan money to so-called commodity stabilization corporations. There would be a corporation for each commodity, such as wheat, corn, or cotton. Each of these corporations would be empowered to buy a commodity on the open market and store it for future sale. In essence, the idea was to buy surpluses in an attempt to maintain prices.

The program never really had a chance. Put into operation just as the stock market collapsed and other countries began dumping grain on the market, any federal money going into the market had very little impact. The price of wheat, for example, fell from $1.05 a bushel in 1929 to 68 cents by 1930 despite the efforts of the government-financed purchase program. At this point, the Federal Farm Board switched tactics and began urging farmers to produce less, hoping to reduce the output rather than trying to buy up the surplus. But the plan had no leverage behind it. There was no means to require farmers to cut production, and the fear that some farmers would "cheat" and continue to produce killed the idea. In fact, agricultural production in 1932 was greater than it had been in 1929, and that was with farm prices well below the costs of production.

A month after the stock market crash, President Hoover arranged a series of meetings at the White House with the nation's leading business leaders. What he wanted from them were assurances that they would not reduce wage rates, lay off workers, engage in price cutting, or lower production. The businessmen agreed to do so if labor would agree not to strike or demand higher wages. The American Federation of Labor then signaled that it would cooperate. The assumption was that if all held to their pledges there would be no significant shrinkage in consumer purchasing power.

It was a flawed assumption. Workers did what they had always done during times of economic crisis: they tightened their belts. They cut back on expenditures and saved their money. Facing unemployment, they grew cautious. Concerned about declining sales, businesses began to cut back on production and sell off their inventories. They soon began to reduce investment in new plants and equipment and started to lay off workers. Without an income, workers stopped buying. Hoover also asked the nation's mayors and governors not to reduce public expenditures on planned public projects like schools, roads, and libraries. But public officials could not keep their promises very long either. As business activity declined, tax revenues shrank, and state and local budgets became tight. Overwhelmed with demands for relief, governments abandoned planned construction projects and began to lay off public employees. Voluntary cooperation in both the production and public sectors had failed.

Hoover tried two other experiments in voluntary cooperation—in banking and unemployment relief—in an effort to halt the expanding economic and social crisis. Banks were in trouble. Many had made bad loans, and even though they still held securities and property as collateral on those loans, they could not collect on the loans or turn that collateral into cash. Under pressure from Hoover, bankers organized the National Credit Corporation (NCC) with a fund of $500 million contributed by the nation's bigger banks. Once again, bankers, not the government, would come to the aid of other bankers. With this new fund of cash, the NCC could purchase assets in banks that were on the verge of insolvency. Fear would be abated, depositors would feel reassured, and the financial sector would regain the confidence to make new loans. But the NCC proved to be too conservative, unwilling to spend more than a fraction of its cash reserve to assume the questionable assets of shaky banks. Voluntary cooperation had failed Hoover again, and bank failures continued to rise.

The same fate befell the effort to provide basic relief—food and shelter—to millions of people who were without work. Most working-class and middle-class families had no savings to fall back on when the Depression hit. They faced mortgages and bills they could not pay, possible foreclosure or bankruptcy, and, at worst, destitution. Hoover had hoped that the nation's private charities and disaster relief agencies like the Red Cross, the Salvation Army, and the Community Chest could hold the line against the suffering that accompanied unemployment, but their task soon proved overwhelming. Looking to bolster that effort, Hoover created the President's Committee for Unemployment Relief to conduct advertising and public relations campaigns to increase private charitable contributions. But Hoover opposed any broader role for the federal government, especially in the area of direct relief to those who were unemployed. As Hoover saw it, such federal intervention would discourage charitable giving, undermine voluntary cooperation, and destroy self-reliance by offering a "dole" and creating a class of dependent citizens. Most historians today agree that Hoover was not the "do-nothing" president during the early years of the Great

Depression that many of his earlier critics made him out to be, but he was hidebound by his philosophy. As one historian noted: "His faith in volunteeristic approaches to economic planning and his abhorrence of an interventionist federal government" limited his ability to take constructive action to meet the crisis (Dumenil 1995, 307).

Document: " 'Much-Surprised' City Officials Ousted by Women" (1920)

As commonly noted in most general accounts of the 1920s, the coalition of women's groups and organizations that had come together to achieve woman suffrage in 1920 failed to realize the expectations of that triumph. Male politicians, impressed with the mobilization shown by women and respectful of the potential power of the "woman's vote," initially gave their interests serious attention. But as it became clear that women were not going to vote as a bloc, male politicians relaxed their concern and reduced their attention to women's issues. The following article offers a glimpse of what might have been.

" 'Much-Surprised' City Officials Ousted by Women"

Pessimists who predicted that, once women were given the vote, they would soon chase mere men into political extinction, may "point with alarm" to the recent feminist revolution in Yoncalla, Oregon. The women of the little town have risen in their wrath, stirred by the alleged inefficiency of the municipal officials, and swept every masculine office-holder out of his job. . . . The women worked secretly, and when the blow fell, on Election day, the superseded mayor and his ousted assistants were too much shocked to make any statement beyond admitting that they were "much surprised." The town has a population of 323. . . in which the men outnumber the women almost two to one, but the women persuaded so many of the sterner sex of the justice of their cause that their all-woman ticket was elected by a safe majority. They are now starting to show the native residents "how a town should be governed."

[According to a reporter for the Portland *Oregonian*]

Their policy, in a general way, according to their announcements, will be to depart just as far as possible from the methods and measures of their male predecessors.

The triumph of the women at the polls was a noteworthy *coup*. They were dissatisfied with the way things had been running along and they decided to elect their own officials. . . .

The women had a good many grievances. They maintained that the mayor and councilmen were not progressive; that they were letting the streets and sidewalks go unrepaired; that the lighting facilities were inadequate; that no effort was made to check automobile speeders, and that affairs generally were not what they should be in an up-to-date and forward-looking community. They might have summed it all up by saying that the officials were lazy, so far as public business went, but they put it more diplomatically.

The new officials are the real leaders among the women of the city. Mrs. Mary Burt, elected mayor, is . . . a university graduate . . . and has long been active in the affairs of the town. She is a Republican.

No one in Yoncalla was more surprised at the turn of events than Jesse R. Laswell, the retiring mayor. This surprise was due in no small part to the fact that Mrs. Laswell was elected to the council. The mayor says he had no knowledge of the step to overthrow his administration, let alone the fact that his wife was on the opposing ticket.

Other women elected to the council were Mrs. Edith R. Thompson, wealthy property-owner and active in women's clubs; Mrs. Bernice Wilson, pioneer school-teacher, wife of the Yoncalla postmaster; and Mrs. Nettie Hannan, wife of a retired capitalist.

After the first surprise Mayor Laswell congratulated the victors and said that they would have the assistance and advice of the retiring officials, altho he did not believe they would need it. Mrs. Burt, mayor-elect, says the women are not yet ready to announce their policies for promoting the welfare of the city.

"We intend to study conditions and do all in our power to give Yoncalla a good, efficient government," she asserted. "At the worst we can't do much worse than the men have done."

The women will go about their new duties in a serious frame of mind, for they believe that the success or failure will be watched with interest by their newly enfranchised sisters in all parts of the country.

Source: " 'Much-Surprised' City Officials Ousted by Women," *Literary Digest* 67 (December 4, 1920): 52, 54.

Document: "Shall Women Be Equal before the Law?" (1922)

The following two selections offer opposing views on the need for an Equal Rights Amendment. Elsie Hill, chair of the National Council of the Woman's Party, sees the proposed amendment as necessary if women are ever to achieve full equality with men. Opposing that view is Florence Kelley, secretary of the National Consumers' League, who sees the proposed amendment as a direct threat to protections that women need in the current industrial environment. Kelley's comments should be considered in their historical context. Faced with a recalcitrant labor movement and the entrenched doctrine of freedom of contract, Kelley and other social reformers confronted formidable obstacles that narrowed their options and molded their strategies.

"Shall Women Be Equal before the Law?"

Yes!

The removal of all forms of the subjection of women is the purpose to which the National Woman's Party is dedicated. Its present campaign to remove the discriminations against women in the laws of the United States is but the beginning of its determined effort to secure the freedom of women. . . . Its interest lies in the final release of woman from the class of a dependent, subservient being. . . .

The laws of various States at present hold her in that class. They deny her a control of her children equal to the father's; they deny her, if married, the right to her own earnings; they punish her for offenses for which men go unpunished; they exclude her from public office and from public institutions to the support of which her taxes contribute. These laws are not the creation of this age, but the fact that they are still tolerated on our statute books and that in some States their removal is vigorously resisted shows the hold of old traditions upon us. Since the passage of the Suffrage Amendment the incongruity of these laws . . . has become more than ever marked. . . .

The shocking humiliating nature of many of the legal discriminations makes it imperative not to endure unnecessary delay and a common-sense regard for economy of the precious resources of life drives one to seek a better technique.

[Proposed] Women shall have the same rights, privileges, and immunities under the law as men, with respect to the exercise of suffrage; holding of office or any position under the government, either State or local or for which government funds or subsidies are used, and with respect to remuneration for services in such office or position; eligibility to examination for any position affected by civil-service regulations; jury service; choice of domicile, residence, and name; acquiring, inheriting, controlling, holding, and conveying property; ownership and control of labor, services, and earnings within and without the home, and power to recover damages for loss of such labor, services, and earnings; freedom of contract, including becoming a party in any capacity to negotiable instruments or evidence of indebtedness, or becoming surety or guarantor; becoming parties litigant; acting as executors or administrators of estates of decedents; custody and control of children, and control of earnings and services of such children; grounds for divorce; immunities or penalties for sex offenses; quarantine, examination, and treatment of diseases; and in all other respects.

No!

Sex is a biological fact. The political rights of citizens are not properly dependent upon sex, but social and domestic relations and industrial activities are. All modern-minded people desire that women should have full political equality and like opportunity in business and the professions. No enlightened person desires that they should be excluded from jury duty or denied the equal guardianship of children, or that unjust inheritance laws or discriminations against wives should be perpetuated.

The inescapable facts are, however, that men do not bear children, are freed from the burdens of maternity, and are not susceptible, in the same measure as women, to poisons now increasingly characteristic of certain industries, and to the universal poison of fatigue. These are differences so far reaching, so fundamental, that it is grotesque to ignore them. Women cannot be made men by act of the legislature or by amendment of the Federal Constitution. . . . The inherent differences are permanent. Women will always need many laws different from those needed by men.

The effort to enact. . . [a] blanket bill in defiance of all biological differences recklessly imperils the special laws for women as such, for wives, for mothers, and for wage-earners. . . .

If women are subject to the *same* freedom of contract as men, will not women wage-earners lose the statutory eight-hour day, rest at night, and one day's rest in seven, which they now have under statutes that . . . limit their freedom of contract? . . .

Why should wage-earning women be thus forbidden to get laws for their own health and welfare and that of their unborn children? Why should they be made subject to the preferences of wage-earning men? Is not this of great and growing importance when the number of women wage-earners, already counted by millions, increases by leaps and bounds from one census to the next? And when the industries involving exposure to poisons are increasing faster than ever? And when the overwork of mothers is one recognized cause of the high infant death-rate? And when the rise in the mortality of mothers in childbirth continues?

Source: "Shall Women Be Equal before the Law?" *Nation* 114 (April 12, 1922): 419–21.

6

RECREATIONAL LIFE

"AIN'T WE GOT FUN?"

One aspect of the consumer culture that grew by leaps and bounds during the 1920s was commercial entertainment and recreation. The title of the popular 1921 song "Ain't We Got Fun?" seemed to underscore the new emphasis on pleasure as most Americans began to enjoy an increasing amount of leisure time. The average workweek for most members of the working and middle classes had dropped from an average of approximately sixty hours in the 1890s to roughly forty-six hours in 1919 and then to forty-four hours by 1929. Although not as evenly distributed as previously thought, real wages and salaries for most workers were on the rise, while the cost of living recorded only a modest increase. With increased leisure time and more disposable income, recreational activities and even paid vacations, previously a pleasure only for the wealthy, were now a possibility for the families of many salaried workers. The amount of money spent by Americans on amusement and recreation increased by 300 percent during the decade.

Most historians of the Jazz Age view the 1920s as one in which there was a pronounced shift in values and behavior. As one historian put it, Americans moved away from "the Victorian 'production' ethos of work, restraint, and order" toward one that embraced "leisure, consumption, and self-expression as vehicles for individual satisfaction" (Dumenil 1995, 57). As work became increasingly regimented for blue-collar workers on the assembly line and more routinized for white-collar workers trapped behind an office desk, it became more alienating. As it did, and as the Lynds found in *Middletown*, workers increasingly sought satisfaction outside the "job" in consumption and leisure. And the choices seemed limitless. Fun-seekers could embrace the mass media as radio "listeners" and movie "viewers"; enjoy the latest musical recordings or step out to nightclubs and dance to jazz; play golf or tennis; attend a variety of mass spectator sporting events like baseball, college football, or boxing; take a motorized excursion; or become totally fascinated by a dizzying number of fads and crazes that swept through the decade.

RADIO

Most historians date modern radio programming to 1920 when Westinghouse engineer Frank Conrad began transmitting phonograph music from the company's headquarters in East Pittsburgh, Pennsylvania. Local amateur wireless operators (there were more than 6,000 nationally by 1920) began picking up his signal, and soon newspapers were touting his regular Saturday evening programs. Several months later, a local retailer looking to capitalize on the phenomenon began offering $10 receivers so others could listen in. Then, on election night 1920, Westinghouse station KDKA, which had just obtained a government license to operate a general broadcasting service, transmitted the results of that day's presidential election between Warren G. Harding (R) and James M. Cox (D). The company quickly established other stations outside the Pittsburgh area with the idea of using the broadcasts to generate a demand for radio equipment and then realize a profit from the sale of radio sets. Seeking to regain its leading position, the Radio Corporation of America (RCA) soon purchased Westinghouse's radio patents and operations to become the predominant corporate player in the industry. Eight months after the initial KDKA broadcast, RCA decided to promote the sales of its radio receivers by broadcasting a major sporting event—the heavyweight boxing championship match between Jack Dempsey and Georges Carpentier from Jersey City, New Jersey. RCA set up a transmitting station and installed receivers in hundreds of theaters along the East Coast. An estimated 300,000 fight fans (including 100,000 gathered around loudspeakers in New York's Times Square) listened to the bout on July 2, 1921. Phenomenal growth followed. By the end of 1922 there were 576 licensed radio stations operating in the United States, while the sale of radios and radio equipment grew from a $60 million business in 1922 to an $842 million business by 1929.

Programming: Something for Everyone

At first, radio programming featured local talent and mirrored local interests. In a big city like Chicago one might listen to an ethnic nationality program or a broadcast by a church group, labor organization, or fraternal order. Neighbors, friends, and coworkers would often gather at a common place to share their entertainment. As such, at least in its early days, radio "helped to promote 'ethnic, religious, and working-class affiliations'" (Dumenil 1995, 82). But the creation of national radio networks (NBC in 1926 and CBS in 1927), with scores of affiliated stations across the country carrying their network's programs, quickly supplanted local programming. Heavy play of a certain song on commercial radio could spark a national craze for that tune and turn performers into national celebrities. When NBC ran its first four-hour broadcast in November 1926—featuring a New York orchestra, a Chicago soprano, and the comedian Will Rogers—the audience was estimated at 12 million. Many radio stations also began airing live "remote" broadcasts from venues like opera houses, concert halls, and hotel ballrooms. Soon listeners were tuning in to the same corporate-sponsored musical programs and hearing many of the same radio personalities. In the process, radio accelerated the homogenization of popular culture in this country. As a new mass medium, radio influenced how Americans spent their leisure time, what products they purchased, and how they perceived the world around them. Neighbors and friends might hold "radio parties," young people might gather to dance to jazz music, and families might tune in on Sunday morning to listen to a religious sermon by a nationally known preacher. Scheduling one's day around one's favorite radio program was not uncommon. According to one survey done in 1929, more than one-third of American families owned a radio set, and 80 percent of those reported that they listened to their sets every day. By 1930 an estimated 51 million listeners tuned in to nightly radio programs.

Although a wide variety of programming would eventually fill out radio's daily broadcast schedule, music was its mainstay. Live performances of parlor piano and vocal music that was recently popular provided the most common selections, but stations soon supplemented more popular tunes with opera and orchestral performances. By 1924 technological improvements in radio components allowed for the production of better-quality sound than phonographs and gave classical music a further boost. In 1927 CBS began regular broadcasts of the Chicago Civic Opera and established its own symphonic orchestra that same year. But intense voices like high sopranos could play havoc with the tubes on sensitive radio transmitters. Ironically, it was radio's early limitations that encouraged a new softer style of singing that soon became known as "crooning" and made big stars out of female singers like Vaughn De Leath and male singers like Rudy Vallee and Bing Crosby.

Radio promoted the popularity of other types of music as well, such as jazz and country. At first, radio did not feature jazz, a music with roots in Dixieland, ragtime, and the blues and commonly identified with black Americans. Many, at least at first, considered jazz as not altogether "respectable" because of its origins in southern black communities; its spontaneous, improvisational style; its pulsating rhythm; or its association with Prohibition-era speakeasies. Ironically, most intellectuals connected to the Harlem Renaissance were dismissive in their attitude toward jazz as well. Embarrassed by its lowly origins, they were somewhat contemptuous of the new music as not being racially promotable as "high culture." Instead, they "tended to view it as folk art—like the spirituals and the dance—the unrefined source for the new art" (Huggins 1973, 10). As a result, most radio stations were reluctant to broadcast it. But as jazz migrated out of New Orleans to Kansas City, Chicago, and New York and grew in popularity throughout the urban North during the 1920s, resistance eased.

One individual who had a great deal to do with changing attitudes toward jazz among white society was Paul Whiteman, the bandleader of the most commercially successful dance orchestra of the 1920s. Trained as a classical musician, Whiteman combined jazz and classical elements to create a synthesis that became known as "symphonic jazz." Seeking to make jazz music more accessible to white audiences, Whiteman stated that he wanted to "remove the stigma of barbaric strains and jungle cacophony" and "make a lady of jazz" (Drowne and Huber 2004, 204). A turning point in this effort came when Whiteman commissioned composer George Gershwin to write a jazz composition for piano and orchestra. In a special performance billed as "An Experiment in Modern Music" at Manhattan's Aeolian Hall on February 12, 1924, Whiteman's orchestra, with Gershwin as piano soloist, performed "Rhapsody in Blue" and gained for jazz almost instant respectability. Although jazz critics might disparage Whiteman's "soft" jazz and his carefully arranged compositions, and continue to tout the innovative (primarily African American) practitioners of "hot" jazz who emphasized spontaneity and improvisation, Whiteman made jazz popular to radio programmers seeking to please a "middlebrow" audience.

One other musical genre that radio helped to popularize in the 1920s was country music. Initially regarded as ill-defined folk music and often referred to as "hillbilly," southern radio stations began to experiment with a variety of fiddle tunes, gospel songs, and other forms of folk music. In April 1924, the Sears, Roebuck station WLS in Chicago began to sponsor a fiddle-and-square-dance music program called *The National Barn Dance*. A year and a half later, station WSM in Nashville, Tennessee, introduced a variety show that it named *The Grand Ole Opry*. Popular among listeners, WSM quickly expanded the show to a four-hour broadcast on Friday and Saturday nights that could be heard throughout the South and Midwest. Innovations in style, in this case combining fiddle, guitar, mandolin, and banjo, soon evolved into new musical forms like bluegrass.

Aside from musical programs, radio provided millions of Americans with other reasons to tune in. One could hear local and national news; get weather forecasts, stock market reports, sports scores, and home improvement or cooking tips; or listen to political speeches or the coverage of special events like the Scopes Trial in 1925 or Charles Lindbergh's return to the United States after his historic transatlantic flight in 1927. For the farmer, the radio had one other utility. It lessened rural isolation. Soap operas, cliffhanging adventure stories, and musical programs all served to relieve the tedium of the day. The radio helped rural folks compensate for the "deficiencies" in rural life and advanced urban culture to the countryside. By the end of the decade, radio shows were becoming more sophisticated with children's shows, detective stories, and variety features. Particularly popular were serial dramas and situation comedies that featured a cast of characters and a constantly unfolding story line that could generate the loyal audience that advertisers coveted.

One of the most popular radio shows of the late 1920s and early 1930s was a fifteen-minute program called *Amos 'n' Andy*.

Originally a ten-minute feature that first aired on Chicago station WGN on January 12, 1926, as *Sam 'n' Henry*, the popular show moved to another Chicago station in 1928 and reinvented the central characters as *Amos 'n' Andy*. Having worked as farm laborers in the South, the two protagonists decide to set out, much like the sojourners in the Great Migration, for a new life in Chicago where they had heard that high-paying jobs were just waiting to be taken. In a serial format, the two likable title characters, exemplars of rural naiveté, attempted to come to terms with the perplexing problems that always confronted newcomers to the big city. The program, sponsored by Pepsodent Toothpaste and airing each weeknight between 7:00 and 7:15, starred two white vaudevillians named Freeman Gosden and Charles Correll. Gosden and Correll wrote all the scripts themselves and furnished the voices for the members of Amos and Andy's fraternal lodge, the Mystic Knights of the Sea (essentially a den of amiable swindlers), and for a host of other characters, including their rascally friend "the Kingfish." They did the entire program in what to anyone familiar with minstrel shows or blackface vaudeville comedy would have recognized as "Negro dialect" and showed no concern for bad grammar or malapropisms.

Reactions to the show varied. Some African Americans criticized the show as demeaning to their race and objected to the portrayal of the major characters as lacking education, common sense, business savvy, and ethics. But although the characterizations were racist and the humor reinforced racial stereotypes, the show was still immensely popular. A number of critics thought that the show's main appeal rested with its "ability to capture the essence of day-to-day human existence." One radio columnist thought the pair "speak a universal tongue" and found their adventures to be "natural, they are life itself." Another writer agreed that the show possessed a "wealth of living qualities." "Who does not see his neighbor, or even himself, when he listens to this comic pair before the 'mike'" (Ely 1991, 144–45). When NBC picked up *Amos 'n' Andy* in 1929 and turned it into a national broadcast, the radio program quickly became a national phenomenon. The show spawned a daily *Amos 'n' Andy* comic strip, a candy bar, toys, phonograph records, two books, and a film. At the height of the show's popularity in the early 1930s, an estimated 40 million fans tuned in each night, which amounted to roughly 60 percent of all radio listeners and almost one-third of the nation's population.

MOTION PICTURES

Motion pictures, like radio, had a tremendous impact on the daily lives of Americans during the 1920s. As Michael Parrish has stated, "In an age of mass consumption which emphasized the importance of self-fulfillment, the products purchased . . . became as important to each person's identity as the more traditional bonds of ethnicity, religion, and work." In this new modern era, the mass media (movies and magazines especially) helped to market a new commodity: "celebrities, men and women who both represented and transcended their culture, whose feats remained out of the ordinary, yet whose lives somehow manifested the fears, hopes, and anxieties of everyman and everywoman struggling for recognition in a cold universe." From Hollywood celebrities to sports heroes, the marketing of personalities became an essential part in maintaining the myth of individualism in American culture. And as Parrish noted, "The American appetite for vicariously participating in their lives proved nearly inexhaustible" (Parrish 1992, 158–59).

Cecil B. DeMille

One Hollywood director who understood the yearnings of the average American was Cecil B. DeMille. Whereas D. W. Griffith had dominated prewar cinema with a series of melodramas that emphasized Victorian morality, DeMille assumed directorial leadership immediately after the war with a series of films that "spoke directly to the prosperity, upward mobility, and erotic yearnings of the Jazz Age." It has been suggested that DeMille instinctively understood that postwar America was going through a period of rising expectations in which "the prewar working classes (with whom American film had found its first major audience) were becoming middle class and the middle classes were aspiring to even higher levels of consumption and taste." Based on those assumptions, DeMille, through his films, began to instruct Americans aspiring to upward mobility on how to dress, dine, decorate the interiors of their homes, and make love. In depicting his characters recreating and dancing, socializing and entertaining, and dressing and undressing in style, DeMille provided a visual panorama of the rituals of consumption. As such, Hollywood became a major arbiter of taste during the 1920s. Between 1918 and the mid-1920s, DeMille, working in close collaboration with his chief scenario writer Jeannie Macpherson, also produced at least a dozen comedies that celebrated a luxurious style of sophisticated sexuality that included the themes of divorce and extramarital sex that would have been taboo in the prewar era. And DeMille was not alone. Joined by directors Erich von Stroheim, Rex Ingram, and George Medford ("*The Sheik*" starring Rudolph Valentino), Hollywood also "emerged in the American consciousness as the major source of imagery and energy for the sexual revolution that was by then in full sway" (Starr 1985, 321, 323). But in a society that had already outlawed liquor, overt sexual license could easily overstep its moral bounds. After a series of sensational Hollywood scandals involving sex, liquor, drugs, suicide, and even murder, there was a reaction. In its wake (as discussed in Chapter 1), the major studios decided to repair Hollywood's damaged image by creating the Hays Office to monitor immorality in film and by establishing the Hays Code that listed actions that could not be portrayed on the screen.

The Most Popular Form of Commercial Entertainment

During the 1920s motion pictures became the most popular form of commercial entertainment in the United States. By 1922, moviegoers purchased an average of 40 million movie tickets each week (a number that would rise to 95 million by the end of the decade). By mid-decade, nearly every small town had at least one movie theater, while big cities like Chicago and New York had hundreds of them. By 1928 there were an estimated 28,000 movie theaters in the country. Looking for an afternoon's or evening's entertainment, going to a movie was a bargain. For the price of a ticket (usually 10–50 cents), a patron might see a newsreel, maybe a comedy short or two, and then a feature attraction. Prior to the advent of "talkies" in 1927, actors conveyed their emotions through a form of pantomime acting, while subtitles conveyed dialogue and helped to explain the plot. Most neighborhood theaters had a pianist or organist who supplied musical accompaniment, while the larger, big-city movie palaces offered full orchestras to heighten the overall experience. These large picture palaces (termed "atmospherics") showcased expansive lobbies; plush carpeting; statuary and paintings, often exotic Spanish, Moroccan, or Byzantine styling; and ceilings that featured moving clouds and twinkling stars. Typical of the type was Grauman's Egyptian Theater in Hollywood, which opened in 1923 and was designed as an archaeologically correct film temple that featured a courtyard and lobby of brightly colored murals, hieroglyphics, statuary and sarcophagi, and a "profusely decorated proscenium [the arch that separates the stage from the auditorium] hovering over the screen like a baldachino above a baroque altar . . . to create an overall effect of mystic reverence, as one might feel in an ancient Egyptian temple" (Starr 1990, 100).

The Star System

Even before World War I, changes in filming techniques designed to create more suspense and emotion increasingly placed more attention on individual actors. As a result, a star system developed in which a few film actors were able to capitalize on their popularity and command fantastic salaries. It was not long before the Hollywood star system grew to become a cultural phenomenon. The desire of film fans to know more about the private lives of their screen idols generated the publication of more than two-dozen mass-circulation fan magazines such as *Motion Picture, Screenland*, and *Photoplay* that offered fans the latest in news, gossip, and scandal. Commenting on this phenomenon, historian Kevin Starr stated:

> On screen and off, their looks, their clothes, each detail of their personal histories (true or concocted) linked Hollywood stars directly to the deepest aspirations of their mass audience. . . . Through its star system Hollywood took ordinary Americans—which by and large the stars themselves were, in terms of talent and frail humanity—and endowed them with a quality of transcendence that flattered star and audience alike. . . . [The stars] touched ordinariness with a glamour of appearances and possibilities for which each individual in the audience of millions secretly yearned, sitting in a movie theater of an evening or on a weekend afternoon in a respite from routine, dreaming of the someone or something that might await them in the day, the week, the month, the year ahead. (Starr 1985, 320)

Looking to capitalize on the new fascination with celebrity, studios aggressively promoted their film stars. Studio publicists, knowing that publicity sold tickets, kept stars in the public eye through a constant stream of press releases, publicity stunts, interviews, and personal appearances. The most popular film personalities of the period included golden-curled Mary Pickford ("America's Sweetheart"), who continued to portray innocent young girls in films like *Pollyanna* (1920); Douglas Fairbanks, the dashing hero of a number of swashbuckling adventures such as *The Mark of Zorro* (1920); Lon Chaney (the "Man of a Thousand Faces"), who thrilled viewers with

his grotesque character-
izations in films like *The
Hunchback of Notre Dame*
(1923) and *The Phantom of
the Opera* (1925); Rudolph
Valentino (the "Great
Lover"), who emerged as
the great male sex sym-
bol of the 1920s in films
like *The Sheik* (1921);
Greta Garbo, a Swedish-
born actress who came
to the United States in
1925 and immediately
became a fan favorite as
a mysterious, alluring
sex symbol in a series of
Hollywood films such as
Flesh and the Devil (1927)
opposite matinee idol
John Gilbert; and Clara
Bow (the "It Girl"), the
epitome of the sexy Jazz
Age flapper who became
a screen sensation with
the movie *It* (1927).

As early silent movie directors like D. W.
Griffith modernized filming techniques
and instructed actors to act in a more life-
like manner, films began to convey more
suspense and emotion, and to focus the
audience's attention more directly on the
individual actors. As a result, a star system
developed in which a few actors were able
to capitalize on their popularity and command fantastic salaries. At the top of that
"star" list were Douglas Fairbanks and
Mary Pickford (shown here), who, along
with Charlie Chaplin, cofounded United
Artists. (Library of Congress)

Comedy

One very popular film
genre of the 1920s was
comedy, and two of its
most creative stars were
Harold Lloyd and Buster
Keaton. Lloyd's forte resided in physical comedy that involved the
self-created problems confronting an innocent "everyman" (wearing horn-rimmed glasses and a straw hat) aspiring to move up in
the world but constantly forcing him into improbable situations.
His best-remembered film, *Safety Last* (1923), is centered around a
publicity stunt (a climb up the outside wall of an eight-story building by a "human fly") that Lloyd had arranged as a promotion for
the department store at which he is employed. When the human

fly is unable to perform his feat, Lloyd (who did most of his own stunts) decides to scale the wall himself. In his climb, he is impeded by pigeons, a tennis net, a painter's board, a gigantic clock, a mouse, and a weather gauge until safely reaching the roof. As film historian Robert Sklar wryly commented, "One could hardly ask for more graphic satire on the theme of 'upward mobility.'" Buster Keaton, known as the Great Stone Face for his deadpan expressions, made a series of memorable film comedies during the decade. *The General* (1926) is considered by many film historians to be the greatest silent comedy ever made. In that picture, Keaton displays a blend of comic ineptitude and mechanical ingenuity to perform daring feats, correct wrongs, clear his name, and win back his love interest. As Sklar has noted, "Where Lloyd accepted middle-class order and made comedy from the foolish antics of the man on the make, Keaton's existence within the same social setting was predicated on a recognition of not his but *its* absurdities. His comedy always had as its goal the restoration of order in the face of society's errors and false judgments" (Sklar 1975, 117, 119).

The greatest genius of the silent film era, and the actor with perhaps the largest fan base, was the British-born comedian Charlie Chaplin. The son of hard luck, vaudevillian parents, Chaplin understood poverty and even spent time in a poorhouse. He began his film career in 1913 as an actor in Mack Sennett's Keystone comedy troupe but soon tired of the chaotic, slapdash, whirlwind action that became the Sennett trademark. Instead, Chaplin chose to develop his own pantomimic style and, in doing so, created the endearing character that moviegoers came to know as "the Little Tramp." With derby hat, diminutive brush moustache, doleful countenance, baggy pants, tight-fitting jacket, oversized shoes, his trademark cane, and snappy gait, Chaplin used comedy to criticize conventions and dogmas and the character of the gentle little tramp to point out the "inequalities and cruelties that afflicted society's little people who lacked property, influence, and status" (Parrish 1992, 164). Chaplin made a number of memorable films during the 1920s, including *The Kid* (1921), *The Gold Rush* (1925), and *The Circus* (1928). In *The Gold Rush*, Chaplin took a gentle poke at the acquisitiveness of society to suggest that "wealth is an illusion; that the happy moments of life are those of anticipation" (Jacobs 1968, 242). As one historian stated, Chaplin's character often waged a "fruitless struggle against the social forces that assaulted and frustrated human dignity and dreams in modern society. He was a romantic, disappointed and betrayed by love; a generous good Samaritan undone by more sinister people; a sensitive soul crushed by bad fortune. Many in the postwar era of social dislocation and moral ambiguity could identify with those roles" (Parrish 1992, 165).

MUSIC

Two of the most popular musical forms of the 1920s were the blues and jazz, and both of these indigenous American genres reflected the widening African American influence on popular culture in this country.

The Blues

One musical form that reflected the experiences common in the lives of many working men and women, especially in the South, was the blues. Black blues musician and songwriter W. C. Handy said that he first heard the blues around 1903 in the Mississippi Delta, but different regional styles of blues music seemed to develop at the same time in East Texas and the Carolina Piedmont. Others, who understood the blues more as a state of mind than a musical genre, doubted that it could be dated precisely. As one New Orleans blues fiddler remarked, "The blues? Ain't no first blues! The blues always been" (Painter 2006, 159).

The roots of the blues can be found in the religious music and work songs of African Americans that drew on a common store of feelings. In the early twentieth century, the blues (distinguished by its three-line verse with an AAB rhyme scheme) could be heard on street corners; in cafes and bars; at house parties, country dances, and fish fries; and in various work camps. Those who played for money traveled a circuit of "joints," road houses, dance halls, and honky-tonks that could be found throughout the South. Most of those who played and sang the blues were poor, without property, and illiterate. Constantly on the move, they felt a certain freedom from being tied to the land by debt or to a labor system that was often brutally coercive. This physical freedom seemed to enhance their freedom of expression, and most blues musicians took the opportunity to stir things up. Many middle-class blacks resented the primitive stereotypes that the blues seemed to reinforce. Many churchgoers found the blues blasphemous. But many others embraced the genre. The blues took a hard look at daily life. Everyone could relate to the subject matter of the songs: the pain of loneliness, dislocation, or personal loss; being unfaithful in love; the indignity of underpaid labor; poverty; escape through alcohol and drugs; or the threat of violence. Blues singers, as they reflected and philosophized, connected with their audiences through shared experiences.

The first individual to popularize the blues was W. C. Handy who wrote and published his own songs. His early musical compositions, most notably "Memphis Blues" (1912) and "St. Louis Blues" (1914), earned him the sobriquet "Father of the Blues." By the time of World War I, sales of Handy's sheet music had triggered a mania for blues songs. Hoping to capitalize on Handy's popularity, songwriters employed by New York City's music publishing firms (Tin Pan Alley) rushed to turn out dozens of commercial songs with the word "blues" in the title. Although most of these efforts were not "real" blues tunes, a few of the more authentic ones helped to popularize the genre among white listeners. In the mid-1920s, W. C. Handy published an edited collection entitled *Blues: An Anthology* (1926), one of the first studies to discuss the influence of the blues on jazz, popular, and classical music.

In February 1920, Harlem cabaret singer Mamie Smith, backed by her band the Jazz Hounds, recorded "You Can't Keep a Good Man Down" and "This Thing Called Love" for Okeh Records, the first recording by an African American vocalist. The record sold so well that Smith returned to the studio a few months later to record "Crazy Blues" and "It's Right Here for You." With almost no advertising, the record sold 75,000 copies in Harlem in less than one month. It was the beginning of a tradition of commercially profitable records sung by talented black female blues singers.

The earliest well-known female blues singer was Gertrude "Ma" Rainey. She had been a star in southern minstrel shows that traveled by train and followed the cotton and tobacco harvests in the South and Midwest, performing under a large circus tent with a portable wooden stage. Rainey brought an authentic Deep South sound to the blues that became very popular. Soon known as the "Mother of the Blues," Rainey signed a recording contract with Chicago-based Paramount Records (one of several white-owned record companies that sought to tap into a lucrative market that existed among African Americans for what became known as "race records") in 1923. Between 1923 and 1928 Rainey recorded at least ninety-two songs for Paramount (more than one-third of which were her compositions), often accompanied by great jazz musicians. Aggressively promoted by her record company and by black newspapers like the *Chicago Defender*, her records were eagerly purchased by southerners through mail order and by northerners through record stores in black neighborhoods.

Bessie Smith, pictured here in a notable 1936 photograph by Carl Van Vechten and known to most fans as the "Empress of the Blues," sang with a rich, resonate voice that some said she employed like a jazz instrument. Using her soulful music to underscore social problems and racial injustice, Smith became a cultural figure who symbolized racial pride much like Jack Johnson, the prize-fighter, and Marcus Garvey, the prophet of black nationalism. When she toured the country, fans would queue up around an entire city block to hear her sing. (Carl Van Vechten Photographs Collection, Library of Congress)

An even bigger star than "Ma" Rainey was Bessie Smith. Smith had a similar background with a traveling minstrel troupe before signing a contract to sing at Charles Bailey's 81 Theater in Atlanta, Georgia. In the early 1920s she moved North but had trouble breaking into the record industry because it was thought her voice sounded too "rough" and "coarse." She finally caught on with Columbia Records in 1923 and recorded two big hits, "Down-Hearted Blues" and "Gulf Coast Blues." Her compelling voice, coupled with the folk lyrics of the songs, struck a chord with African American record buyers. Her first Columbia record sold 780,000 copies in just six months. Tours of northern cities enhanced her popularity, and black Americans waited in long lines at clubs to hear her vocal rendition of the blues.

"She sang them," said one writer, "with a passionate conviction and stage presence. Her voice was rich and resonant. . . . Like other great Black vocalists, Smith could bend, stretch, and slur notes to achieve a desired effect. She used her voice as a jazz instrument, like the growl of a trombone" (Hine 1993, 1075). Jazz great Louis Armstrong once said of Smith, "She used to thrill me at all times, the way she could phrase a note with a certain something in her voice no other blues singer could get" (Hine 2000, 411). By the mid-1920s, Smith was using some of the most talented jazz musicians in the country in her recording sessions to vastly improve the quality of her recordings. Between 1925 and 1930 Smith gave special attention to social topics in her songs like poverty, unemployment and hard times, drinking, bootlegging and gambling, prison, injustice, and the mistreatment of women by men, issues that especially affected the African American population. With the onset of the Great Depression, Smith's career began to decline. Talking pictures signaled the end of vaudeville, while the popularity of radio undercut record sales and forced Columbia Records to terminate her contract in 1931. During one of her final recording sessions for Columbia, Smith recorded her prophetic "Nobody Knows You When You're Down and Out." Many music historians today still regard her as the greatest female blues singer of all time.

Jazz

The most influential form of popular music in the 1920s was jazz. Jazz has been described as "an unwritten, polyphonic music characterized, at least originally, by blues accents and collective improvisation, in which musicians each embellished the melody" (Drowne and Huber 2004, 200). Jazz bands commonly featured cornets, clarinets, trombones, drums, saxophones, and piano, and the music was said to have been around since the mid-1890s among African American and creole musicians in New Orleans. During the first two decades of the twentieth century, the music moved North with the black migration to Chicago and New York before spreading throughout the United States. Some early jazz musicians performed on steamboats plying the Mississippi River and in vaudeville shows on the all-black musical circuit before moving on to urban dance halls, nightclubs, and speakeasies in cities like Chicago. It was, however, a five-piece ensemble of white musicians from New Orleans who called themselves the Original Dixieland Jazz Band that made the first commercial jazz recordings—"Livery Stable Blues" and "Dixie Jazz Band One Step"—in 1917. Largely because of discriminatory racial practices in the recording industry, black musicians were not given the opportunity to make any jazz records until 1922 when Edward "Kid" Ory and his band recorded "Ory's Creole Trombone" and "Society Blues" in Los Angeles. But as jazz music gained in popularity, and as race records proved to be commercially profitable, record companies began to issue recordings of both races, including such legendary black jazz groups as King Oliver and his Creole Jazz Band, Clarence Williams's Blue Five, Louis Armstrong and His Hot Five (and later Hot Seven), and Fletcher Henderson and His Orchestra. Although record sales soared, African American musicians were largely excluded from performing on early commercial radio. Band leader Duke Ellington finally changed that policy when he signed a contract with CBS that put his orchestra on nationwide radio in 1928.

By the mid-1920s, versions of jazz were being played in road-houses and dance halls all across the country. It has been estimated that more than one hundred dance bands traveled the mid-section of the country, from Missouri to Colorado and from Texas to Nebraska, playing one-night gigs. Known as "territory bands," these small groups, often too poor to afford buses, would crowd into old cars for the long trips between engagements with their instruments tied to their vehicle. There were even "all-girl" orchestras on the road with names like the Hollywood Redheads, the Twelve Vampires, and the Parisian Redheads (all of whom were actually from the state of Indiana). As one veteran of this circuit remembered it, "People didn't think anything about going a hundred and fifty to two hundred miles to dance back in those times" (Ward and Burns 2000, 124). At the same time, radio and phonograph records (Americans purchased more than 100 million of them in 1927) were bringing jazz music to locations that were too remote even for territory bands. And the music itself was beginning to change. By mid-decade a style of music known as "hot jazz," featuring individual solos by extremely gifted individuals and hard-driving rhythms, became very popular. King Oliver's Creole Jazz Band, which played at the Lincoln Gardens café on Chicago's South Side and included the best jazz musicians to come North from New Orleans, and Fletcher Henderson's Orchestra, which performed at the Savoy in Harlem, were two of the best. One man who played for both, and who is regarded as the greatest jazz musician of the 1920s, was cornetist and trumpeter Louis Armstrong whose innovative solos and technical brilliance dazzled audiences. Between 1925 and 1928, Armstrong recorded a series of sixty-five songs for Okey Records as the leader of his own bands, the Hot Five and the Hot Seven, that have become hot jazz classics.

Harlem Nightlife

By the late 1920s, the hub of jazz music had shifted to New York City where most of the major recording companies were located, and the epicenter of this new jazz mecca was Harlem. Nightclubs and cabarets located above 125th Street in Manhattan began to attract a wealthy white clientele who wanted to drink, dance, and listen to "exotic" African American music after the downtown clubs had closed. And, according to the account of one social chronicler, it was a spectacle.

> You saw throngs on Lenox and Seventh Avenues, ceaselessly moving from one pleasure resort to another. Long after the cascading lights of Times Square had flickered out, these boulevards were ablaze. Lines of taxis and private cars kept driving up to the glaring entrances of the night clubs. Until nearly dawn the subway kiosks poured crowds on the sidewalks. The legend of Harlem by night—exhilarating and sensuous, throbbing to the beating of drums and the wailing of saxophones, cosmopolitan in its peculiar sophistications—crossed the continent and the ocean. (Miller 2014, 516)

Of the eleven major nightclubs in Harlem listed in *Variety* in 1929, no nightspot offered more excitement than the Cotton Club at the corner of Lenox Avenue and 142nd Street. Originally known as the Club Deluxe when it was purchased by bootlegger Owney Madden and a group of hoodlums in 1923 to peddle illegal alcohol, extensive remodeling quickly turned the second-story hangout into a swank supper club that could seat 700. The Cotton Club's entertainers and waiters were black, but the customers were white. Awash in racial condensation, the club featured an antebellum motif. As singer Cab Calloway described the room, "The bandstand was a replica of a southern mansion, with large white columns and a backdrop painted with weeping willows and slave quarters. The band played on the veranda of the mansion, and . . . down a few steps, was the dance floor, which was also used for the shows" (Miller 2014, 514). The floor shows featured songs, dances, and "lots of light-skinned, lightly-clad chorus girls billed as 'Tall, Tan and Terrific'" (Ward and Burns 2000, 147).

Between 1927 and 1931, Duke Ellington's Orchestra performed as the house band at the Cotton Club. Ellington, regarded as the premier composer of jazz music at the time, created a popular jazz style that became known as the "Jungle Sound" and recorded a number of popular compositions with his orchestra such as "Black and Tan Fantasy," "Creole Love Call," and "Mood Indigo." According to one account, "Ellington's driving, rhythmic music pulled audiences out of their seats to do the Shimmy, the Shuffle, the Black-Bottom, the Turkey Trot, and the Charleston." After signing a nationwide radio contract in 1928, the band became immensely popular. As one band member remembered, "We'd play a set, people would come up to the bandstand and tell us they heard us on the air, in Walla Walla, Washington; Elko, Nevada; Boise, Idaho; Austin, Texas; and places like that." As one writer put it, "The music of New York became America's music" (Miller 2014, 517).

Broadway Musicals

Another form of entertainment that was popular throughout the Big Apple was musical theater. Sets were elegant, costumes glamorous, and dance numbers elaborate. It has been said that musicals became a favorite form of entertainment during the decade and paved the way for the spectacular Hollywood movie musicals of the 1930s. Popular musicals like *No, No, Nanette* (1925) included songs like "Tea for Two" and "I Want to Be Happy," while the more serious *Show Boat* (1927) featured an outstanding musical score written by composer Jerome Kern and lyricist Oscar Hammerstein II and featured hits like "Ol' Man River" and "Make Believe." In 1921, *Shuffle Along* became the first musical to be written, produced, directed, and performed entirely by African Americans. *Shuffle Along* included hit musical numbers like "Love Will Find a Way" and "I'm Just Wild about Harry," written by the songwriting team of Eubie Blake and Noble Sissle, and launched the careers of a number of black performers including Florence Mills, Josephine Baker, and Paul Robeson. There were 19 black floor shows produced on Broadway in 1923, and Manhattan had over 200 dance halls. Notable were the Savoy, which featured a 200-foot-long dance floor, and the Manhattan Casino, which could accommodate up to 6,000 dancers.

Mexican Music—the *Corrido*

If music played a central role in the recreational life of urban, African American communities like Harlem, the same might be said for urban, Mexican American communities like the one in Los Angeles. According to historian George Sánchez, "The constant sound of Mexican music—music that ranged from traditional Mexican ballads to newly recorded *corridos* depicting life in Los Angeles—was everywhere. A burgeoning Mexican music industry flourished in the central and eastern sections of the city during the 1920s, largely hidden from the Anglo majority." The only exception to that generalization would be the small number of Anglo residents of Los

Angeles who liked to listen to "traditional" Mexican music as it provided a "nostalgic backdrop to the distinctive 'Spanish' past of the city" (Sánchez 1993b, 171, 180). Over one-third of the Mexican families in Los Angeles owned radios (as a predominately working-class community, they often purchased the equipment "on time"), while a smaller number (3 percent) owned phonographs. As Sánchez has noted, when immigrant musicians arrived in Los Angeles from central and northern Mexico (much as black migrants had done from the South), they created an environment for musical innovation and ultimately fueled the growth of a recording industry.

The musical style that was most popular during this period was the *corrido*. With roots in the Mexican Revolution, where important events, political leaders, and rebels were often immortalized in song, these *corridos* found their way into Mexico's urban centers where they were "codified and transformed from folk expression to popular songs." As this music migrated along with the musicians to urban centers like Los Angeles, it became popular as an urban art form for a couple of reasons. First, the urban *corrido* reminded those who had migrated from rural areas in Mexico of their provincial origins and "gave urban dwellers a connection to the agrarian ideal which was seen as typically Mexican." Second, most *corridos* appealed to a latent nationalism "at a time when the pride of Mexican people, places, and events was flourishing." As a style of composition, the *corrido* could be easily adapted to a new environment and different situations. The music was intended to tell a story to its listeners, "one that would not necessarily be news but rather would 'interpret, celebrate, and ultimately dignify events already thoroughly familiar to the *corrido* audience.'" *Corrido* musicians (most of whom continued to work at blue-collar jobs while they struggled to survive as musicians) were expected to make the story relevant to the working-class Mexican immigrant audience living in Los Angeles, and this "adaptive style was particularly well suited for the rapidly expanding Los Angeles Mexican community of the 1920s and the ever-complex nature of intercultural exchange in the city" (Sánchez 1993b, 177, 178).

The first commercial recording of a *corrido* in the United States was "El Lavaplatos," which was performed in Los Angeles on May 11, 1926, by Los Hermanos Bañuelos. This *corrido* tells the story of a Mexican immigrant who dreams of striking it rich in the United States but, instead, runs into economic misfortune. Finally, after being forced to take a job as a dishwasher, the singer laments:

"Goodbye dreams of my life, goodbye movie stars, I am going back to my beloved homeland, much poorer than when I came" (Sánchez 1993b, 178). Not surprisingly, the same national record companies that had begun to produce race records featuring black blues music now began to search for Chicano musicians and singers to tap into the potential ethnic market among Mexicans. Although radio resisted broadcasting Spanish-language music for most of the decade, as advertisers and large corporations came to exert more control over programming, a market for Spanish-language music began to open up. Reticent to jump in with both feet, American radio programmers often scheduled Spanish-language broadcasts during "dead" airtime—early morning, late night, or weekends—which was not turning a profit. Although not ideal, many Mexican immigrants tuned in to such broadcasts while they got ready for their early morning shifts at work. By the late 1920s, the hours dedicated to Spanish-language broadcasts had greatly expanded.

One entrepreneur who promoted Spanish-language music while taking full advantage of the opportunity to tap into the lucrative Spanish-language music market was Mauricio Calderón. During the 1920s, he established the Repertorio Musical Mexicana, which served as a clearinghouse for phonographs and Spanish-language records and operated under the slogan, "The only Mexican house of Mexican music for Mexicans." Then, when radio started to expand its ethnic programming, Calderón operated as a broker who negotiated with stations, paying them a flat rate for cheap, "off-hour" broadcasting time. He then sold this time to advertisers looking to reach the thousands of working-class Mexican immigrant families within the range of the station's signal. Also giving a boost to the Mexican music industry in the city was the boom in Chicano theater during the 1920s. It has been estimated that over thirty Chicano playwrights moved to Los Angeles during the decade, producing a variety of shows ranging from melodrama to vaudeville. The Spanish-speaking population in the area was able to support five major theater houses with programs that changed daily, and at least seventeen other theaters that supported Spanish-speaking theatrical companies on a more irregular basis.

DANCE

Dancing, whether it be at nightclubs, dance halls, speakeasies, or private social clubs, became a passion during the Jazz Age. Records were readily available and radios had become increasingly affordable, while the influence of Hollywood movies had never been greater. All one had to do was to diligently watch the dancers one saw on the movie screen. Fred and Adele Astaire popularized tap dancing, while Broadway entertainers and movie stars taught everyone how to fox-trot. Matinee idol Rudolph Valentino showed how to do the tango in *The Four Horsemen of the Apocalypse* (1921), while Gilda Gray popularized the "shimmy" in *The Ziegfeld Follies of 1922*. As dance became seen as the key to popularity, many—young and older alike—signed up for lessons at local dance studios. For those seeking a more private approach, Arthur Murray created a mail-order dance instruction course that taught customers the basic steps by using a lesson booklet with footprint patterns and simple instructions. By 1925, an estimated five million people had learned to dance at home with the help of Arthur Murray.

Far and away the most popular dance of the decade and the symbol of the carefree spirit and fervor that characterized the period was the Charleston. Although its origins are unclear, dancer Elizabeth Welch is credited with introducing it into the popular culture in the all-black musical revue *Runnin' Wild* (1923) and touching off a nationwide dance craze between 1923 and 1926. The dance involved turning one's knees and toes inward in rapid fashion, and hospitals reported increasing numbers of people complaining of "Charleston knee." Soon dance venues across the country were staging dance contests, while popular songwriters were hard at work producing new Charleston songs for a dance-mad public. One other dance fad that eventually overtook the Charleston in popularity was the Black Bottom, first introduced in the all-black musical *Dinah* (1923) although it did not become a sensation until white dancer Ann Pennington performed it in *The George White Scandals of 1926*. Jazz musician Jelly Roll Morton wrote the tune "Black Bottom Stomp," a reference to Detroit's Black Bottom area.

MASS SPECTATOR SPORTS

The act of living vicariously that was so much a part of the motion picture audience was perhaps even greater for fans drawn to the world of sport. During the 1920s watching or listening to amateur or professional sports contests became a national pastime, while the worship of a rather long list of larger-than-life social heroes exceeded any previous era. With more leisure time and disposable income, and assisted by radio broadcasts and newspaper sports columns, mass spectator sports became hugely popular and transformed individuals like Babe Ruth, Red Grange, Jack Dempsey, Bill Tilden, Helen Mills, Bobby Jones, Gertrude Ederle, and Johnny Weissmuller into the status of national celebrities. And like much of the commercialization of the decade, sports became a big industry, with sports owners, promoters, agents, and media outlets all looking to capitalize on the phenomenon.

Baseball

Major league baseball had been popular before the war and a big business even then. But the sport was still in its "primitive" stage where competition among teams was ruthless, where owners bought and sold players like virtual indentured servants, and where conditions and pay were exploitative. Such an environment was ripe for scandal, and it happened in 1919 when players for the Chicago White Sox, fed up with what they regarded as low pay and sweatshop-like conditions, decided to rebel and accepted gambler's money to throw the 1919 World Series. The ensuing trial of the so-called Black Sox resulted in eight players—including star outfielder "Shoeless Joe" Jackson—being banned from baseball and the appointment (like the motion picture industry) of federal judge Kenesaw Mountain Landis as baseball commissioner with a mandate to clean up the sport. Rule changes followed as well. Pitchers were prohibited from "scuffing" baseballs with sandpaper or smearing them with dirt, licorice, or tobacco juice, which gave the pitcher an advantage by making the thrown ball more difficult to hit and harder to see. Umpires were now instructed to immediately replace a soiled ball with a spotless one. The changes—coupled with the baseball having been made livelier as manufacturers wound the yarn within them more tightly—shifted the balance to the hitter and enabled hitters to hit the ball farther. The stage had been set for George Herman "Babe" Ruth.

Ruth had grown up in a poor South Baltimore neighborhood to abusive parents. Wild as a youth, he was committed to the St. Mary's Industrial School for Boys where he learned to play baseball. After signing a professional contract with the Boston Red Sox, Ruth was traded to the New York Yankees in December 1919. In his first season with his new club, he hit fifty-four home runs (more than were hit by fourteen of the other fifteen major league teams), and more than a million fans came to the Polo Grounds to see him do it. As manager Miller Huggins commented, the average fan "likes the fellow who carries the wallop" (Ward and Burns

1994, 159). The next year Ruth boosted his home run total to fifty-nine, and the Yankees won the pennant. Two years later, as gate receipts climbed, the Yankees opened a new 62,000-seat stadium in the Bronx that became known as "the House that Ruth Built." Although a star on the diamond, Ruth's off-field exploits were less than admirable. He hit the nightspots and hung out with celebrities, while his escapades with liquor and women became so notorious that Commissioner Landis once suspended him for forty days. But the fans seemed not to mind. His "very raffishness, combined with an absence of guile that bordered on naiveté, made him an almost perfect symbol of a big business that embraced the country's simple, rural past as well as its hedonistic urban present" (Parrish 1992, 171).

But baseball was bigger than Babe Ruth, and radio had a lot to do with that. When the World Series was broadcast on radio for the second time in 1923, the announcer, sitting in a box seat close to the field, spoke into a large microphone to an estimated five million listeners. In Chicago, which had a loyal Cubs following and a competitive ballclub, the impact of radio was just as great. As one baseball historian described the scene:

> Across the sprawling city the announcers' voices squawked through windows and doors still open in the warm late-summer afternoon, down quiet side streets and alleys, inside stores and barbershops and the ice cream parlors that fronted for the ready availability of beer. No other program—no music, no comedy, no soap opera, no news—aired during the Cub game. The flat Midwestern deliveries of the play-by-play men were the common denominator of a city where sociologists had recorded the presence of at least twenty-eight spoken tongues. (Ehrgott 2013, 2)

Listeners of these broadcasts included not merely the seven million residents of Chicago and its suburbs but also millions more in a six-state region of the upper Midwest. As one fan wrote from somewhere in the rural hinterland, "Don't stop it [the broadcasts], I have a radio [battery-powered radios were not uncommon] in the field with me. I plow one turn, sit down for a cool drink out of the jug and listen to the score. It's grand." On Ladies Day, female fans reaching numbers of 20,000 or more poured into Wrigley Field to watch a Friday afternoon home game. They "applauded foul balls enthusiastically, adopted and discarded favorites, and hounded the chosen ones for autographs; the boldest flappers forwarded their phone numbers to the dugouts." Saturdays and Sundays brought more women to the ballpark as paying customers who had learned baseball on Friday afternoons or by listening to the broadcasts while doing household chores. Joined by their husbands and families, the park frequently sold out on weekends, and latecomers (numbering up to 4,000) might have to settle for standing-room-only admission behind a rope stretched deep in the outfield (Ehrgott 2013, 2, 3, 50).

Strict policies of racial segregation, however, prohibited many talented African American ballplayers from joining professional baseball. As a result, black ballplayers had created loosely organized associations of their own dating back to the 1890s. In 1919, the year of the infamous Chicago race riots, Andre "Rube" Foster, the owner and manager of the Chicago American Giants, decided to create the National Negro Baseball League (NNBL) to "keep Colored baseball from the control of whites" and "do something concrete for the loyalty of the race." Foster, previously an outstanding black pitcher, now became black baseball's "first great impresario" (Ward and Burns 1994, 157). Teams in the NNBL faced a number of problems—segregated hotels and passenger trains and high fees for the use of white-owned ballparks when those teams were on the road—but the venture proved to be a success. With standout stars like pitchers "Smokey Joe" Williams and "Bullet Joe" Rogan and center fielder Oscar Charleston, the NNBL drew more than 400,000 black fans during the 1923 season. The success of the NNBL quickly caught the attention of white businessmen who formed a rival organization, the Eastern Colored League, and the two leagues staged the first Negro World Series in 1924, which was won by the Kansas City Monarchs of Foster's league.

College Football

College football was tremendously popular during the 1920s. As schools began to set rules and insist on fairness and safety, they drained a good deal of the excessive violence from the sport and made it more respectable. Changes in the style of play increased fan appeal, and coaches, like Knute Rockne at Notre Dame, revolutionized the game by perfecting the faster-paced, forward pass offense. At the same time, college football lost some of its elitism as the sport expanded from the eastern schools of the Ivy League to larger universities in the Midwest and on the Pacific Coast. With college and university enrollments nearly doubling during the 1920s, the popularity of college football increased by leaps and bounds. As universities made the connection between strong football programs, gate receipts, and alumni donations, they moved in the direction of erecting bigger and bigger stadiums to accommodate their enthusiastic supporters. Yale built a new stadium that seated 60,000. Stanford University soon upped the ante to 86,000, only to be outdone by the University of Michigan's huge 102,000-seat shrine to the gridiron. Soon, dozens of colleges and universities could boast of their own 60,000- to 80,000-seat stadiums. Extensive radio broadcasting of college games and the reshowing of game highlights in movie theaters further broadened college football's fan base. In 1927 alone, more than 30 million spectators across the nation spent more than $50 million on college football tickets. By the end of the decade, ticket receipts for college football exceeded those of professional baseball.

The most exciting college football player of the 1920s was a young University of Illinois halfback by the name of Harold "Red" Grange, whom sportswriters dubbed "the Galloping Ghost." A three-time All-American, Grange first captured national attention in 1924 when he scored four touchdowns on runs of 93, 67, 56, and 44 yards in the first twelve minutes of a game against the University of Michigan. The following year, he became the first athlete to be featured on the cover of *Time* magazine. After playing his final college game in 1925, Grange signed a contract with the professional Chicago Bears football team that paid him a salary and a share of gate receipts that amounted to at least $100,000 a year (equivalent in purchasing power to over $1.4 million in 2018). The investment was well worth the money as Grange began to attract hundreds of thousands of fans to professional games (the National Football League [NFL] had been organized in 1922) and helped put the struggling NFL on solid financial footing while giving it some legitimacy. During his time as a professional football star, Grange also starred in two silent films, *One Minute to Play* (1926) and *Racing Romeo* (1927), as well as a serial about college football called *The Galloping Ghost* (1931).

Boxing

In 1920 professional boxing still carried the stigma of a brutal, lowbrow sport that served as a magnet for gamblers and "toughs." But, as the decade progressed, state legislatures began to lift bans and restrictions, while state boxing commissions took steps to curb some of the more brutal aspects of the sport and clean up its image. As a result, boxing gained in popularity among all classes of people and became, with the help of big-time boxing promoters like George "Tex" Rickard, a big business.

The public's desire for vicarious participation in the world of boxing during the 1920s reached a peak in the heavyweight matches between Jack Dempsey and Gene Tunney. The two fighters were a study in contrasts. Dempsey, the current champion, was a roughneck from the Colorado mines who had ridden the rails and lived in hobo jungles, "whose vicious fighting style, stemming from a well of lower-class discontent, had earned him the title 'The Manassa Mauler'" (Cashman 1998, 198). "Like bad boy [Babe] Ruth, who hailed from the wrong side of the tracks, Dempsey was a bit of an outlaw, a hero to those who carried a lunch bucket to work, who toiled with their hands, and who dreamed of striking it rich" (Parrish 1992, 174–75). Tunney, the challenger, was handsome, educated, well read, and a former marine who could come across as aloof and pedantic yet had the air of a gentleman. To those in the crowd who tended to be more middle class, affluent, and female, he could do no wrong. Quick, graceful, and agile, he was a thinking man's fighter.

The two pugilists battled twice. In their first match in Philadelphia in 1926, which Tunney won by a unanimous decision, over 120,000 spectators paid to see the fight, which was waged outdoors in the rain. Gate receipts totaled nearly $2 million. In the rematch a year later at Chicago's Soldier Field with 145,000 fans in attendance, the gate reached $2.6 million. Nearly 400 newspapermen covered the bout at ringside surrounded by 9 governors, a dozen mayors, over 20 Broadway stars, members of European royalty, congressmen and senators, and a number of "captains" of industry who occupied 100 or so "front-row" seats. NBC radio announcer Graham McNamee described the fight to 50 million American listeners. In the seventh round, with Tunney ahead on points, Dempsey knocked the champion to the canvas. But Dempsey delayed retreating to a neutral corner, and the referee did not begin his count until Dempsey did so. By that time five or six seconds (some said it was closer to ten or twelve) had elapsed. Tunney got up at the count of nine, danced away from Dempsey for the rest of the round, and eventually won another unanimous decision. Boxing fans still debate the "outcome" of the famous "long count."

Golf, Tennis, and Swimming

There were two sports—golf and tennis—in which increasing numbers of Americans participated as well as spectated. Golf, previously a game only for the affluent, enjoyed a boom in popularity among the middle class during the 1920s. Frederick Lewis Allen estimated that there were two million recreational golfers who played the game in 1920, a number that increased to more than three million by 1930. According to Allen, "More men were playing golf than ever before—playing it in baggy plus-fours, with tassels at the knee and checkered stockings" (Allen 2010, 179). As the ability to play the game became an essential component of the aspiring business executive, the country club became ever more important as a center of social life in hundreds of communities. But golf was also popular as a spectator sport, with fans attending tournaments and following their favorite idols—Walter Hagen, Gene Sarazen, and Bobby Jones—in the newspapers as never before. The biggest golfing sensation of the decade was Bobby Jones, who dominated the sport as an amateur between 1923 and 1930, a period during which he won 13 of the 21 national championship tournaments he entered. In 1930, at the age of twenty-eight, he won the Grand Slam by capturing the U.S. Amateur, U.S. Open, British Amateur, and British Open all in the same year. Feeling that no more challenges remained, he then abruptly retired from competitive golf in 1930.

Tennis, like golf, also enjoyed a surge in popularity during the 1920s. More men and women took lessons or casually played the game, and by the end of the decade, many cities had built public courts to accommodate enthusiasts. Both male and female stars captured the public's attention during the decade and, like golf, the skill and artistry of the major stars made what had been purely elite sports interesting to the masses. William "Big Bill" Tilden became a national tennis idol with his powerful serves, his finesse and grace on the court, and his comeback style of play that whipped fans into a frenzy. He became the first American to win the Wimbledon title in 1920, a feat he repeated in 1921 and 1930. He also won the U.S. Open Singles Championship six years in a row (1920–1925) and again in 1929, and the Clay Court Championship in singles six times (1922–1927) during the decade. Tilden's popularity convinced promoters to build a new stadium at Forest Hills, New York, to accommodate the huge crowds that he drew to the sport. Not to be eclipsed from the tennis spotlight was Helen Wills who used a more methodical style of play to win the women's title at the U.S. Open in 1923 at the age of seventeen. Between 1923 and 1933 Wills won seven U.S. Open championships, eight Wimbledon tournaments, and four French Open titles and was virtually unbeatable.

The sport of swimming also produced two spectacular champions during the 1920s whose fame encouraged tens of thousands of Americans to take up swimming at municipal pools throughout the country. In 1926, nineteen-year-old Gertrude Ederle made headlines around the world when she became the first woman to swim the twenty-one-mile English Channel in fourteen hours and thirty-one minutes, a time that bested the previous men's record by nearly two hours. The accomplishment earned her a ticker-tape parade in New York City on her return. In assessing the feat, one Northwestern University swimming coach remarked that gender-restrictive attitudes were changing: "Physical education has brought about an evolution of common sense that has wrought a complete turnover, not only in woman's physical condition but in her whole mental attitude" (Brown 1987, 43). Ederle won a gold medal and two bronze medals at the 1924 Olympics in Paris, a year in which she also held eighteen world swimming records. Just as notable was Johnny Weissmuller, who never lost a freestyle race during his amateur swimming career. Weissmuller won three gold medals at the 1924 Olympics and two more at the 1928 Olympics in Amsterdam. At the time he retired from amateur swimming in 1929, Weissmuller had won fifty-two U.S. national championships and had set sixty-seven world records. A sensation in the pool, Weissmuller went on to win further fame as an actor playing Tarzan in a dozen Hollywood movies beginning with *Tarzan, the Ape Man* in 1932.

FADS AND CRAZES

The growing influence of radio, motion pictures, advertising, and mass circulation magazines and newspapers during the 1920s created a nationwide entertainment industry that seemed capable of generating enthusiasm for anything new or out of the ordinary. And it appeared as if Americans would try anything to entertain themselves. As a result, a series of fads and crazes captured the attention of Americans like never before. Three of the tamer crazes of the decade were crossword puzzles, mah-jongg, and miniature golf.

Crossword Puzzles, Mah-Jongg, and Miniature Golf

Crossword puzzles are said to date back to at least 1913 but did not gain widespread popularity until 1924 when Richard Simon and Max Schuster began a publishing venture by issuing the world's first collection of word puzzles called *The Cross Word Puzzle Book*. Sold with a pencil attached to each copy, the book became an instant best seller and touched off a nationwide craze. The Baltimore and Ohio Railroad placed dictionaries on its trains for the convenience of puzzlers. College teams competed in tournaments, while thousands of fans in New York cheered two crossword finalists in a national contest. The University of Kentucky even offered a course in crossword puzzles because, as one administrator stated, they were "educational, scientific, instructive and mentally stimulative, as well as entertaining" (Editors of Time-Life Books 1998, 176). By 1926 the fad itself had run its course, but the crossword puzzle was here to stay.

The Chinese game called mah-jongg also proved to be tremendously popular as a leisure pursuit when it was first introduced to the United States in 1922. Resembling both dominoes and dice, the game is played by four people using a set of 144 decorated tiles, originally manufactured only in China where beautiful, handcrafted sets with inlaid tiles could cost as much as $500. By 1923 an estimated 10–15 million Americans were hooked on the game, while ladies' tea clubs occasionally tried to enhance their experience by playing the game attired in Chinese silk robes and embroidered slippers. That same year more people bought mah-jongg sets than radios. When Chinese suppliers could not keep up with the growing demand for sets, American companies began making and marketing cheaper sets with simplified rule books. The game's popularity soon convinced newspapers to begin running daily columns devoted to the rules and strategies of the game.

Another game that became a national craze in the late 1920s was miniature golf (also called "Tom Thumb" golf and "pygmy" golf). Most accounts credit Garnet Carter, the owner of a hotel and golf course on Lookout Mountain near Chattanooga, Tennessee, for building the first layout in 1927 as a way to generate publicity for his resort. The miniature course proved to be so popular with guests that he soon began charging them to play. By the end of the decade it was estimated that four million people were playing on any one of nearly 40,000 miniature golf courses across the country. Putting through windmills, tiny castles, and clown's faces proved to be so popular that Hollywood movie studios worried about the fad cutting into their ticket sales.

Marathon Dancing and Flagpole Sitting

Two fads that were not so tame were dance marathons and flag-pole sitting. One of the enduring images from the 1920s is that of an exhausted couple leaning against each other on the dance floor as they desperately try to keep "dancing" longer than the other competitors so they can win the prize. The fad apparently began in 1923 when Alma Cummings set a record of twenty-seven hours of non-stop dancing at a contest held in New York City. That feat sparked a craze, and soon there were contests being held in cities across the country to see if anyone could break the record. By the end of 1923, the record for nonstop dancing by a couple had reached 182 hours and 8 minutes. Promoters then took the competitions to the next stage by adding emcees, orchestras, and dozens of vendors selling everything from hot dogs to sore feet remedies. Dance marathons could drag on for weeks, and radio broadcasters and tabloid newspaper coverage hyped these spectacles and allowed listeners or readers to follow the daily drama. The most famous of the dance marathons took place at New York's Madison Square Garden in 1928. Billed as the "Dance Derby of the Century," more than 100 couples competed for the $5,000 first prize. Thousands of spectators paid the $2.20 admission fee to watch, but after 428 grueling hours (nearly 18 days) the Board of Health stopped the contest when one contestant collapsed and had to be hospitalized. Rather than fade, the popularity of dance marathons actually increased during the following decade when unemployed Americans eagerly competed for badly needed cash prizes.

One additional endurance craze that briefly mesmerized the country during the decade was flagpole sitting. The most famous flagpole sitter of the era was undoubtedly Alvin "Shipwreck" Kelly, a former boxer and Hollywood stuntman. Kelly started the fad when he spent thirteen hours and thirteen minutes atop a flagpole as part of a publicity stunt to attract crowds to a Hollywood theater. Soon fame-seekers across the country were out to break the record. As Kelly's celebrity increased, businessmen and promoters hired him to stage exhibitions at store openings, amusement parks, and county fairs across the country. To provide himself some comfort, Kelley balanced on a small, padded disk-seat, thirteen inches in diameter, and sometimes used stirrups for his feet to help him maintain his balance. He took five-minute catnaps every hour and subsisted on liquids hoisted up to him on ropes. In 1930, 20,000 spectators watched Kelly break his own record by sitting atop a flagpole on the Atlantic City boardwalk for 1,177 hours (more than 49 days).

Emile Coué

Another fad that swept the country for a brief period occurred when millions of Americans became fascinated with the ideas of Emile Coué, a French psychotherapist who made two lecture tours in the United States in 1923 and 1924. During the late nineteenth century, those who promoted the gospel of success took their cues from Horatio Alger and proclaimed that the keys to personal success (broadly defined) came through hard work, sobriety, and thrift. In contrast, by the early 1920s the popularization of Freudian thought (though only vaguely understood) drew attention to one's subconscious mind, described by one writer as a reservoir of "intelligence and power" (Dumenil 1995, 87). This opened the door to the idea that anybody could summon his or her innate ability through an exercise of will. Coué, the author of the best-selling book *Self-Mastery through Conscious Autosuggestion* (1922), built on that assumption and suggested that people could improve their mental health and happiness, boost their confidence and motivation, and become more successful if they simply engaged in a daily program of self-hypnosis that focused on the verbal repetition of a simple maxim: "Day by day, in every way, I am getting better and better." Willing to run with the latest fad, millions of Americans during the middle of the decade decided to give Coué a try.

Document: John R. McMahon, "Unspeakable Jazz Must Go!" (1921)

Despite the growing popularity of jazz music during the 1920s, many Americans considered it to be a threat to the nation's social order. Defenders of more "traditional" moral values blamed jazz for the rebellious behavior of young people and charged that its "sex-exciting" music encouraged immorality. The following excerpt is from an interview with Fenton T. Bott, the "director of dance reform" of the American National Association Masters of Dancing.

"Unspeakable Jazz Must Go!"

"Jazz dancing is a worse evil than the saloon used to be!" . . .
"Jazz is worse than the saloon! Why?" I asked.
"Because it affects our young people especially," said Mr. Bott. "It is degrading. It lowers all the moral standards. . . . [I]t also leads to undesirable things. The jazz is too often followed by the

joy-ride. The lower nature is stirred up as a prelude to unchaperoned adventure."

"This strikes especially at the youth of the nation, and the consequences are almost too obvious to be detailed. When the next generation starts on a low plane, what will its successors be?" . . .

"Is there anything bad about jazz music itself?" I asked.

"There certainly is! Those moaning saxophones and the rest of the instruments with their broken, jerky rhythm make a purely sensual appeal. They call out the low and rowdy instinct. All of us dancing teachers know this to be a fact. We have seen the effect of jazz music on our young pupils. It makes them act in a restless and rowdy manner. A class of children will behave that way as long as such music is played. They can be calmed down and restored to normal conduct only by playing good, legitimate music."

"Dancing, as you know, has enormously increased in the last few years. It has become a great public institution in which all classes and ages are interested. We have estimated that about ten per cent of the entire population, or more than ten million people, have become dancers. . . . Anything that is radically wrong with the recreation of so many people must affect all of us."

"Granted," I said. "Now what is the organized dancing profession doing to reform conditions?"

"We are working in several directions," replied Mr. Bott, "but we have an uphill fight. . . ."

"We have a booklet and chart which we send to welfare organizations, owners of dance halls and dancing teachers. The booklet describes the dances approved by our association, and the charts, which are meant to be placed on the walls of the dance halls, show the correct positions and steps for the various approved dances. I am glad to say that the United States Public Health Service has not only commended our booklet but has distributed thousands of copies of it to welfare agencies. High schools throughout the country have been well supplied. This is the third year of publication and to date we have issued about twenty thousand copies. . . ."

"What is the attitude of music publishers?" I inquired.

"Not very helpful, unless they have had a recent change of heart," replied Mr. Bott. "The music written for jazz is the very foundation and essence of salacious dancing. The words also are often very suggestive, thinly veiling immoral ideas. Now, at the 1920 convention of our association we appealed to the music publishers to eliminate jazz music. A representative of the publishers came before us and replied that personally he was against the indecent stuff, being himself a church elder or deacon, but the publishers had to give the public what they wanted. . . ."

"What do parents say to your efforts?"

"Naturally most parents are heartily with the dancing teachers in the effort to discipline youngsters and make them toe the mark of propriety. There are a few exceptions of fashionable mothers, who want their daughters to learn everything up-to-date and snappy and who consider objections to high-society movements as being squeamish."

[As noted by the interviewer]

Among the rules contained in the booklet for dance regulation issued by the organized professionals is one that separates extreme youth from age in public dance places or otherwise. Youngsters under eighteen are not to be admitted at grown-up functions. This coincides with regulations in some high schools and also with civic or state law in some sections. Animal names for dances, such as cat step, camel walk, bunny hug, turkey trot, and so on, are disapproved as of degrading tendency. Rapid and jerky music is condemned, while a medium dance tempo . . . is recommended. There are ten "Don'ts," which may be summarized:

> Don't permit vulgar dance music; don't let young men hold their partners tightly; no touching of cheeks which is public love making; no neck holds; no shimmy or toddle; no steps very long or very short; no dancing from the waist up but rather from the waist down; suggestive movements barred; don't copy stage stuff; don't hesitate to ask offenders to leave the room.

Source: John R. McMahon. "Unspeakable Jazz Must Go!" *The Ladies Home Journal* 38 (December 1921): 34, 115–16.

Document: "Medical Derision of Coué" (1922)

While acknowledging Emile Coué's growing popularity, this editorial excerpt from the Journal of the American Medical Association *takes a rather dim view of the practice of healing by autosuggestion.*

"Medical Derision of Coué"

From Nancy, France . . . comes Coué, who has been setting Britain afire with his curative formula. "Every day, and in every way, I get better and better," the mere repetition of which . . . will ultimately affect the unconscious centers and bring about what it asserts. One can hardly call Coué a faith-healer. His cures, he asserts, are the result of the imagination, which he says is the most powerful influence about us. What the medical world thinks of it all may be gathered from a leading editorial in *The Journal of the American Medical Association* (Chicago), parts of which we quote below.

> The physician who has learned the phenomena of disease at the bedside, and the structural alterations caused by them in the laboratory, will read with his tongue in his cheek a series of small books which have recently reached this country dealing with M. Emile Coué of Nancy, and his method of "curing" disease. . . .
>
> M. Coué, who is not a physician, but, so far as we are informed, a former apothecary, has in later years devoted himself to hypnotism and suggestion. For the last ten years . . . Coué has been publishing his "discovery" and preaching his doctrine in his native land, and during the past winter in England, where he had much notoriety. He calls his little book, a pamphlet of less than a hundred small pages, "Self-Mastery by Conscious Autosuggestion." According to him, autosuggestion is . . . an original endowment. We possess it at birth, and in it resides a marvelous and incalculable power. If we know how to practice it consciously, it is possible to avoid provoking in others bad autosuggestions; to provoke good ones instead, thus bringing physical health to the sick and moral health to the neurotic and erring, and to guide into the right path those whose tendency is to take the wrong one.
>
> He and his admirers and protagonists have published testimonials of cures of virtually all the ills to which the flesh is erroneously alleged to be heir, but which it unfortunately and frequently displays. He does it in a very simple way; that is, he doesn't do it at all; the patient does it. The patient tranquilizes himself, makes his mind as nearly blank as possible, and says articulately, preferably in a semi-detached and dreamy sort of way, "Every day in *every* way I grow better and better." The second "every" must be emphasized, and that the verbigerating articulator does not get mixed in "his love," he is recommended to make use of an improvised rosary, that is, a string with twenty knots tied in it, and in this he must "autosuggest" every morning before rising, and every night on getting into bed. He is very insistent that there is no supernatural element in the cure. The imagination does it all.
>
> When M. Coué functions personally in the cure, the program is somewhat more elaborate. He tells his patients, in groups, . . . that they will sleep soundly, that their dreams will be pleasant, that

troubles and worries will melt away, that they will awake to sing, not sigh, that there will be no more fears, no more thoughts of unkindness, and that shyness and self-consciousness will vanish.

For M. Coué, the unconscious self is the grand director of all our functions, and when the grand director nods, our functions go wrong. The will is its sinister motivator. The imagination turns the face of the unconscious self toward the East. Hence, train the imagination; never seek to reeducate the will. "If you can persuade yourself that you can do a certain thing, provided it is possible, you will do it however difficult it may be." . . .

Meanwhile, purveyors of cloudy stuff, like M. Coué, cure many persons who are ill or who comport themselves as if they were ill, and for this we are . . . grateful. But to accept any of his "laws" as established, or as consistent with the established principles of psychology, is quite impossible; such acceptance would conflict with common sense and with the facts of pathology, which are as firmly established as facts can be.

Source: "Medical Derision of Coué," *The Literary Digest* 74 (October 28, 1922): 21–22.

7

RELIGIOUS LIFE

It is commonplace to assert that the Great War eroded prior intellectual certainties and absolutes, and this was certainly the case with religion. But the 1920s was also very much a decade of contested values, one in which the hold of traditionalism constantly vied with the pull of modernism. The 1920 census revealed that, for the first time, more Americans lived in the city than in the country and, as this emerging urban society looked to dominate cultural values, traditionalists found ample cause for concern. Born into an era in which Protestant leaders upheld Victorian morality and extolled the ideals of temperance and sexual repression, many Americans found their worldview under assault by a new culture of sensation. The new icons of the Jazz Age were the licentious speakeasy, the sexually liberated flapper, dissonant jazz music, suggestive dances, and lurid motion pictures. Could the old-time religion hold its place?

THE STATE OF RELIGION IN THE 1920s

In generalizing about the importance of religion in the daily lives of Americans, most observers seemed to agree that the vast majority of people still identified with a religious denomination and that membership in one of the religious groups was generally taken for granted (although only about 55 percent of the adult population were actually church members). In their study of *Middletown,* Robert and Helen Lynd noted that five forms of religious service—Sunday morning and evening preaching services, Sunday School, mid-week prayer meeting, and Sunday evening young people's meeting—"remain, fundamentally unchanged since the nineties, the outstanding features of the worship of Protestant Middletown" (Lynd and Lynd 1956, 398). They also counted, in 1924, forty-two churches representing twenty-eight different Christian denominations (there was one Jewish congregation) in a city of fewer than 40,000 inhabitants. Churches seemed to prosper financially as well, partly as a result of aggressive membership campaigns. With money to spend, many urban churches initiated ambitious building programs to erect new churches or to expand their operations to include facilities for social and educational programs. But while church *membership,* in general, had tended to keep pace with population growth, and religious observance had changed very little, overall church *attendance* declined as the popularity of Sunday golf, motoring, movies, and sporting events complicated loyalties. It was not uncommon to hear ministers complain that poor attendance had left many of their new sanctuaries only half filled on Sunday mornings and had forced them to drop Sunday-evening services altogether.

In an effort to keep religion "relevant," organizations outside the church decided to "fight fire with fire" and increase their involvement in social activities that centered on the young. The Young Men's and Young Women's Christian Associations provided not only places for limited religious instruction but also venues for activities of a more secular nature like swimming, basketball, movies, and an active club life for their members. The various organizations commonly engaged in athletic competitions and, according to the Lynds, it would not have been surprising at all to find a 1924 newspaper headline that read: "Methodists Are Jolted 16 to 13" or "Christians and Disciples Are Victorious." The better part of one annual meeting of a leading business-class church was reserved for the presentation of athletic sweaters to the boys of the Sunday School League. Churches quickly followed suit with their own social clubs and recreational activities. But, as the Lynds noted, the effort to keep young people engaged in the church was an uphill struggle. One young woman who belonged to one of the most successful Sunday School clubs remarked that "seventy-five per cent of the Sunday School classes in Middletown are organized socially or they couldn't keep going. We have a party every month with a regular program, games, and a feed." Another young woman in a similar class at a fashionable church told the Lynds: "Our Sunday School class is *some* class. Our teacher is Mrs. _____, and she gives us some slick parties out at her place. Two of the girls in our [senior] class got kicked out of their clubs a year ago for smoking—*that's* the kind of class we have!" (Lynd and Lynd 1956, 399). Having noted the attempts by various congregations to expand the social and recreational scope of their activities in an effort to stay "current," the Lynds were left with the sobering finding that only 11 percent of males and 18 percent of females attended Sunday-morning church services.

Although most people identified with some religious denomination and rarely questioned their dominant Christian beliefs, there seemed to be a growing sense of uncertainty at least among some parishioners. In their study of *Middletown*, the Lynds found a persistence of traditional religious beliefs among the working class and "a disposition to believe their religion more ardently and to accumulate more emotionally charged values around their beliefs." They also concluded that religion appeared to hold a more prominent place as "an active agency of support and encouragement" among that particular demographic. On the other hand, the business class demonstrated much more ambiguity and showed "an outwardly conforming indifference" to matters of a religious nature. As one prominent resident noted, "I've joined the church because who am I to buck an institution as big as the church, and anyway it seems necessary to conform, but I guess my pastor knows all right how little my heart is in it." Another business-class wife commented, "People are questioning and wondering now about religious matters. There are just a lot of things you have to try not to let yourself think about." According to the Lynds, even those with enough education to arrive at some kind of synthesis of the new and the old often expressed doubt and uneasiness. As one high school science teacher commented "in a bewildered tone" after listening to a sermon on evolution and religion,

> I wish he had said something about Jonah. A whale's throat is *so* small it simply *couldn't* swallow a man. Of course it might have kept Jonah in its mouth, but I don't see how—all *that* time! And then he never said himself what he thought about evolution. He just said that you *could* believe in it and still be a Christian. I don't see that that helps much. (Lynd and Lynd 1956, 317, 329, 330, 331)

In his classic popular history of the 1920s, Frederick Lewis Allen sensed the same tendencies. "Something spiritual," he said, "had gone out of the churches—a sense of certainty that theirs was the way to salvation." And although religion was a topic that was vigorously discussed, the intensity of the discussion itself suggested that "for millions of people religion had become a debatable subject instead of being accepted without question among the traditions of the community." In his book *Preface to Morals* (1929), writer Walter Lippmann made the same point and suggested that church attendance was declining because people were not so certain that they were going to meet God when they went to church. Allen concurred, "In the congregations, and especially among the younger men and women, there was an undeniable weakening of loyalty to the church and an undeniable vagueness as to what it had to offer them" (Allen 2010, 170). He might have noted that there was also a pronounced discrepancy among women and men in their likeliness to be church members, with 62 percent of white women and 73 percent of African American women so engaged compared to only 49 percent and 46 percent of their male counterparts.

THE RISE OF RELIGIOUS UNCERTAINTY

A number of reasons have been offered to explain the mental uneasiness that seemed to surround religion during the 1920s. As mentioned, the strain of the war was a primary factor. Frederick Lewis Allen saw it as contributing to a "general let-down in moral energy" (Allen 2010, 170). Some took that argument a step farther and suggested that the disillusionment connected to the war generated a new cynicism in society that worked to undermine belief. Others found causation in the emerging secularization of society and placed special emphasis on the expansion of a more cosmopolitan urban culture. Some saw a direct connection between prosperity and the increased emphasis on materialism. The enthusiasm for business seemed to have an impact as well; businessmen and advertisers increasingly used a religious vocabulary to promote their new ventures and, in the case of Bruce Barton, to reconcile business with Christianity. Charles Fiske, in his *Confessions of a Puzzled Parson* (1929), spoke directly to this point. "America," he said, "has become almost hopelessly enamored of a religion that is little more than a sanctified commercialism; it is hard in this day and this land to differentiate between religious aspirations and business prosperity" (Dumenil 1995, 170–71). Still others found an explanation in the way that society had turned away from social reform, in general, and abandoned the Social Gospel movement that had been an integral part of the Progressive Era.

Perceptive observers like Walter Lippmann, however, found the primary cause of spiritual uncertainty located in the "expanding scientific understanding of the universe, scholarly analysis of the history of mankind and its religions, and the fluid conditions of urban industrial life." "This is the first age," he stated, "in the history of mankind when the circumstances of life have conspired with the intellectual habits of the time to render any fixed and authoritative belief incredible to large masses of men" (Dumenil 1995, 173). As the liberal Presbyterian minister Dr. Harry Emerson Fosdick noted, "The men of faith might claim for their positions ancient tradition, practical usefulness, and spiritual desirability, but one query could prick all such bubbles: Is it scientific?" Frederick Lewis Allen agreed and noted that the "prestige" of science was "colossal." He also noted that "millions of people were discovering for the first time that there was such a thing as the venerable theory of evolution" (Allen 2010, 171, 172).

The Impact of Darwinism

At the center of the religious debate in the 1920s was a book, *On the Origin of Species by Means of Natural Selection, or the Preservation of Favored Races in the Struggle for Life*, published in 1859 by Charles Darwin, an English naturalist. The volume, based on Darwin's empirical observations and hypothetical deductions, caused not only a revolution in scientific thinking but also a radical reexamination of the content of Christianity. Instead of arguing that God had created species that were fixed, Darwin suggested that species were mutable, that they could change, and, based on the fossil record, that they could evolve from earlier species.

One of the most contentious points in Darwin's argument was his theory of natural selection—the idea that species evolved as a result of a struggle for existence that made animals with certain traits more likely to survive and reproduce than others. Many opponents were morally offended by a natural law that operated so randomly, seemed so cruel and wasteful, and offered no hope to the "unfit." In addition, natural selection seemed to contradict what was termed the "argument from design," the idea that the natural world was a revelation of God's workings and proof that there was a God in Heaven. But Darwin "now seemed to be suggesting that nature revealed a God who was either cruel and wasteful or absent altogether" (Moran 2002, 5). And that was not all. Darwin's theory also conflicted with traditional religious belief: it was incompatible with the story of creation as presented in Genesis—that God created the world and populated it with living creatures in six days and that Adam and Eve were the first humans on Earth.

Modernism versus Fundamentalism

Darwin's theory also generated a clash within the church between theological liberals or "modernists," who chose to reconcile science and faith, and a rising movement of fundamentalist Protestants who saw no room for accommodation whatsoever. Modernists like Shailer Mathews at the University of Chicago took the position that the Bible employed symbols and allegory to convey God's meaning. They tended to embrace scientific discoveries (including evolution) and saw these advances as part of God's ongoing revelation to his followers. Following the literal words of the Bible was not as important as uncovering what Mathews called the "spirit and purpose" of Jesus Christ's moral teachings. Conservative Protestants or fundamentalists disagreed. As William Jennings Bryan, one of the leaders in this group, asserted in a 1923 article, "The Bible is either the Word of God or merely a man-made book." "When all the miracles and all the supernatural are eliminated from the Bible it becomes a 'scrap of paper.'" "When the Bible ceases to be an authority—a divine authority—the Word of God can be accepted, rejected, or mutilated, according to the whim or mood of the reader" (Moran 2002, 12). To Bryan, society stood on the verge of moral anarchy. The perceived increase in immorality and the turning away from active participation in the church, especially by the young, seemed to confirm that, for many Americans, the messages of the Bible had lost their meaning.

The Fundamentalist Movement

The Fundamentalist movement began to come together early in the twentieth century when some religious leaders grew concerned that the churches were becoming controlled by modernists. The movement actually got its name from a series of popular pamphlets that appeared between 1910 and 1915 under the general title "The Fundamentals." Written by conservative theologians, the pamphlets focused on church doctrines (e.g., the virgin birth, the resurrection of Jesus, and the literal reading of the Bible) that they believed were being threatened by unorthodox modernist thinking. To guarantee a wide circulation, two wealthy oil men from

Los Angeles subsidized the publication of three million copies. The Great War seemed to add a new urgency to the fundamentalist position as many interpreted German aggression as an attempt to fulfill the Darwinian notion of survival of the fittest. With renewed motivation, more than 6,000 conservative Christians gathered in Philadelphia in 1919 for the first conference of the World's Christian Fundamentals Association (WCFA), an organization created by William Bell Riley, pastor of the First Baptist Church of Minneapolis. Their mission was to return the churches and the nation to the path of righteousness. It was not long before the WCFA had developed an institutionalized network of Bible institutes and local associations, supplemented with newspapers and periodicals, to challenge the modernist point of view. The movement appeared to have its greatest strength in the rural South and the Midwest, but there were also pockets of strength in the North and in the cities. The movement also appeared to have its greatest appeal among lower-middle-class and working-class believers. Followers united behind several basic principles—the virgin birth, the bodily resurrection of Christ, atonement, miracles, and a literal interpretation of the Bible.

The evolution controversy that came to a head in the famous Scopes Trial in Dayton, Tennessee, in 1925, had a great deal to do with the participation of one individual: political icon William Jennings Bryan. Bryan had grown up in a pious household. On Sunday he attended both his father's Baptist church and his mother's Methodist church until he converted to the Presbyterian Church at a revival meeting during his fifteenth year. As one historian noted, "Bryan always interpreted political reform as part of the Christian mission to move man closer to God's vision of earthly perfection." The antievolution crusade of which he became a leader was completely consistent with this vision. It was during and immediately after World War I that Bryan, the famous orator and three-time presidential candidate, really focused his attention on the "threats" posed by evolutionary theory. As Bryan saw it, Darwin's theory of evolution, and the Social Darwinian argument later perfected by Herbert Spencer and William Graham Sumner, provided a rationale for warfare ("survival of the fittest"), undermined the cause of social reform (no help for the weak), and contradicted biblical revelation. Taken together the theories eroded faith in God. And Bryan was convinced that the theory of evolution and the scientific education that accompanied it were weakening Christian belief, especially among the young. By the early 1920s Bryan had come to the conclusion that the "unproven hypothesis of evolution is the root cause of nearly all the dissention in the church" (Moran 2002, 14, 18). It had to be stopped. And he thought he was the person to do it. Bryan pressed his antievolution argument in dozens of books and articles, while his syndicated weekly column, "Bible Talks," appeared in over one hundred newspapers that reached over 20 million readers. He had a national reputation as an orator and gave hundreds of speeches to audiences across the country. He also had the political prestige to enable him to gain invitations to speak before nine different state legislatures in the South and Midwest. With an army of loyal followers and the assistance of a number of popular evangelists like former major-league baseball player Billy Sunday who traversed the country giving emotional antievolution sermons to hundreds of thousands of the faithful, the Bryan-led antievolutionist crusade quickly coalesced into a militant resistance.

By the early 1920s the battleground for the debate over evolution had shifted from within the church to the public schools. In 1890 about 200,000 youths (less than 5 percent of high-school-age teenagers) attended secondary school. By 1920, that number had jumped to nearly two million students per year. The tremendous growth in the number of public schools brought thousands of impressionable young people into contact with evolutionary science for the first time. That contact upset many parents and religious conservatives. Suddenly, evolution, along with sex education and questions about whether history textbooks were sufficiently patriotic in tone, triggered a new concern over the content of the curriculum in the public schools.

The antievolutionists mounted their first concerted effort to rescue the schools from Darwinism in the winter of 1921–1922 when, under pressure, the Kentucky legislature considered a law to ban the teaching of evolution in the public schools. Although that effort failed by a narrow margin, the idea soon spread to North Carolina, Florida, Oklahoma, and Tennessee. In January 1925, John Washington Butler, a farmer, Primitive Baptist, and representative in the Tennessee legislature from rural Macon County, proposed a bill to prevent the teaching of evolution in the public schools of the state. The measure made it a crime to teach "any theory that denies the story of the Divine creation of man as taught in the Bible, and to teach instead that man has descended from a lower order of animals." The bill easily passed the Tennessee House of Representatives by a vote of 71–5 and the state senate by a margin of 24–6.

Historian Lawrence Levine has suggested that supporters of the law did not really desire to overturn modern education as much as they "craved the comfort of statutory symbols which would settle the question of whose version of the good society was legitimate." When Governor Austin Peay signed the bill into law on March 23, 1925, he told the legislature: "I can find nothing of consequence in the books now being taught in our schools with which this bill will interfere in the slightest manner. Probably the law will never be applied." All that the backers of the bill (which had wide public support throughout the state) intended, he said, was to record "a distinct protest against an irreligious tendency to exalt so-called science, and deny the Bible in some schools and quarters" (Levine 1993, 199).

The Scopes Trial

One organization that was not amused by the action of the Tennessee legislature was the American Civil Liberties Union (ACLU), which felt the law violated freedom of speech. It immediately decided to challenge the law in court and ran advertisements in Tennessee newspapers offering to provide free legal counsel for anyone willing to act as a plaintiff. The only response to their call came from the small town of Dayton in eastern Tennessee, where a small group of the town's boosters thought they had found a way to revitalize their town's declining economic fortunes through the publicity that would come from the trial. They looked for a teacher to join their plot. The man they found was a substitute science teacher named John Thomas Scopes. Scopes was young, single, recently arrived in town and unlikely to stay very long. He was also principled, believed that the law was a threat to academic freedom, and saw the trial as more of an opportunity for public debate over that issue than as a criminal proceeding. As a result, he dutifully admitted to a local law enforcement officer that he had taught a class on evolution from the state's officially adopted biology textbook and submitted to arrest for violation of the so-called Butler law. The town's boosters immediately contacted the ACLU and alerted the newspapers.

At this point things began to spiral out of control. Under prodding from William Bell Riley and others at the WCFA, William Jennings Bryan agreed to assist the prosecution as an acknowledged expert on the Bible. Bryan's involvement brought Clarence Darrow, perhaps the nation's most famous criminal trial lawyer, into the

For 12 days during sweltering heat in July 1925, eager onlookers packed
the courthouse in Dayton, Tennessee, while hundreds of thousands of
listeners followed the famous Scopes trial on radio station WGN from
Chicago. At issue was whether or not a state could ban the teaching of
Darwin's theory of evolution in the public schools. Leading the defense
was the famed trial lawyer Clarence Darrow, pictured here wearing sus-
penders, surrounded by the rest of his legal team. (Library of Congress)

proceedings as an attorney for the defense. Only a year before, Darrow had defended Nathan Leopold and Richard Loeb, two intelligent teenagers from wealthy families, who had brutally murdered
a fourteen-year-old boy named Bobby Franks apparently for the
sole reason that they wanted to see if they could commit the "perfect crime" and get away with it. A pair of eyeglasses inadvertently
left near the body of the murder victim ultimately led police to the
two young men who then confessed to the crime. For this mon-
strous act, prosecutors demanded the death penalty. But Darrow
sought mercy for the two defendants "by attributing their actions
to misguided Social Darwinist thinking" and got their sentences
reduced to life in prison (Larson 1997, 72). Some regarded Darrow's
"victory" as humane, but others could only see a miscarriage of justice. For Bryan, the trial symbolized a larger concern. Leopold and

Loeb were examples of the moral depravity that could be created when young men had too much education and not enough morality rooted in religious belief. In a sense, if Darrow were to prevail again and have the court allow Darwinism to enter the schools, it risked producing more young men and women without any moral compass.

Personalities dominated the spotlight at Dayton and elevated the trial to a national stage. It was almost like a movie scripted by Hollywood—Bryan, the symbol of agrarian America, the righteous defender of the faith, and the spokesperson for democratic majoritarianism, pitted against Darrow, the urbane iconoclast standing as the defender of science and reason. As the major personalities readied themselves for what cynics would call the "Monkey Trial," the town got ready to host an event that was already being hyped in the national media. Approximately 200 reporters descended on the town to cover the event and wired over two million words of copy during the eight-day trial. It was estimated that over 2,300 daily newspapers in the country carried accounts of the trial. Western Union ran telegraph wires into the courtroom for instant transmission of the proceedings and kept a score of key operators at the ready in Dayton to transmit news reports. A movie camera platform was set up in the courtroom and newsreel crews dispatched miles of film from Dayton, while the *Chicago Tribune*'s station WGN set up the nation's first radio network hookup and sent daily broadcasts of the trial.

Looking to capitalize on the event, the Dayton Club announced that it would spend $5,000 in advertising to promote local businesses during the trial and give every visitor a souvenir badge featuring a monkey wearing a straw hat. As sightseers poured into Dayton to witness the event, the town quickly assumed a carnival atmosphere. Street performers, traveling evangelists, soapbox preachers, hot dog and lemonade vendors, and sidewalk singers crowded Main Street, while Dayton's merchants decorated their shops with pictures of monkeys and chimpanzees. Other enterprising individuals set up stands to sell antievolution literature. A notable example of the latter was well-known evangelist T. T. Martin, who did a brisk business selling copies of his book *Hell and the High Schools*.

Although several topics—academic and scientific freedom, parental and states' rights, and the separation of church and state—were at issue, religion quickly came to dominate the discussion in the courtroom. Who was right? Darwin or the Bible? Darrow had intended to introduce a number of scientists and theologians to prove the validity of evolutionary science and to argue that evolution and Christianity were compatible, but Judge John T. Raulston blocked the presentation of their testimony in open court. When that tactic failed, Darrow called Bryan to the stand as an authority on the Bible. At that point, because of the oppressive summer heat and the fear that the second-story courtroom floor would no longer support the weight of all the people, Judge Raulston moved the trial outside to the courthouse lawn for the afternoon of Bryan's testimony. There, before a crowd of 3,000 onlookers, Darrow began his questioning. At times the exchanges became quite heated. At one point, Darrow said to Bryan: "You insult every man of science and learning in the world because he does not believe in your fool religion." Later in the trial, Bryan bitterly responded: "I am simply trying to protect the word of God against the greatest atheist or agnostic in the United States!" Before Judge Raulston decided to stop the questioning, Darrow had humiliated Bryan with questions pertaining to some of the more miraculous events in the Old Testament. Did a whale swallow Jonah? Is it possible that Joshua could command the sun to stand still? More damaging than Bryan's defense of the Bible as the literal truth were his confessions of ignorance regarding basic points of scientific and theological knowledge. Newspapers across the nation reprinted Darrow's cross-examination of Bryan, and "many editorialists agreed that 'it has brought about a striking revelation of the fundamentalist mind in all its shallow depth and narrow arrogance'" (Moran 2002, 49–50, 150, 156). In the end, Scopes was found guilty and fined $100. The defense then took the case on appeal to the Tennessee Supreme Court where, on January 15, 1927, the court upheld the constitutionality of the Butler law but set aside Scopes's conviction on a legal technicality. Because of the court's decision, Darrow and the ACLU no longer had a conviction that they could appeal to a higher court.

In the Aftermath of the Trial

In the immediate aftermath of the trial, two states, North Carolina and Kentucky, considered but narrowly defeated antievolution measures, while Mississippi followed Tennessee and enacted a ban on the teaching of evolution in 1926. The following year, however, the legislatures in nineteen states considered bills banning Darwin from the schools, but all such efforts failed. The only other state to take action was Arkansas where voters approved an antievolution statute by popular referendum in 1928. By 1930 it appeared that the push for state-enacted antievolution legislation had lost its momentum. Antievolutionists, however, found that there were other weapons to be wielded. The 1930s saw the development of fundamentalist colleges (Bryan College in Dayton was one of those) and schools, conferences and camps, radio ministries, and missionary societies. At the county level, hundreds of school boards, primarily in the South, took action to ban evolution and prevent the hiring of teachers who might be sympathetic to Darwinism. Impacting students perhaps to an even greater extent were the actions taken by a half dozen states and innumerable localities to purchase special editions of science textbooks in which publishers had agreed to excise all references to evolution.

The common interpretation of the Scopes Trial was that the antievolutionists had been exposed as poorly educated and narrowminded religious zealots and that their cause had been badly damaged in the court of public opinion. But the trial also showed that religion deeply mattered to millions of Americans in the 1920s and underscored the anxieties that accompanied the scientific challenges to traditional faiths. Although the divisions have been oversimplified into competing dualities that tend to ignore diversity, the trial pointed out just how badly the country had become polarized—between believer and doubter, antimodernist and modernist, and rural and urban. Historian Lawrence Levine has argued, however, that it is important to understand that the "cultural regionalism" exemplified by Prohibition, the Ku Klux Klan, and Protestant fundamentalism was "psychic and not purely geographic in character." Supporters of all three movements could be found in the cities as well as the countryside. But their allegiance always had a rural cast to it. According to Levine,

> The large numbers of urban migrants from rural, small-town America faced a difficult, often impossible, cultural adjustment which left them bereft of identity. They, perhaps even more than those who remained behind, craved a lost sense of community and longed for a reassertion of the old moral values. Though they were technically urbanites ... they were psychically attuned to the cultures from which they had emigrated. They supported prohibition, fundamentalism and the Klan precisely because these movements promised a real or symbolic flight from the new America back to the familiar confines of the old. (Levine 1993, 197)

The antievolution movement showed just how committed many Americans had become in their defense of traditional values in the face of rapid and extensive social change.

The Westward Migration of Religious Fundamentalism

Early twentieth-century Los Angeles had a reputation as a city of middle-class, Christian respectability. Hollywood had yet to cloak the town with an aura of glamour and more than a suggestion of sin, and the booms in oil, real estate, and tourism were just beginning to have their acquisitive impact on the southland. As one historian described the city at that time, "Its leading citizens were still largely sober sons of the Puritans, not far removed from their Eastern and Middle Western forebears" (Mowry 1963, 38). By 1906 the city could boast that it had more churches for its size than any other city in the United States. Historian Kevin Starr described the City of the Angels at that time as "an openly Christian community." This tendency continued into the postwar era as well. Journalist Louis Adamic claimed that Los Angeles could count 142,000 of its inhabitants (roughly a tenth of the population) on the active rolls of its Protestant churches in the mid-1920s. He also noted that the numbers were scattered among some 300 congregations. To another observer, this statistic gave the impression that Christianity still "ranked as the city's leading industry after real estate and motion pictures" (Starr 1990, 134, 135).

The mass migration to Southern California during the 1920s also expanded the base for the spread of religious fundamentalism in Los Angeles. Local writer Louis Adamic coined the term "Folks" to describe the hordes of newcomers—largely migrants from the Midwest, many of whom were of retirement age, who trekked to Los Angeles after World War I. Visiting the city in the late 1920s, writer Hamlin Garland was "greatly interested in the floods of Middle Westerners filling the streets. The throngs of women shopping, and the cords of men in the park, were all American, of familiar form and coloring." Under the general direction of agencies like the Federation of State Societies of Los Angeles, created in 1913 largely through the efforts of Charles H. Parsons, a former Iowan, many of these newcomers either joined or formed state-based associations as a way to reestablish a sense of stability and community in their new environment. Meeting annually to hear speakers, play games, and enjoy musical entertainments, thousands flocked to various picnic grounds for a day of fun and reunion. The activities of the Iowa Society were perhaps most notable. According to one writer,

> A gathering of the Iowa Society is a sight to think about. A huge park, or other open space, is taken over, and the map of Iowa laid out upon it, each county in its proper place, being marked by a flag-pole and pennant. When the erstwhile Iowans arrive in their Dodges and Chevrolets—and 125,000 is not an uncommon figure for the attendance—each family rallies round its own flag amid its former neighbors, and holds high carnival, with reunion, reminiscence, fried chicken and hard-boiled eggs.

"They were in truth," noted writer Hamlin Garland, "incredibly unaesthetic and yet they were worthy, fine serious folk who do not believe in drinking, smoking, or philandering." Other commentators did not pick up on the same Gothic dignity. In the words of Louis Adamic,

> No matter where one goes and what one does, one cannot get away from The Folks in Los Angeles. They are everywhere and their influence is felt in well-nigh every phase of city life. They are simple, credulous souls; their bodies are afflicted with all sorts of aches and pains, real and imaginary; they are unimaginative and their cultural horizons are sadly limited—and as such they are perfect soil to sprout and nourish all kinds of medical, religious and cultural quackery. (Starr 1990, 132)

By the 1920s the religious climate of the city had changed. Journalist Willard Huntington Wright noted the shift as early as 1913 and commented that the city abounded with

> "leading citizens" from Wichita; honorary pallbearers from Emmetsburg; Good Templars from Sedalia; honest spinsters from Grundy Center—all commonplace people, many of them with small competencies made from the sale of farm lands or from the lifelong savings of small mercantile businesses. These good folks brought with them a complete stock of rural beliefs, pieties, superstitions, and habits. . . . They are a sober and phlegmatic people. . . . They are victims of the sonorous platitude . . . and they vote for their pastor's choice of candidate.

Wright also noted a tendency toward cults and various forms of religious quackery as part of the city's changing temperament: an attraction to "faddists and mountebanks—spiritualists, mediums, astrologists, phrenologists, palmists and all other breeds of esoteric wind-jammers." In 1926 another writer noted the same thing and that organizations like Children of the Sun Church, the Pre-Astral Fraternity of Love, and the Nature-Way Medical College for Drug-less Healing were "the sick survivors of New England transcenden-talism" arriving in Los Angeles from Boston by way of Chicago. "The milder climate enables them to keep the illusion that they have conquered disease through spiritual power" (Starr 1990, 133–36). Joining what he called the "literary habit of the hour," journalist George P. West seconded this theme and harshly noted that along with the "moderately prosperous who represent the virtue of the Middle West," the Southern California climate "has attracted a vast assortment of odds and ends of humanity—poor souls in sick bod-ies, victims of all manner of starvations and suppressions and per-versions. Every weird cult and -ism flourishes on the patronage of these pitiful refugees" (West 1922, 327).

Tapping into this new demographic were a growing number of evangelists. The Fundamentalist movement had produced a num-ber of nationally known preachers who gained fame spreading the gospel. During the 1910s and 1920s, the Iowa-born evangelist Wil-liam "Billy" Sunday, a former professional baseball player for the Chicago White Stockings, toured the country staging revival meet-ings that incorporated techniques from modern show business. The events featured audience participation, large choirs, and circus-like parades led by marching bands. Meetings no longer took place in large tents but in temporary wooden church-like venues that were called tabernacles. Sunday also worked with a vaudeville-like troupe that included perhaps twenty other onstage performers. Millions of Americans flocked to hear "Billy" Sunday's wise-cracking ser-mons that featured the use of baseball terminology along with an emotional denunciation of the evils of modern society—drinking, prostitution, card playing and gambling, and the teaching of evolution—all while being exhorted to live like Christians.

Pentecostalism

An offshoot of Protestant fundamentalism was Pentecostalism. Adherents believed in the Bible as the literal truth and the central role accorded Jesus, but they also believed in faith healing and speak-ing in tongues, which, to them, signified the presence of the Holy Spirit. Pentecostalists and fundamentalists both believed that the modern world was sinful and that the emphasis on moneymaking, materialism, excessive leisure, and science had led many Christians astray. Pentecostalism had special appeal to many working-class and poor Americans, especially those from the Midwest and South.

Aimee Semple McPherson

One of the most famous evangelists of the 1920s was Aimee Semple McPherson, a Pentecostal preacher and media celebrity who proved that an emotional Bible-based religion could incorporate the incongruous elements of modern-day Hollywood and be phenomenally successful. Aimee Kennedy was born in Ontario, Canada, in 1890 and raised on a farm by religious parents. She eventually abandoned the strict Methodism of her father for the salvationist theology (the idea that everyone was ultimately redeemed) of her mother, the daughter of a Salvation Army captain. When she had a crisis of faith in her teens, a young Scotch-Irish Pentecostal evangelist by the name of Robert Semple helped her reaffirm her faith in Christianity. Aimee and Robert were married in 1908 when Aimee was seventeen. The couple traveled in eastern Canada and the United States conducting revivals, and Aimee became a preacher of the Pentecostal Full Gospel Assembly in 1909. The following year the Semples journeyed to China as missionaries, but Robert died from typhoid fever just before the birth of their first child. Returning to the United States with her young daughter, Aimee Semple went to work for the Salvation Army and continued to preach as an evangelist. In 1912 she married Harold McPherson, a grocery salesman, and the couple moved to Providence, Rhode Island, where Aimee tried to settle into the life of a housewife.

After the birth of a second child, however, Aimee became restless in her marriage and the lure of the pulpit became too difficult to resist. In 1915 she conducted her own revival service and began to practice faith healing. For the next several years, she toured the East Coast in her "gospel" touring car as a traveling evangelist, pitching her tent along the way and preaching a mix of Pentecostalism, Holy Rollerism, and what she called the Foursquare Gospel—divine healing, regeneration, baptism in the Holy Spirit, and the Second Coming of Jesus Christ. After divorcing Harold McPherson, Aimee, along with her two children and her mother, traveled to Los Angeles by automobile (later remembered as a biblical journey to reach the City of the Angels), stopping en route to preach but actually looking to start a new life in the Mediterranean climate of Southern California along with thousands of other migrants. When she arrived in Los Angeles in 1918 she had $100 in her purse, a tambourine, and a slogan emblazoned across the side of her car that read "Jesus Is Coming Soon—Get Ready." She started preaching in a small rented room but quickly signed a lease on a small church. Before long, she was preaching to standing-room crowds at the Philharmonic Auditorium, the largest assembly hall in the city. Revivals that she conducted in Denver, Colorado, in 1921 and 1922 filled the local coliseum with a crowd of 12,000 worshippers every night for a month.

It did not take long for "Sister Aimee" to adapt to her new material environment. By 1923 she had a following of 30,000 and was able to open the Angeles Temple at the northwest corner of Echo Park at a cost of $1.5 million. With a seating capacity of 5,300, it was said to be the largest class A church building in the United States. She raised most of the money for the Temple herself from revival tours in California, the Midwest, and Australia. She and her mother held the deed to the property. Next to the church were a Bible school and an administration building from which she directed the Foursquare Gospel program, which eventually enrolled 240 affiliated churches along with a ministry of affiliated preachers and congregations joined primarily by the power of her church-owned radio station KFSG (Kall Four Square Gospel). Sister Aimee worked to create a feeling of intimacy with her radio audience. During her broadcasts she invited listeners to put their hands on their radio and kneel in prayer with her. According to one writer, "Hundreds of thousands of people were electrified with the certainty that the broadcasts represented God's invasion into their personal lives. Thousands believed they were miraculously healed" (Dumenil 1995, 179).

A flamboyant personality on the stage, Sister Aimee also projected Hollywood glamour, sex appeal, and an actress's voice. Contemporaries noted her "electric quality" and "animal magnetism" and concluded that "she has It, and plenty of it." According to one observer, her ministry had "a brass band bigger and louder than Sousa's, an organ worthy of any movie cathedral, a female choir bigger and more beautiful than the Metropolitan chorus, [and] a costume wardrobe comparable to Ziegfeld's" (Brown 1987, 178). Although she became famous for her theatrical sermons in which she would illustrate biblical messages with elaborate stage sets and actors starring herself as the leading performer, Aimee McPherson was also very much a woman of show *business*. She also managed a rescue mission, a home visitors' organization, and a publishing house. She even constructed a "prayer tower" in which volunteers worked twenty-four hours a day answering requests for special prayers. Along with success came money, a mansion, a shiny new car, and elegant clothes. When she took her revival on the road, she now traveled by train and stayed in first-class hotels.

Sister Aimee's preaching style was crafted to appeal to her audience. "A glance about shows that they are largely represented by the Middle-West farmer or small-townsman and his family who have come to form so large a proportion of Los Angeles' population. On every hand are old men and women, seamed, withered, shapeless, big jointed from a lifetime of hard labor" (Moran 2002, 207). She knew that most of her followers had a limited background, that they were, in general, credulous, and that they loved movies and fantasy. As a result, she linked costuming to her sermonizing—dressing like a football player to carry the ball for Christ, riding into the Temple on a motorcycle dressed in a policeman's uniform so she could place sin under arrest, or clad as a pitchfork-wielding farmer so that she could chase the devil from the stage. "In a mock battle between God and the devil, heroic Christians fired holy artillery at Satan, who floated across the battlefield in a hot-air balloon while a giant scoreboard kept tally" (Parrish 1992, 134). At times she would dress as a nurse to pray for the sick. As Sister Aimee acted, preached, and prayed, the mighty Angelus Temple organ thundered away, joined by a brass band and a well-trained female choir. One historian commented that the Temple resembled a motion-picture theater more than a church, while another writer described her evening service as being much like a vaudeville program. On the outside of the church, a huge illuminated cross could be seen for miles, while an electric marquee over the entrance announced in lights Sister Aimee's next sermon.

Like a number of other Hollywood celebrities in the 1920s, Aimee Semple McPherson became mired in scandal. In her thirties and at the height of her success, Sister Aimee developed an attraction to one Kenneth Ormiston who was employed at the Temple as a stage engineer. Unfortunately, he was also a married man. On May 18, 1926, Sister Aimee was last seen while swimming in the Pacific Ocean near Venice, California. Concerned parties assumed that she had drowned, but an extensive search failed to turn up a body. About five weeks later, two days after an all-day memorial service at the Angeles Temple, Sister Aimee suddenly appeared in the small Mexican town of Agua Prieta. She claimed that she had been kidnapped and that she had escaped from a shack in the desert where she was being held captive. Investigative reporters were quickly on the case and soon claimed that the whole episode was a ruse. Allegedly, Sister Aimee had run off with Kenneth Ormiston and spent part of her time in a cottage in Carmel, California. She escaped going to trial on charges of conspiracy to produce false testimony when the city's district attorney decided at the last minute that he could not conclusively prove that the whole affair had been nothing more than a romantic tryst. Whereas many of her faithful followers believed her denials and stuck with her throughout her public ordeal, others saw her as a modern-day version of Nathaniel Hawthorne's Hester Prynne "whose scarlet A bespoke both angelism and adultery" (Starr 1990, 139). A large part of the public, however, could only offer ridicule.

Aimee Semple McPherson's influence was tied up in her message of hope and salvation that many lower-middle-class white Protestants wanted to hear. It might be noted in passing that Robert Shuler, another Los Angeles evangelist with his own magazine and private radio station (KGEF) that started with 200,000 listeners and then increased by 100,000 new listeners a year during the late 1920s, based his phenomenal popularity on a psychology of resentments (against Jews, Catholics, movies, evolution, jazz, and dancing) that also appealed to the same lower-middle-class white Protestant base. Sister Aimee, however, did not attack; she encouraged. Her Foursquare Gospel emphasized "a personalized encounter with conversion, healing, the second coming, and redemption." Her healing ministry was especially important. For many of the Folks who had migrated to Southern California in the hopes of improving their health, she encouraged them to cast aside their crutches. They had come looking for betterment, and she preached salvation in the present. As one historian rather harshly commented, for many of the "inconspicuous" "rural nobodies from the eccentric borderlands of evangelical American Protestantism, [s]he helped them become somebodies in Los Angeles" (Starr 1990, 139, 143).

RELIGION IN THE AFRICAN AMERICAN COMMUNITY

The experience of the Folks in Southern California shows that the firm hold that religion had on rural migrants could thrive in an urban environment. For hundreds of thousands of African Americans who migrated to northern cities during the teens and twenties, the experience was not dissimilar. As noted in Chapter 2, the process of transplanting oneself to a new environment was jarring. As a result, one of the resources that many African Americans drew on as they tried to adjust to their new urban surroundings was religion. Many migrants to Harlem and elsewhere in the urban North gravitated to established black churches. In Chicago, Olivet Baptist grew by 5,000 members between 1916 and 1919. In Harlem, St. Philips's Protestant Episcopal Church (the wealthiest black church in the United States), the Abyssinian Baptist Church of Adam Clayton Powell Sr. (with its imposing 2,000-seat sanctuary), St. Mark's Episcopal Church, and the African Methodist Episcopal Zion Church all relocated to Harlem from other parts of the city in the decade before World War I. Some of these churches took over the buildings of white congregations, while others built new structures of their own. These rather elite black churches were notable for more than their elaborate facilities. They also conducted well-organized social and recreational activities for their congregations and generated a number of community-related programs that ranged from helping

One resource that many African Americans drew upon as they acclimated to new urban surroundings was religion. Many migrants to Harlem and elsewhere gravitated to established congregations, some of which had taken over the buildings of white congregations, while others built new structures of their own. These rather elite black churches (like the Baptist Temple of New York shown in this 1920 cornerstone ceremony) conducted well-organized social and recreational activities, and generated a number of community-related programs. (Bettmann/Getty Images)

the poor and the needy to adult education and day care. It has been suggested that these black churches helped make Harlem a black community.

Many transplanted black migrants from the South, however, did not feel comfortable in these large urban churches. Much of this dissatisfaction was class based. Dominating the larger churches was an emerging black middle class. Although they may have been sympathetic to the plight of the migrants, they were also "embarrassed" by them and their inelegant manner. These class differences could also be seen in the different styles of religious worship. Southern rural churches tended toward a more emotional style of worship with unrehearsed singing and a great deal of bodily movement. In response, many migrants created their own small "storefront" churches (they would number in the hundreds by the 1930s) to lessen the sense of anonymity and feel that they were part of a more closely knit religious family. As one parishioner explained after leaving the first urban church she joined, it was "too large—it don't see the small people. . . . The preacher wouldn't know me, might could call my name in the book, but he wouldn't know me otherwise. Why, at home whenever I didn't come to Sunday school they would always come and see what was the matter." Many of the storefront churches were organized as Baptist or Methodist, but there were a number of Holiness-Pentecostal churches as well. Lucy Smith, much like Aimee Semple McPherson, was well known for her divine healing and optimistic message. She eventually started the All Nations Pentecostal Church in Chicago. In offering an explanation as to what attracted her followers, she stated: "The members of my church are troubled and need something to make them happy. My preaching is not about sad things, but always about being saved. The singing in my church has 'swing' to it, because I want my people to swing out of themselves all the mis'ry and troubles that is heavy on their hearts." The emphasis on music seems to run counter to a general disapproval of the hedonistic sounds of ragtime and jazz that so characterized the era, but as one observer noted, "They sang the blues in church; the words were religious, but it was the blues" (Dumenil 1995, 182, 183). In fact, a case can be made that the blues and jazz music performed in nightclubs during the 1920s was transformed into urban gospel music in the 1930s.

The large number of migrants to the big cities also encouraged the proliferation of numerous cult religions that were seen as alternatives to mainstream Protestantism. Spiritualist churches would fall into this category, offering a form of personal counseling that served as a mechanism for positive, optimistic thinking. Mother Leafy Anderson had her own church in New Orleans that became a major spiritualist center. Other cults rallied around charismatic individuals that assumed God-like status. One such individual was George Baker Jr., known to his followers as Father Divine. Although he did not achieve widespread notoriety until the onset of the Great Depression, he had actually begun his ministry years before. Father Divine took "New Thought" ideas—that God dwelt within every individual, the power of positive thinking, and the healing power of individuals—and put them together with Holiness-Pentecostal religious enthusiasm to create his own theology that became known in the 1930s as the Peace Mission Movement. He started communal living colonies and preached a gospel that emphasized hard work, honesty, sobriety, equality, and adherence to a strict moral code that included sexual abstinence. He also offered practical help to those looking for work or needing a meal and shelter.

Other nontraditional groups began to advance the notion that African Americans needed to find a faith that was not connected to a Protestantism that had been imposed on them by white Americans. Some centered on the idea that blacks were, in fact, the first Jews of the Bible and the real chosen people. Others, like Timothy Drew, who took the name Nobel Drew Ali, founded the Moorish Science Temple of America and crafted his own version of Muslim faith. He soon had a large following in Chicago, Detroit, and other urban centers in the 1920s. When Nobel Drew Ali died in 1929, Wallace D. Fard took over his Detroit operation to create the Nation of Islam. His teachings that black people were the true Muslims attracted many poor residents in Depression-era Detroit. Common threads in all of these groups were strict moral codes, a strong sense of community, and a racial pride and identity that became associated with black nationalism.

The most important black nationalist movement during the 1920s was Marcus Garvey's Universal Negro Improvement Association, primarily a social and economic organization that fostered black pride, encouraged self-help, and advocated racial separatism. Although not a religious movement per se, it did have a strong religious emphasis. Meetings were styled much like church services with hymns, prayers, and sermons, and racial pride was very much a part of the religious message. Garvey wanted his followers to reject white images of God and Jesus. Part of the larger message was a vision of Africa that was rooted in the biblical prophecy of Psalms 68:31: "Princes shall come forth from Egypt; Ethiopia shall soon stretch forth her hand to God." Garvey promised that Africa would regain its prior glory and that resurrection would lead to the redemption of all blacks. Garvey "offered hope, not of individual salvation, but of corporate salvation." His crusade has been called the first genuine mass movement of African Americans, and, as one historian noted, it accomplished that "in part by channeling the commitment and dedication associated with the black church. Fusing racial pride to a sense of spiritual and secular mission, Garveyism constituted a powerful civil religion for many African Americans" (Dumenil 1995, 184, 185).

RELIGION IN THE HISPANIC COMMUNITY

Some indication of the hold that religion had on rural-based, Mexican immigrants and how they adapted their beliefs to a strange new urban environment can be found in early twentieth-century Los Angeles. Mexican immigrants to Southern California brought a wide variety of religious convictions and attitudes with them. Some came with strong anticlerical views, which were often reinforced on arrival in the United States. Because Mexicans did not bring a significant number of their own clergy with them, they found that they were often served by priests of other ethnicities, especially Irish. As one historian has noted, "Even among the large majority of Mexicans who remained at least nominally Catholic, religious reference points were often intertwined with an ethnic identity that existed outside of the official framework of the Catholic Church" (Sánchez 1993b, 152). Compounding problems for the established Catholic Church in Los Angeles were two other factors: many working-class migrants had grown up in areas of Mexico where their local communities had been served by no Catholic clergy, while almost all of the peasant migrants practiced a "folk Catholicism" that was replete with the rituals associated with the culture of rural Mexican villages.

Religious attitudes and practices in the United States were very much shaped by the environment in which new immigrants found themselves. In south Texas and New Mexico, for example, newcomers most often resided in communities where Mexican Catholics were a numerical majority. In Los Angeles, however, the city was dominated by Protestant denominations, and, as one historian noted, "Though the wide variety of creeds gave Los Angeles an aura of tolerance, the city actually provided an arena of stiff competition between Catholics and Protestants" (Sánchez 1993b, 154).

The dilemma facing both denominations was how to respond to the newcomers.

The Protestants responded first, creating programs designed to provide needed services in the barrio and dispensing charity to the poor in hopes that such contact would open the door for conversion. The Methodists went a step further and instituted programs designed to train Mexican youth for industrial occupations. The thinking was that if Mexicans were taken out of the fields and placed in more modern, industrial occupations, they might be more willing to adopt the Protestant faith that many associated with economic progress and a strong work ethic. These early twentieth-century efforts aimed at conversion were supplemented by the development of the Americanization movement that characterized the second decade of the century. Around the time of World War I, it was not uncommon to find school boards instituting Americanization and citizenship classes in schools that were predominately Mexican. In many cases, the materials used in these classes came from Protestant denominations that had crafted pamphlets and other instructional material specifically for that purpose.

A number of Protestant churches believed that conversion could be won through good works and friendliness. In 1915 the Methodist-Episcopal Church established the All Nations Foundation on East Sixth Street in the downtown area of Los Angeles. All Nations provided a variety of services, including an employment agency, a craft shop, a music department and choral club, medical care, a sewing club for girls and a sports club for boys, and a Children's Home for Mexican orphans. In 1918 Robert McLean Jr. assumed the post of superintendent of Mexican Work for the Presbyterian Church in Los Angeles and promoted a program of proselytization coupled with social service. The church set up free night classes in English and domestic science, and established an employment agency, a free first-aid clinic, a kindergarten for the children of working mothers, and a summer youth program. At least a small amount of religious instruction came with each of the programs.

The fear of Protestant proselytizing prompted the Catholic Church to take action. In 1918 Irish-born Bishop John Cantwell organized an Immigration Welfare Department within the Association of Catholic Charities to coordinate outreach activities among the Mexican immigrant population of Los Angeles. In 1920 Cantwell established the first medical clinic in the diocese at the Santa Rita Settlement House, servicing a neighborhood in which 89 percent of the residents were Mexican American. During the previous year social workers at the settlement serviced 770 families through home visits by nurses and volunteers. In the predominantly Mexican neighborhood of Boyle Heights, a small religious chapel run by Father Ramirez coordinated the efforts of the Mexican Ladies of Charity, a church group comprising sixty young women from prominent Mexican families who visited homes to give religious instruction to children and instruct mothers in domestic science.

Neither the Protestant nor Catholic churches, however, were able to meet the needs of the Mexican immigrants entering the United States in the early twentieth century. Programs stressing "Americanization" simply failed to appeal to the majority of Mexican newcomers. Most immigrants believed that they would eventually return to Mexico, and even those who had decided to stay rarely wanted to give up their ethnic heritage. They were willing to accept medical services and employment opportunities but held fast to their cultural values.

When the depression of 1920–1921 compromised some of these social service efforts, the Catholic Church switched gears. Deciding not to try and compete with various Protestant denominations in providing social services, the Catholic Church shifted its emphasis to teaching Catholic doctrine and tradition (still done within the context of Americanization). As Bishop Cantwell noted, "These people [the recent Mexican immigrants] are already Catholic by nature and inheritance and need only a friendly and guiding hand to make them good citizens and better Catholics" (Sánchez 1993b, 159). To further that effort, the Catholic Church began to disseminate booklets written in Spanish that treated, in very simple fashion, the subjects of doctrine and devotion and established the Confraternity of Christian Doctrine, an organization of lay volunteers, to offer religious instruction to Catholic children. Catholic Church authorities also believed that through religious instruction Mexicans would reject attempts from the Protestant Church to lure them away from Catholicism. Volunteers were divided into two groups—"Fishers" and "Teachers." Fishers visited the homes of families to encourage the children to attend their local catechism center, while Teachers offered instruction in the doctrines and practices of the Catholic Church in more formal classroom-like settings. The assumption behind these programs was that Mexicans arrived in the United States without proper religious training and that the folk Catholicism to which they had been subjected in Mexico was deficient and unprogressive.

The established churches in Los Angeles confronted another major problem when it came to making a strong religious connection with recent Mexican immigrants. Their new life in the city was dominated by secular activities. Leisure-time pursuits cut into more staid church-sponsored activities. In addition, having moved away from the village-dominated influence of the Catholic Church, many immigrants, barely instructed in the faith to begin with, quickly developed a more personal and familial view of religion. With so many things to do in an urban center like Los Angeles, more and more Mexican Americans drifted away from formal religious practice, even though they still regarded themselves as Catholics. The decline in church attendance, a trend similar to the rest of the American population, underscored this lessening of enthusiasm. One study showed that although nearly 80 percent of the Mexican population identified themselves as members of the Catholic Church, only half of that number attended mass. A census taken among Catholic priests in the 1920s showed that fewer than 40 percent of Mexican women and children came to church on Sunday, while the percentage for Mexican men was only 27 percent. Removed from its community-based context in Mexico, religion appealed less to men. As George Sánchez has commented, "In the United States, with its myriad churches and growing secularism, participation in Catholic ritual rapidly became an empty shell" (Sánchez 1993b, 164, 165). Bonifacio Ortega, a twenty-eight-year-old street paver, expressed a common attitude: "I am Catholic, but the truth is that I hardly follow out my beliefs. I never go to church nor do I pray. I have an amulet which my mother gave to me before dying. This amulet has the Virgin of Guadalupe on it and it is she who always protects me" (Monroy 1999, 50).

The numbers suggest that one other trend was taking place as religion shifted to the personal and familial. Public religion was gradually becoming "feminized" in the Los Angeles Mexican community. This process could be seen on two levels as the Catholic Church began to allocate much of the religious work in the city to both religious and lay women, while Mexican families themselves began to relegate the religious part of the family's activities to the women. The daughter of one Mexican family, like many others, noted that family members went their separate ways on Sunday. "My mother and I go to Church almost every Sunday. My brother . . . never goes, but he believes in God and in religion even though he doesn't carry it out. My sister . . . goes to Church very regularly and we pray every night." One husband commented that he was "very Catholic" in Mexico and "went to church there every Sunday . . . but here she [his wife] goes alone" (Sánchez 1993b, 165, 166).

The inability of the Catholic Church to provide enough facilities (there were not enough Catholic churches in East Los Angeles to serve the rapidly expanding population), coupled with the absence of Chicano priests and a Spanish liturgy, left many Mexican immigrants with no alternative other than practicing a Catholicism centered in their own homes. According to historian Sánchez, "The widespread presence of home altars and personal displays of religious sentiment was the urban equivalent of the 'folk Catholicism' so often chided by critics of Mexican rural practice." "You may find," explained one Mexican immigrant, "a Catholic picture in every room of our house, but you will seldom see us in the religious services at the parish." These expressions of spirituality, increasingly supervised by the women of the family, were, according to Sánchez, "the base of a new religious consciousness shaped in Los Angeles, as it was developing throughout the Southwest" (Sánchez 1993b, 166).

Document: G. Bromley Oxnam, "The Mexican in Los Angeles from the Standpoint of the Religious Forces of the City" (1921)

In 1918 the City Missionary Society of the Methodist Church in Los Angeles sent a young pastor by the name of G. Bromley Oxnam into the east-central section of the city to establish a church settlement house known as the Church of All Nations, a position he maintained until 1927. It was Oxnam's mission to help the newly arrived and needy Mexican population. Combining social welfare with a desire to Americanize these recent immigrants, Oxnam was cognizant that he needed to break down the "antisocial conditions" that prevented Mexicans from seeking citizenship. The following excerpt, written before the Mexican population in the city had tripled by the end of the next decade, offers a glimpse of his plan.

"The Mexican in Los Angeles from the Standpoint of the Religious Forces of the City"

There are approximately 30,000 Mexicans in the city of Los Angeles, composed largely of three distinct groups: the descendants of the original settlers of California, known as "Californians" or

"Spanish"; the refugee, representing the cultured classes of pre-Revolution days in Mexico; and the laborer, constituting the large majority of the Mexican population. . . . The laborer, however, presents a compelling social challenge constituting at once the most serious foreign problem in Los Angeles and the city's largest Americanization opportunity.

Large numbers of Mexicans are crossing the border at the present time, but as yet this influx has not materially affected the Los Angeles situation. The results, therefore, of the recent study conducted by the writer for the Interchurch World Movement will show clearly the social conditions prevailing among the Mexicans, with which the religious forces of the city must deal in building a new program that seeks the complete transformation of the community life.

. . . . The condition of. . . [Mexican housing] is classified as follows: Good, 5 per cent; fair, 40 percent; poor, 45 per cent; very bad, 10 per cent. Of the houses . . . 35 per cent are shacks. The worst conditions obtain in the house courts. . . . The houses are constructed of rough 1 × 12 ft. pine boards with battened cracks. Thin partitions of similar construction separate the habitations, which consist of two rooms—one used for living and sleeping, the other for the kitchen. Lack of privacy, inadequate toilet facilities, and overcrowding characterize the courts throughout.

Another serious factor revealed is the high rate of adult illiteracy. Of this group, 55 per cent of the men and 74 per cent of the women can not speak English; 67 per cent of the men and 84 per cent of the women can not read English, and 75 per cent of the men and 85 per cent of the women can not write English. . . .

Sickness and disease reap a frightful toll among the poorer classes of Mexicans. . . . Poor and insufficient food, overcrowding and lack of ventilation, lack of facilities for cleanliness, ignorance of personal hygiene coupled with low wages have contributed largely to the tuberculosis menace [more than twice the city average] mentioned, and likewise have developed the high infant mortality rate [nearly three times the city average] prevailing among the Mexicans. . . .

The result of bad housing, illiteracy, and disease is seen clearly in the records of the Los Angeles County Charities. The Mexican, representing but one-twentieth of the population, contributes nearly one-quarter of the poverty cases handled by the county. Sickness and disease were listed as the major causes in 67 per cent of the cases studied. . . .

The foregoing conditions constitute the challenge flung at the organized religious forces of Los Angeles by the Mexican population. . . . [The Churches] frankly face the fact that 80 per cent of the Mexicans have virtually refused to become American citizens, and have come to the conclusion that the anti-social conditions prevailing are a major cause of this refusal. The churches have accepted this challenge and at present are drafting a long time program, seeking the removal of all anti-social forces and the substitution therefor of forces making for more abundant living. The Protestant Churches have invested more than $350,000 in property, buildings and equipment to carry on religious and social work among the Mexicans. . . . While the Protestant membership is comparatively small, the institutions are actually serving a constituency of 3,000 families or a total population of between ten and fifteen thousand people. These churches are employing sixty-three social workers and direct the activities of several hundred volunteer workers. The Roman Catholic Church is likewise serving a large constituency through regular churches, and is rendering splendid service at Brownson House, a Catholic social settlement. . . .

To meet the housing situation, official representatives of the various denominations have drafted a program calling for the purchase of tracts of land and the erection of model dwellings to be sold to Mexicans on easy terms which will properly finance the project. . . .

It is further planned to support the home teacher movement in the public schools, to continue all settlement classes in English and to develop a series of home charts to be used in teaching English and religious matters. It is felt this endeavor will contribute much toward the solution of the adult illiteracy problem. The churches also plan to support the request of the housing commission that it be given authority to inspect one-family dwellings. This is felt to be essential if the campaign against sickness and disease is to be successful. Several churches plan to employ district nurses, some are maintaining clinics and milk stations, and are generally agreed that a preventorium should be provided by the County to which children from tubercular homes may be sent when conditions make adequate prevention in the home impossible. . . . It is believed that this ministry of constructive friendliness will break down the barrier between the American and the Mexican and . . . develop a willingness on the part of the Mexican to become an American citizen.

Source: G. Bromley Oxnam. "The Mexican in Los Angeles from the Standpoint of the Religious Forces of the City," *Annals of the American Academy* 93 (January 1921): 130–33.

GLOSSARY

Acculturation—the process of adopting the cultural traits or social patterns of another social group.

Americanization—the process of assimilating to the customs and institutions of the United States.

Anarchism—a doctrine advocating the abolition of government as a prerequisite for full social and political liberty.

Anti-Semitism—discrimination against or prejudice or hostility toward Jews.

Barrio—a crowded inner-city area inhabited primarily by a Spanish-speaking population.

Black capitalism—the idea that African Americans should build wealth and create opportunity through the development and ownership of their own businesses.

Blacklist—a list of individuals who have been targeted by employers because of unacceptable activities or behavior; primarily a means used to target union organizers who would be fired from a job and then denied employment elsewhere.

"Bootlegger"—one engaged in the illegal business of transporting (smuggling) alcoholic beverages where such transportation is forbidden by law (Prohibition).

Civil liberty—the freedom to exercise basic rights such as speech or assembly without unwarranted interference by the government.

Companionate marriage—the idea of marriage based on sexual intimacy with birth control as a necessary part. Couples could separate at any time, and property rights would be determined based on the economic standing of both parties. The intention was to adapt marriage to a growing youth culture and the emphasis on women's independence and civil equality.

Comstock Law—an 1873 law that sought to ban from the U.S. Mail all "obscene, lewd, or lascivious" literature, including information about birth control.

Consent decree—an agreement approved by the court in which a corporation ceases an activity alleged by the Justice Department to be illegal (e.g., an antitrust violation) in return for the government dropping its suit.

Corrido—a Mexican ballad or folk song about struggle against oppression and injustice in which musicians would make it relevant to a working-class Mexican audience.

Crop-lien system—the process by which a tenant farmer or sharecropper gave a lien (claim) on his crop to the "furnishing" merchant as collateral for credit granted at the store. Such farmers often became trapped in a cycle of debt from which they never escaped (debt peonage).

Cultural pluralism—a condition in which minority groups participate fully in the dominant society while maintaining their cultural differences; usually accompanied by the belief that society benefits from such a condition.

Dole—a term used by Herbert Hoover to suggest that direct federal assistance to the unemployed during the Depression would undermine self-reliance and create a class of dependent citizens.

Eugenics—the study of the possibilities of improving the human population by discouraging the reproduction by certain people or ethnic groups deemed to have undesirable traits.

Feminist—someone who advocates social, political, and economic rights and opportunities for women.

Flapper—a young woman who, during the 1920s, behaved and dressed in a boldly unconventional manner and was usually characterized with bobbed hair; slim, short dresses; cloche hats, long, beaded necklaces; and rolled stockings.

Fundamentalism—the movement in American Protestantism that arose in the early twentieth century as a reaction to modernism that stresses the infallibility of the Bible in matters of faith.

Ghettoization—the process of segregating or isolating an ethnic or racial group to a specific residential area.

Great Migration—the process by which nearly half a million African Americans migrated from the rural South to northern cities in the period before, during, and after World War I. The migration transformed the racial demographic of the nation.

Harlem Renaissance—a cultural flowering that developed among a group of African American poets, novelists, painters, and sculptors in Harlem who probed racial themes and tackled the question of what it meant to be black in America during the 1920s and 1930s.

Hyphenated American—pertaining to a person or group of mixed origin or identity.

Labor injunction—a judicial order requiring a person or persons (e.g., a labor union) to refrain from taking a particular action (e.g., a strike).

Lost generation—a group of American writers who came of age during World War I. Spiritually shattered by that experience, they became disillusioned with life and alienated from the dominant cultural values of the 1920s. Many chose to live as expatriates in Paris.

Mores—folkways of central importance that embody the fundamental moral views of a group.

Nativism—hostility shown toward immigrants because of perceptions that their presence in this country would undermine the existing system of values and threaten the American way of life.

Naturalization—the process of obtaining the rights and privileges of citizenship.

New Negro—the title of a 1925 book by Alain Locke in which he suggested that the recently transplanted African migrant from the South possessed a new vision of hope that he or she could obtain social and economic freedom. The term was also used during World War I and immediately after to describe a more self-assertive black person.

"Normalcy"—the campaign slogan of presidential candidate Warren G. Harding in 1920 in which he promised to move the nation away from Wilsonian crusading and back to a steady, stable order of things without excess.

Oligopoly—the tendency toward the concentration of corporate wealth and power in the hands of a relatively few corporate entities.

Parity—the system of regulating the prices of farm commodities (usually through government price supports) so that farmers would be able to realize the same purchasing power that they had in the prosperous period before World War I.

Protectionism—the practice of trying to develop domestic industries by protecting them from foreign competition through duties (tariffs) imposed on imports.

Scrip—a certificate given to workers in place of cash that could be exchanged only for goods at a company-run store. It allowed a company to sell goods at inflated prices and essentially made employees dependent on the company.

Social Darwinism—the idea that human progress is the result of a process of natural selection or natural competition that weeds out the weak and selects the strong. In its popular form, it became known as "survival of the fittest."

"Speakeasy"—a saloon or nightclub selling alcoholic beverages illegally, as during Prohibition.

Syndicalist—a person who advocates taking possession of the means of production through general strikes or sabotage.

"Trickle-down"—the idea that tax breaks to the wealthy will encourage new investments and bring about higher productivity. With economic growth stimulated, workers would eventually see benefits come to them in the form of job creation or higher wages.

Welfare capitalism—a paternalistic program whereby employers would offer workers various benefits in return for promises not to form or join a union.

BIBLIOGRAPHY

Allen, Frederick Lewis. 2010. *Only Yesterday: An Informal History of the 1920s*. New York: HarperCollins.

Arnesen, Eric. 2001. *Brotherhoods of Color: Black Railroad Workers and the Struggle for Equality*. Cambridge, MA: Harvard University Press.

Asinof, Eliot. 1990. *1919: America's: Loss of Innocence*. New York: Donald I. Fine.

Berg, A. Scott. 1998. *Lindbergh*. New York: G. P. Putnam's Sons.

Berlin, Ira. 2010. *The Making of African America: The Four Great Migrations*. New York: Viking Penguin.

Bernstein, Irving. 2010. *The Lean Years: A History of the American Worker, 1920–1933*. Chicago: Haymarket Books.

Bodenner, Chris. 2006. "Harlem Renaissance." Issues and Controversies in American History. Infobase Publishing. Web. February 6, 2013. http://icah.infobaselearning.com/icahfullarticle.aspx?ID=107275

Borough, Reuben W. 1968. "The Little Judge." *Colorado Quarterly* 16: 371–82.

Brown, Dorothy M. 1987. *Setting a Course: American Women in the 1920s*. Boston: Twayne.

Buck, Christopher. 2013. "Harlem Renaissance." *The American Mosaic: The African American Experience*. ABC-CLIO. Web. March 31, 2013.

Buhle, Mary Jo, Teresa Murphy, and Jane Gerhard. 2009. *Women and the Making of America*. Upper Saddle River, NJ: Prentice-Hall.

Cashman, Sean Dennis. 1998. *America Ascendant: From Theodore Roosevelt to FDR in the Century of American Power, 1901–1945*. New York: New York University Press.

Chambers, John Whiteclay II. 1992. *The Tyranny of Change: America in the Progressive Era, 1890–1920*. New York: St. Martin's Press.

City of Phoenix. 2006. Planning and Development Department: Historic Preservation, Hispanic Historic Property Study. "Migration, Marginalization and Community Development, 1900–1939." https://www.phoenix.gov/pdd/historic/historicmaps/historic-property-surveys

Collins, Gail. 2003. *America's Women*. New York: HarperCollins.

Cott, Nancy F., ed. 2000. *No Small Courage: A History of Women in the United States*. New York: Oxford University Press.

Cowan, Ruth Schwartz. 1976. "The 'Industrial Revolution' in the Home: Household Technology and Social Change in the 20th Century." *Technology and Culture* 17: 1–42.

Cowan, Ruth Schwartz. 1983. *More Work for Mother: The Ironies of Household Technology from the Open Hearth to the Microwave*. New York: Basic Books.

Danbom, David B. 1979. *The Resisted Revolution: Urban America and the Industrialization of Agriculture, 1900–1930*. Ames: Iowa State University Press.

Danbom, David B. 2006. *Born in the Country: A History of Rural America*. Baltimore, MD: Johns Hopkins University Press.

Daniel, Pete. 1996. *Standing at the Crossroads: Southern Life in the Twentieth Century*. Baltimore, MD: Johns Hopkins University Press.

Dawley, Alan. 1991. *Struggles for Justice: Social Responsibility and the Liberal State*. Cambridge, MA: Harvard University Press.

Dos Passos, John. 2003. *Novels 1920–1925*. Edited by Townsend Ludington. New York: Library of America.

Dray, Philip. 2010. *There Is Power in a Union: The Epic Story of Labor in America*. New York: Random House.

Drowne, Kathleen, and Patrick Huber. 2004. *The 1920s*. Westport, CT: Greenwood Press.

Dumenil, Lynn. 1995. *The Modern Temper: American Culture and Society in the 1920s*. New York: Hill and Wang.

Dumenil, Lynn. 2007. "The New Woman and the Politics of the 1930s." *OAH Magazine of History* 21: 22–26.

Editors of Time-Life Books. 1998. *Our American Century: The Jazz Age, the 20s*. Alexandria, VA: Time-Life Books.

Ehrgott, Roberts. 2013. *Mr. Wrigley's Ball Club: Chicago and the Cubs during the Jazz Age*. Lincoln: University of Nebraska Press.

Ely, Melvin Patrick. 1991. *The Adventures of Amos 'n' Andy: A Social History of an American Phenomenon*. New York: The Free Press.

Farrell, John A. 2011. *Clarence Darrow: Attorney for the Damned*. New York: Vintage Books.

Fass, Paula S. 1977. *The Damned and the Beautiful: American Youth in the 1920s*. New York: Oxford University Press.

Filippelli, Ronald. 1984. *Labor in the USA: A History*. New York: Alfred A. Knopf.

Fitzgerald, F. Scott. 1931. "Echoes of the Jazz Age." *Scribner's Magazine* 90: 459–65.

Fitzgerald, F. Scott. 1980. *The Great Gatsby*. New York: Charles Scribner's Sons.

Fitzgerald, F. Scott. 2012. *F. Scott Fitzgerald: Two Novels and Nineteen Short Stories*. New York: Fall River Press.

Freedman, Estelle B. 1974. "The New Woman: Changing Views of Women in the 1920s." *Journal of American History* 61: 372–93.

Fried, Richard M. 2005. *The Man Everybody Knew: Bruce Barton and the Making of Modern America*. Chicago: Ivan R. Dee.

Gebhard, David. 1967. "The Spanish Colonial Revival in Southern California, 1865–1930." *Journal of the Society of Architectural Historians* 26: 131–47.

Glickman, Lawrence B. 2007. "Rethinking Politics: Consumers and the Public Good during the Jazz Age." *OAH Magazine of History* 21: 16–20.

Goldman, Eric F. 2001. *Rendezvous with Destiny: A History of Modern American Reform*. Chicago: Ivan R. Dee.

Gordon, Linda. 2009. *Dorothea Lange: A Life beyond Limits*. New York: W.W. Norton.

Gowans, Alan. 1986. *The Comfortable House: North American Suburban Architecture, 1890–1930*. Cambridge, MA: MIT Press.

Green, Donald J. 2010. *Third-Party Matters: Politics, Presidents, and Third Parties in American History*. Santa Barbara, CA: Praeger.

Green, Harvey. 1992. *The Uncertainty of Everyday Life, 1915–1945*. New York: HarperCollins.

Griswold del Castillo, Richard. 1984. *La Familia: Chicano Families in the Urban Southwest, 1848 to the Present*. Notre Dame, IN: University of Notre Dame Press.

Gutman, Herbert G. 1976. *The Black Family in Slavery and Freedom, 1750–1925*. New York: Random House.

Hemingway, Ernest. 1995. *A Farewell to Arms*. New York: Scribner.

Hemingway, Ernest. 2003. *The Sun Also Rises*. New York: Scribner.

Henstell, Bruce. 1984. *Sunshine and Wealth: Los Angeles in the Twenties and Thirties*. San Francisco: Chronicle Books.

Herald, Jacqueline. 1991. *Fashions of a Decade: The 1920s*. New York: Facts on File.

Hine, Darlene Clark, ed. 1993. *Black Women in America: An Historical Encyclopedia*. Brooklyn, NY: Carlson Publishing

Hine, Darlene Clark, William C. Hine, and Stanley Harrold. 2000. *The African-American Odyssey*. Upper Saddle River, NJ: Prentice-Hall.

Howes, Kelly King. 2006. *The Roaring Twenties: Almanac and Primary Sources*. Farmington Hills, MI: Thomson Gale.

Huggins, Nathan Irvin. 1973. *Harlem Renaissance*. New York: Oxford University Press.

Hughes, Langston. 1926. "The Negro Artist and the Racial Mountain." *The Nation* 122: 692–94.

Hughes, Robert. 1997. *American Visions: The Epic History of Art in America*. New York: Alfred A. Knopf.

Jacobs, Lewis. 1968. *The Rise of the American Film: A Critical History*. New York: Teachers College Press.

Kahn, Roger. 1999. *A Flame of Pure Fire: Jack Dempsey and the Roaring Twenties*. New York: Harcourt Brace.

Kallen, Stuart A., ed. 2002. *The Roaring Twenties*. San Diego: Greenhaven Press.

Kazin, Michael. 2006. *A Godly Hero: The Life of William Jennings Bryan*. New York: Anchor Books.

Kennedy, David M. 2004. *Over Here: The First World War and American Society*. New York: Oxford University Press.

Kersten, Andrew E. 2007. *A. Philip Randolph: A Life in the Vanguard*. Lanham, MD: Rowman and Littlefield.

Kessler-Harris, Alice. 1982. *Out to Work: A History of Wage-Earning Women in the United States*. New York: Oxford University Press.

Krist, Gary. 2018. *The Mirage Factory: Illusion, Imagination, and the Invention of Los Angeles*. New York: Crown.

Kyvig, David E. 2004. *Daily Life in the United States, 1920–1940*. Chicago: Ivan R. Dee.

Larson, Edward J. 1997. *Summer for the Gods: The Scopes Trial and America's Continuing Debate* over *Science and Religion*. Cambridge, MA: Harvard University Press.

Leach, William. 1993. *Land of Desire: Merchants, Power, and the Rise of a New American Culture*. New York: Random House.

Leuchtenburg, William E. 1958. *The Perils of Prosperity, 1914–1932*. Chicago: University of Chicago Press.

Levenstein, Harvey. 2003. *Revolution at the Table: The Transformation of the American Diet*. Berkeley: University of California Press.

Levine, Lawrence W. 1993. *The Unpredictable Past: Explorations in American Cultural History*. New York: Oxford University Press.

Lewis, David Levering. 1997. *When Harlem Was in Vogue*. New York: Penguin Books.

Lewis, Sinclair. 1920. *Main Street*. New York: Harcourt Brace Jovanovich.

Lewis, Sinclair. 1922. *Babbitt*. New York: Harcourt Brace Jovanovich.

Lewis, Sinclair. 1927. *Elmer Gantry*. New York: Harcourt Brace Jovanovich.

Locke, Alain. 1925. "The Art of the Ancestors." *The Survey* 53: 673.

Lynd, Robert S., and Helen Merrell Lynd. 1956. *Middletown: A Study in American Culture*. New York: Harcourt Brace Jovanovich.

Marchand, Roland. 1985. *Advertising the American Dream: Making Way for Modernity, 1920–1940*. Berkeley: University of California Press.

Martin, Robert F. 2002. *Hero of the Heartland: Billy Sunday and the Transfor-mation of American Society, 1862–1935*. Bloomington: University of Indiana Press.

McGerr, Michael E. 1986. *The Decline of Popular Politics: The American North, 1865–1928*. New York: Oxford University Press.

McGerr, Michael E. 2003. *A Fierce Discontent: The Rise and Fall of the Pro-gressive Movement in America, 1870–1920*. New York: Oxford Univer-sity Press.

Mencken, H. L. 1921. "On Living in the United States." *The Nation* 113: 655–56.

Miller, Donald L. 2014. *Supreme City: How Jazz Age Manhattan Gave Birth to Modern America*. New York: Simon & Shuster.

Miller, Nathan. 2004. *New World Coming: The 1920s and the Making of Mod-ern America*. Cambridge, MA: Da Capo Press.

Monroy, Douglas. 1999. *Rebirth: Mexican Los Angeles from the Great Migra-tion to the Great Depression*. Berkeley: University of California Press.

Moran, Jeffrey P. 2002. *The Scopes Trial: A Brief History with Documents*. Boston, MA: Bedford/St. Martin's.

Mowry, George E. 1963. *The California Progressives*. Chicago: Quadrangle Books.

Ngai, Mae M. 2007. "Nationalism, Immigration Control, and the Ethnora-cial Remapping of America in the 1920s." *OAH Magazine of History* 21: 11–15.

Osofsky, Gilbert. 1965. "Symbols of the Jazz Age: The New Negro and Harlem Discovered." *American Quarterly* 17: 229–38.

Osofsky, Gilbert. 1996. *Harlem: The Making of a Ghetto*. New York: Ivan R. Dee.

Painter, Nell Irvin. 2006. *Creating Black Americans: African-American His-tory and Its Meanings, 1619 to the Present*. New York: Oxford Univer-sity Press.

Parrish, Michael. 1992. *Anxious Decades: America in Prosperity and Depres-sion, 1920–1941*. New York: W.W. Norton.

Piott, Steven L. 2011. *Daily Life in the Progressive Era*. Santa Barbara, CA: ABC-CLIO.

Riley, Glenda. 2007. *Inventing the American Woman: An Inclusive History*. Wheeling, IL: Harlan Davidson.

Robertson, Stephen, Shane White, Stephen Garton, and Graham White. 2010. "This Harlem Life: Black Families and Everyday Life in the 1920s and 1930s." *Journal of Social History* 44: 97–122.

Rosenberg, Rosalind. 1992. *Divided Lives: American Women in the Twentieth Century*. New York: Hill and Wang.

Ruiz, Vicki L. 1993. "Star Struck: Acculturation, Adolescence, and the Mex-ican American Woman, 1920–1950." In *Building with Our Hands: New Directions in Chicano Studies*, edited by Adela de la Torre and Beatriz M. Pesquera, 265–71. Berkeley: University of California Press.

Ruiz, Vicki L. 1998. *From out of the Shadows: Mexican Women in Twentieth-Century America*. New York: Oxford University Press.

Sánchez, George J. 1993a. *"Go after the Women: Americanization and the Mexican Immigrant Woman, 1915–1929."* In *Mothers and Motherhood: Readings in American History*, edited by Rima D. Apple and Janet Golden, 475–94. Columbus: Ohio State University Press.

Sánchez, George J. 1993b. *Becoming Mexican American: Ethnicity, Culture, and Identity in Chicano Los Angeles, 1900–1945*. New York: Oxford University Press.

Shannon, David A. 1965. *Between the Wars: America, 1919–1941*. Boston, MA: Houghton Mifflin.

Sklar, Robert. 1975. *Movie-Made America: A Cultural History of American Movies*. New York: Random House.

Starr, Kevin. 1985. *Inventing the Dream: California through the Progressive Era*. New York: Oxford University Press.

Starr, Kevin. 1990. *Material Dreams: Southern California through the 1920s*. New York: Oxford University Press.

Stricker, Frank. 1983. "Affluence for Whom? Another Look at Prosperity and the Working Classes in the 1920s." *Labor History* 24: 5–33.

Sullivan, Mark. 1996. *Our Times: America at the Birth of the Twentieth Century*. Edited by Dan Rather. New York: Scribner.

Sutton, Matthew Avery. 2007. *Aimee Semple McPherson and the Resurrection of Christian America*. Cambridge, MA: Harvard University Press.

Topp, Michael M. 2005. *The Sacco and Vanzetti Case: A Brief History with Documents*. Boston, MA: Bedford/St. Martin's.

Wade, Wyn Craig. 1987. *The Fiery Cross: The Ku Klux Klan in America*. New York: Oxford University Press.

Ward, Geoffrey C., and Ken Burns. 1994. *Baseball: An Illustrated History*. New York: Alfred A. Knopf.

Ward, Geoffrey C., and Ken Burns. 2000. *Jazz: A History of America's Music*. New York: Alfred A. Knopf.

Ward, John W. 1958. "The Meaning of Lindbergh's Flight." *American Quarterly* 10: 3–16.

Watts, Steven. 2006. *The People's Tycoon: Henry Ford and the American Century*. New York: Vintage Books.

West, George P. 1922. "These United States—XIII: California the Prodigious." *The Nation* 115: 325–28.

Williamson, Joel. 1984. *The Crucible of Race: Black-White Relations in the American South since Emancipation*. New York: Oxford University Press.

Yellis, Kenneth A. 1969. "Prosperity's Child: Some Thoughts on the Flapper." *American Quarterly* 21: 44–64.

Zeitz, Joshua. 2006. *Flapper: A Madcap Story of Sex, Style, Celebrity, and the Women Who Made America Modern*. New York: Crown Publishers.

Websites

Best of History Websites. http://www.besthistorysites.net
Clash of Cultures in the 1910s and 1920s. https://ehistory.osu.edu/
exhibitions/clash/default
Digital History. http://www.digitalhistory.uh.edu/
"Edna St. Vincent Millay." The Academy of American Poets. http://
www.poets.org/poet.php/prmpid/160
"Eyewitness to History—America in the 1920s." http://www.eyewitness
tohistory.com/snpmech.htm
The F. Scott Fitzgerald Society. http://www.fitzgeraldsociety.org/
"Henry Ford, 1863–1947." A Science Odyssey: People and Discoveries.
http:pbs.org/wgbh/aso/databank/entries/btford.html
"The Jazz Age: Flapper Culture and Style." http://www.geocities.com/
flapper_cultureLibrary of Congress. "Prosperity and Thrift: The
Coolidge Era and the Consumer Economy." http://lcweb2.loc
.gov/ammem/coolhtml/coolhome.html
National Humanities Center. "America in Class." Primary Resources.
"Becoming Modern: America in the 1920s."
"The Roaring Twenties—Jazz Age Music." http://alephnull.net/20s/cds
.html
"Scopes 'Monkey Trial' (1925)." http://www.law.umkc.edu/faculty/
projects/ftrials/scopes/scopes.htm

INDEX

About the Author

STEVEN L. PIOTT is emeritus professor of history at Clarion University of Pennsylvania. He holds BA and MA degrees from the University of Utah and his PhD from the University of Missouri. His published works include *The Anti-Monopoly Persuasion: Popular Resistance to the Rise of Big Business* (1985); *Holy Joe: Joseph W. Folk and the Missouri Idea* (1997); *Giving Voters a Voice: The Origins of the Initiative and Referendum in America* (2003); *American Reformers, 1870–1920: Progressives in Word and Deed* (2006); *Daily Life in the Progressive Era* (2011); and *Americans in Dissent: Thirteen Influential Social Critics of the Nineteenth Century* (2014). He is a former Fulbright Teaching Fellow at Massey University in New Zealand.